Praise for *Overschooled but Undereducated*

'Abbott and MacTaggart use their findings to show how society's increasing concern about the well-being of adolescence is not to be rectified simply by more schools, ever more prescription about subject content, or more quantification dependent only on more examinations. Yet progress is only possible if, once or twice in a generation, someone confronts us with an image in the mirror that makes us feel that we have grown old and stale prematurely. We have to transform ourselves quickly, or surely we will perish.'

Dr Paul Cappon
President and CEO of the Canadian Council on Learning

'Your message is critically important . . . we're growing a generation many of whom leave education knowing not much about rather little, and who are, for the most part, quite unfitted for the kind of competitive world in which they will find themselves . . . as you rightly state, the very continuation of our society is at stake.'

Professor Charles Handy
Formerly of the London Business School, and author of many books including *The Hungry Spirit*, *The Empty Raincoat* and *The Elephant and the Flea*

'This penetrating exploration burrows through to the heart of the malaise which has stifled so much education into the twenty-first century . . . this is not only a brilliant, lucid and erudite exposé but also a provocative and bold manifesto for change. Everyone involved in education should be familiar with its message – from politicians, policy-makers and administrators to parents, teachers and students.'

Dr Jonathan Long
Principal, United World College of India

'This remarkable work, so individualistic and peppered with fascinating reminiscences and asides, deserves the widest possible readership. It is at the same time profoundly scholarly and eminently accessible. It is nothing less than a tour de force, and it is a privilege to recommend it unreservedly.'

Professor Sir Gustav Nossal

Fellow of the Royal Society and Former President of the World Immunology Association, and of the Australian Academy of Science

'*The principle of "going with the grain of the brain" is so fundamentally right, it's breathtaking in its simplicity and deserves the status of a daily mantra.*'

Martin Pritchard

Educational Consultant, former secondary school assistant headteacher

'*I'm not exaggerating at all when I say that* Overschooled but Undereducated *simply encapsulates and summarizes (in a way that I couldn't hope to do) all the issues, contradictions, frustrations and worries that I've faced over the last 30 years. It's hard to imagine how anyone with a commitment to education, a care for the young, or a concern about the dismal state of our education system could fail to be convinced and inspired or could avoid wanting to sign up as a "Responsible Subversive".*'

Dr Bernard Trafford

Chairman of the Headmasters' Conference

'*I read John Abbott and Heather MacTaggart's book with great interest and almost entire agreement!*'

Sir Eric Anderson

Provost of Eton College

'*The problem lies in a triad of undereducated public, reactionary media and cowardly politics. This pushes us, as the book says, towards either radical change or the status quo. Politicians, looking for short-term solutions, inevitably favour the status quo, which is the cause of all our problems.*'

Keir Bloomer

Former Chief Executive of Clackmannanshire, Scotland

'*This brilliantly rich, historical and philosophical background makes this a landmark work. It is absolutely marvellous that this book is question-rich, because never before have the right questions been more important.*'

Dr Helen Drennen

Principal, Wesley College, Melbourne

'*I see this book as becoming the standard text for teachers-to-be, and necessary reading for anyone taking Masters' programmes in education.*'

Jeff Hopkins

Superintendent, Gulf Islands, Vancouver

'Overschooled but Undereducated *argues that both common sense and science – specifically, new insights into how the brain develops – should force us to overhaul our attitude to those scary teenage aliens slamming doors and grunting.*'

Prue Leith

From the *Spectator*, September 2008

'*I have known for decades that political leadership in education is short-termist and that, metaphorically, we are required to plant hanging baskets when we are called towards forestry. This is just what I believe we need right now, not only as a profession, but as a nation, perhaps even as a species. We can't go on as we have been: so what? That is the question John and Heather so eruditely stalk and lay before our moral and professional conscience.*'

Pete Mountstephen

Primary School headteacher

'*This may well be the most important and significant book that young people and those involved in education will read. It could be, quite literally, life-changing and indeed life-saving! There is a deceptive simplicity in the telling of this narrative: a complex and urgent message is told in elegant, lucid and engaging prose. It should be required reading in schools, at the very least to stimulate debate among young people so that they can become Responsible Subversives before it is too late.*'

Maureen Nitek

Teacher for the Gifted and Talented, The Clarendon College

'Abbott and MacTaggart need to be congratulated on pointing out the errors in the present system, explaining why they are errors, and suggesting how they have evolved. An important and interesting book. It is engagingly written and stimulating in its perceptions and points. It deserves to enjoy a very wide circulation, from which this country would be the beneficiary.'

Lord Neuberger
Law Lord

'Overschooled but Undereducated *is unashamedly a synthesis, a deliberate attempt to destroy the narrow interpretations placed upon education by governments of all political persuasion. This is not merely a good read, or even a cautionary tale, it is a call to arms.'*

Neil Richards
Principal of Atlantic College

'This is an important book; at its heart lies a challenge to government to build its policies on evidence and scientific advances, particularly about the development of the brain, and its implications for adolescence.'

Dr Keith Robinson
Chief Executive, Wiltshire County Council and
Chairman of the Association of County Chief Executives

'Abbott and MacTaggart have provided an accessible, and challenging book, that provides valuable insights into adolescence and the need for an appropriate approach to their preparation for adult life and responsibility.'

The Rt Reverend Peter Price
Bishop of Bath and Wells

Overschooled but Undereducated

Also available from Network Continuum

The Unfinished Revolution: Learning, Human Behaviour, Community and Political Paradox – John Abbott and
  Terry Ryan

Also available from Continuum

The Great City Academy Fraud – Francis Beckett

Also by John Abbott

The Child is Father of the Man: How Humans Learn and Why

*Learning Makes Sense: Recreating Education for a
  Changing World*

Both are available from the 21st Century Learning Initiative

Overschooled but Undereducated

*How the crisis in education
is jeopardizing our adolescents*

JOHN ABBOTT

with

HEATHER MacTAGGART

continuum

Continuum International Publishing Group
The Tower Building, 11 York Road, London SE1 7NX
80 Maiden Lane, Suite 704, New York NY 10038

www.continuumbooks.com

First published 2010

British Library Cataloguing-in-Publication Data
A catalogue record for this book is available from the British Library.

Library of Congress Cataloging-in-Publication Data
Abbott, John.
 Overschooled but undereducated : is the crisis in education jeopardizing our
adolescents? / John Abbott with Heather McTaggart.
   p. cm.
 Includes bibliographical references.
 ISBN 978-1-85539-623-4 (hardcover)
1. Education--Social aspects--1. 2. Education--Aims and objectives--Great
Britain. 3. Education--Great Britain--History. 4. Teenagers--Great Britain--Social
conditions. I. McTaggart, Heather. II.
Title.

 LC191.8.G7A34 2010
 370.941--dc22

2009006370
                         ISBN: 1–8553–9623–8 (hardback)

Typeset by Kenneth Burnley, Wirral, Cheshire
Printed and bound in Great Britain by . . .

Contents

Dedicated to our respective children,
Peter, David and Tom, Leigh, Sheila, Connor and Jessica,
and to all those who, having listened to our lectures,
have gone out determined to find better ways of
supporting adolescents

Foreword

When I first met John Abbott 20 years ago he told me a story: as a young teacher at the prestigious Manchester Grammar School he had led several expeditions of boys to study agriculture in rural pre-revolutionary Iran.

After a week, the village headman felt he knew John well enough to ask him a difficult question: 'These young men,' he said, 'they are so tall, so strong, so beautiful. But what use are they? They cannot reap, they cannot ride a donkey, they cannot make a fire, they cannot even sew or sweep or cook like our girls.'

This stopped young Abbott in his tracks. Not only were these flowers of English youth useless in rural Iran, they were also useless at home. They could not change a plug or boil an egg. They lived their lives unconnected to 'real life' and unnecessary to it. Their mothers made their beds and their lunchboxes, their fathers dished out pocket money, and both parents drove them everywhere. They made no contribution to home life, they did not work in the holidays or weekends, they were not responsible for anything. Little was expected of them, except to conform at school and pass exams.

John Abbott's book is a call to us all – parents, teachers, man on the street and woman in the House of Lords – to change the way we treat children, especially teenagers. Instead of seeing the teenage years as an aberration to be tolerated, we need, he believes, to take advantage of the changes that are going on in the teenage brain, and allow young people to learn as nature intended – by experience and in a multitude of ways. Teenagers must be stretched, they need diverse experiences to jolt them out of apathy and into learning mode.

Abbott argues that both common sense and science – specifically, new insights into how the brain develops – should force us to overhaul our attitude to those scary teenage aliens slamming doors and grunting. And overhaul those attitudes we must – adolescence is an opportunity, not a problem. Understand that, and it changes everything.

It used to be thought that the brain was fully developed by the age of twelve. Not so, says Abbott. 'Far from being fully finished, the teenage brain remains a teeming ball of possibilities, raw material which is wildly exuberant and waiting to be synaptically shaped.' And listening to your iPod while hanging around the park swings won't promote the best synaptic shape. Nor will sitting in a classroom learning (or dozing) by rote. The adolescent brain sloughs off unused circuits and develops the most exercised ones like mad. So to give teenagers the best chance of becoming happy, productive adults, all their circuits need regular workouts. They need to challenge, to be challenged, to experiment; above all, to take risks and learn from experience. If they are prevented from this, they become stuck in a permanent childhood of dependence, caution and clone-like acceptance.

Abbott has another lesson drawn from the traditional habits of other cultures, and indeed from our not-so-distant past. Apprenticeship – learning alongside an experienced older person – is, says Abbott, such a longstanding practice that it is hard wired within the brain of every teenager today. It is what their instincts tell them they should do – as is the idea that they should face difficult tests to win the approval of a mentor. Some African and aboriginal tribes still send their young men off to fend for themselves in the bush, or set them initiation rituals that test them and confirm their worth to the community. Many would argue that National Service did the same.

But even knowing all this, knowing that it's natural for young people to learn through experience, we still expect teenagers to sit quietly in class and do what teacher tells them. And at home we'd like them to stay in their bedrooms and swot. What we are doing, Abbott fears, is stunting the development of the brain and producing overcautious, unimaginative, conservative clones: fine for the days of few bosses and armies of manual workers, fine for passing exams even, but no good for surviving in twenty-first-century life.

Abbott would like learning to happen all over the place, by which he means a lot less in the classroom. He sees the purpose of education as the gradual weaning of the young from dependency so that by the time they are seventeen, our children should be self-motivated learners, equipped with the confidence and judgement to be useful to society.

John Abbott is persistent. For the last 40 years he has been trying, with undiminished vigour, to change the way we teach. He has drawn on anthropology, neuroscience and his own decades of experience to prove his central point: that we have misunderstood the nature of adolescence.

His methods have been extraordinarily successful. But politicians, themselves the product of our educational system, are loyal to at least some version of it. And they are too frightened of the conservative (small 'c') voter, to think big. The British Government, in desperate need of a workable education policy that does not turn out disaffected, incompetent young people, or which fails to develop the creative, imaginative, self-reliant and confident future citizen, should take *Overschooled but Undereducated* very seriously indeed – as should we all.

Abbott has been passionately trying to make us see sense for 40 years. It is high time we listened.

Prue Leith

Acknowledgements

This book could never have been written were it not for the invaluable help of many people. The footnotes testify to the range of writers whose ideas have helped to shape our argument that, by over-schooling young people, society is effectively under-educating children in ways which undermine their natural intelligence. The nature of the reviews so far received testify to the book's widespread significance. We are equally indebted to the comments and suggestions made in the hundreds of discussions that have followed lectures given on this topic across the British Isles, the United States and Canada, and around the world over the past fourteen or fifteen years. None of this would have been possible had it not been for the enthusiasm and commitment of the Trustees of the 21st Century Learning Initiative, especially David Peake, Tom Griffin and Christopher Wysock Wright, whose unflinching support over many years has ensured that this story can now be told.

As joint authors we are indebted to our families for their patience, love and care over the many months that it has taken to draw these ideas together, and especially to Susanne Daws for her patient typing and good-humoured editing of numerous drafts; to Janet Lawley, John Senior, Carolyn Shirley, Vicki Wolfe and Suzanne Anderson for their assistance with the research on which we have drawn; to Terry Ryan for his insistence that this book should be written in the first place; to Anne Abbott for her ability to spot split infinitives, incorrect punctuation and sloppy language; and to David Abbott for the design of the text and the management of the website which supports the book. Beyond these we never cease to be amazed at the dedication of all those who have either read sections of the book in draft form, or who have taken time out to review it in its entirety. We are particularly grateful to Professor Sir Gus Nossal, formerly President of the World's Immunology Association and of the Australian Academy of Sciences for technical advice; to Neil Richards, Principal of Atlantic College and formerly Principal of the Yokohama International School; to Dr Bernard Trafford, Chairman of the Headmasters' Conference; to Dr Helen Drennen, Principal of Wesley College, Melbourne, Australia; and to Dr Paul Cappon, Director General of the Canadian Council on Learning; and Giles Gherson, Deputy Minister of Communications, Ontario. We extend particular thanks to two exceptional primary school headteachers, Nigel Coren of West Sussex and Peter Mountstephen of Bath. Without their support we would have made numerous mistakes. Our thanks to Bridget Gibbs of Continuum, and her team of editorial production assistants, and to Jim Houghton.

Our thanks in advance to all those who are likely to gather around these ideas and create that ferment of interest which we believe is waiting to be united to propel this book into the 'must-read' category of at least 100,000 readers.

Introduction

Civilized society can never be taken for granted since human passions are complex, contrary and potentially self-destructive. 'Human history becomes more and more a race between education and catastrophe'[1] was an essay I was required to write as a seventeen-year-old in the late 1950s. A heavy topic it might now seem to tax the minds of adolescents, but we knew then that we were within a year of being conscripted into the Army, and possibly fighting on some distant battlefield. Our teachers were determined to challenge us to understand why we thought as we did, and why we accepted that our civilization was worth dying for. The age of seventeen was not too soon to show that we were mature enough to become adults.

I was reminded of that essay years later when, lecturing in Africa on the subject of adolescence, an African greeting '*Umbutu*' was explained to me. It is the traditional greeting used when people of different tribes come together. Literally it means, 'How goes it with the children?' It is an enquiry about the 'state' of the next generation. It is every bit as much to do with rearing in the home and community as it is with formal schooling. It is about the preparation and nurture of young people to take over from their ageing parents. It is nothing short of a life-and-death issue, for on that depends the continuation of a way of living, of a civilization. Adolescence, to those Africans, was too important to be ignored.

Indigenous people the world over, from the native tribes of

North America and back to the ancient Greeks, knew something which advanced Western cultures seem to have forgotten – unless their young men and women could prove that they were tough enough to play a full role in adult society, they were simply cast out. Not that any of those societies would have survived if they rejected too many of their young – life was too precious for such a waste. The ongoing survival of the tribe was totally dependent on a supply of responsible and tough new adolescents replacing the worn-out skills of their elders. Although initiation ceremonies were tough, few failed because their entire education up to that time had prepared them to stand on their own feet.

Adolescents in our Western society are nowadays getting an increasingly bad press, from newspaper reports detailing anything from rude and brutish behaviour to random stabbings. It is too easy to assume that the problem lies with them, something that has gone wrong with their internal psychological make-up. That is simplistic, and very wrong. Many adolescents are courteous, responsible, idealistic and as horrified by violent crime as any of us, but too many adults have become so engrossed in their own affairs that they have forgotten to give youngsters the opportunity to prepare themselves to be the next generation of responsible adults. This has gone on now for several generations, so today we are surrounded by many older men and women who have never properly grown up – people who cannot really stand on their own feet. This is becoming an ever more serious issue as the years pass.

Neuroscientists are discovering that adolescence, for reasons this book will explain, is a period of profound structural change in the brain, an integral part of its progression from birth to adulthood. This means that adolescents are especially susceptible to environmental, social and emotional pressures.

Adolescence confuses adults almost as much as it disturbs the individual adolescent. Inquisitive yet confrontational, capable of amazing energy when roused yet frequently infuriatingly laid back, we don't know whether we love them or despair of them. No longer children to be told what to do, they simply blow hot or cold quicker than the rest of us. Apparently lacking adult powers of judgement, they are often as uncertain as to how to behave as are adults in how to respond to them. Curiously, it is often those who had to batter their way through adolescent trauma who are, years later, more successful than those who had an easier passage.

This relatively short book about the development and education of young people raises a quite fundamental question. By misunderstanding teenagers' instinctive need to do things for themselves, isn't society in danger of creating a system of schooling that so goes against the natural grain of the adolescent brain that formal education ends up *trivializing* the very young people it claims to be supporting? This is an unintended, but inevitable, consequence of an outdated design brief (from the shape of schools, the nature of the curriculum, the structure of assessment, and the way teachers teach). By failing to keep up with appropriate research in the biological and social sciences, current educational systems continue to treat adolescence as a problem rather than an opportunity bequeathed to them through the genetic transfer of important mental predispositions to learn in particular ways. These predispositions, once activated, transform the clone-like learning of the pre-pubescent child through adolescence into the self-directed learning of the mature adult.

Our ancestors understood this intuitively and saw adolescence as a special time in life in which both mind and muscle needed to be stretched. Until the late nineteenth century in the

Western world there was no room for youngsters who couldn't do anything properly. Basic skills of reading, writing and arithmetic might be taught in a classroom, but apprenticeship was most people's finishing school, as it still is in some places to this day. It was apprenticeship that gave young people an education for an intelligent way of life. It was the process by which teenagers could both learn useful skills while also modelling themselves on socially approved adults, thus providing a safe passage from childhood to adulthood in psychological, moral, social and economic ways.[2]

Apprentices learned well in those days. They knew the inherent satisfaction of a job well done, and they had the time to refine their skills and learn in depth. However, as factories became ever more productive, and the cult of economic efficiency grew, the craftsman could not compete with such a single-minded focus on profit-making. So the opportunity for apprenticeships decreased and the frustrated energy and high spirits of unemployed youths – too large now to stay sitting in a classroom, and too young to be employed – threatened the social order. By 1904, American psychologists, observing the apparent chaotic and dysfunctional life of adolescents with nothing meaningful to do and no role models to follow, started to define adolescence as a kind of disease brought on, they assumed, by the rapid development of sex hormones. This, they argued forcefully (but simplistically) to politicians willing to be impressed, had to be treated with extended years of schooling to 'protect' teenagers from the risks of adult life until they were mature enough to deal with them on their own.

In this was the birth of the modern secondary school – a kind of holding ground in which the problems of adolescence could be worked through so that eventually youngsters would be mature enough to deal with adult society. School was the exact opposite of apprenticeship. Schoolchildren were required to sit docilely in classrooms, listening to the received wisdom of the teacher and then reproduce that knowledge when tested. Independent and creative thinking was not encouraged, for that threatened the teacher's control of the rest of the class. Young apprentices, on the other hand, had to be so put through their paces that the older they became the less dependent they were on the craftsman, and the more confident they were in demonstrating their ability to solve problems. Every skill learned, every experience internalized, increased the apprentice's sense of autonomy. Recent research in cognitive science and neurobiology makes it obvious that apprenticeship was a culturally appropriate response to the neurological changes in the adolescent brain. Apprenticeship was a form of intellectual weaning whereby the more skilful and thoughtful the apprentice became, the less dependent he or she would be on the teacher. The German philosopher Nietzsche put it succinctly: 'It is a poor teacher whose pupils remain dependent on him.'

If Western society is to survive (and it really is as serious as that), it is essential that all those involved with young people escape from that assumption made 100 years ago by early psychologists, that adolescence is an aberration, an inconvenience, an irrelevance which has to be got over. That is what this book is all about. While the human brain has evolved to enable each of us to function effectively in complex situations – we naturally think big, and act small – modern education has become sidetracked into creating specialists who are well qualified in their own disciplines, but nothing like as good at seeing the wider impact of their actions. Because formal schooling has done its best to neutralize the impact of adolescence, recent generations of young people have been deprived of the strength that comes from knowing that they are not frightened of taking difficult decisions, and if necessary picking up the pieces when things go wrong. We have effectively lost the plot: adolescence is an opportunity, not a threat. Understand that, and it changes everything.

This book has been a long time in the writing. It draws very heavily on the work of Education 2000, a British not-for-profit foundation of which I was Director between 1985 and 1995, and on the subsequent work of The 21st Century Learning Initiative.[3] The Initiative is a transnational research group whose work started in conjunction with the Johnson Foundation at Wingspread[4] in Wisconsin. There a team of some 60 researchers, policy-makers, politicians and practitioners started to bring together thinking from different perspectives to produce a synthesis across the biological and social sciences on the principles of human learning. In late 1999 the Initiative moved its base back to England and in the past eight years has delivered training programmes and given more than 500 lectures in various parts of the United States and Canada, in South America, across Europe and the Near East, Africa, Indonesia, Malaysia, Japan, Korea, Australia and throughout the British Isles. I began to explore many of the arguments in my three earlier books, *Learning Makes Sense*, *The Child is Father of the Man* and *The Unfinished Revolution* with Terry Ryan.[5]

This is a short book intentionally. Extensive work in Canada in conjunction with the Canadian Council on Learning[6] over the past three years, and the energetic and determined enthusiasm of my Canadian co-author, Heather MacTaggart, that I should not lose the urgent message of these findings in too much technical detail, means that this book has been made as reader-friendly as possible. That it is written from an English perspective should not detract from its value to people in other

English-speaking countries,[7] for while their attitudes towards children and the shape of their education systems will inevitably reflect their own national identity, go back only 100 years and the origins of many of these national systems were brought to their shores by immigrants from England.[8] Some readers might wish to speed-read Chapter 5 and much of Chapter 6 so as to get to the meat of the argument from Chapter 7 onwards. They might then find that they would want to return to the more detailed explanation of educational policy at a later stage. All readers will need to interpret the issues raised in the book through the lens of their own circumstances and culture, and knowledge of their own history.

Our task has been to synthesize[9] an array of research from both the physical and social sciences and show how these insights can contribute to a better understanding of human learning, especially as this relates to adolescence. If in any way this has led us to trivialize what is to them their life's work, we apologise unreservedly, and ask them respectfully how they would have expressed the essence of their research in a few words, and still made it possible to complete the jigsaw of a picture.[10]

An education system that truly went with the natural way in which people learn – I call it 'going with the grain of the brain' – would prepare children in their younger and pre-pubescent years for the self-defining struggle that is adolescence. A delightful story illustrates this well. A man, seeing a butterfly struggling on the footpath to break out of its now useless cocoon, bent down, and, with his pocket knife carefully cut away the cocoon and set the butterfly free. To the man's dismay the butterfly flapped its wings weakly for a while, then collapsed and died. A biologist later told him that this was the worst thing he could have done, for the butterfly needed the struggle to develop the muscles to fly. 'By robbing the butterfly of the struggle, you inadvertently made him too weak to live', the biologist explained.

All children need the struggle of adolescence to sort themselves out and put away those childish behaviours which earlier had served them well. Sometimes alone, often with their peers and supported by the guidance of wise and caring adults, adolescents need a careful mixture of guidance and the space to work things out for themselves. Through the struggle of adolescence they develop the strength for adult life. To waste adolescence is to deny future generations the strength that is essential to deal with the ever-changing scenes of life.

Neither our writing of this book, nor your reading of it, is an end in itself. Hopefully the story told here should make you determined to help transform our overschooled but undereducated society. It is not a book which, once read, you should ever be able to put away on the bookshelf. This is a call to action to create 'responsible subversives', people in all walks of life ready to face up to the tragic consequences of our society's failure to understand the significance of adolescence. When that happens, things really will change for the better.

John Abbott

Do not confine your children to your own learning,
for they were born in another time.

Ancient Hebrew proverb

We have not inherited this world from our parents.
We have been loaned it by our children.

Native American tradition

I call therefore a complete and generous education
that which fits a man to perform justly, skilfully and
magnanimously all the offices both private and public,
of peace and war.

John Milton, 1644

. . . the work of the Department for Education and
Employment fits with a new economic imperative of
supply-side investment for national prosperity.

Minister of Education, 2001

1

A Fable: The Whole Story in Fewer Than 2,500 Words

Of all the animals in the woodland, surely it is the deer that most excites human imagination. A peaceful herbivore, the deer's survival over aeons of time has depended on its ability to sniff out danger, and then to run off to safety faster than any other creature. Over millions of years it has developed the sleekest and most powerful combination of bone structure, muscle and tendon, so making it a veritable icon of animal fitness.

It takes all of two years for the young fawn to learn enough about the art of survival from its mother to move off to live on its own. Once responsible for itself, the young deer has learned not to panic when danger approaches, but to stand stock still so as to attract no attention; to sniff the air for the scent of danger; to hold a leg just off the ground to detect the slightest vibration of an approaching predator; and to flex its ears to pick up the faintest of sounds. All those skills have been perfected by its ancestors over vast periods of time and have become part of the instincts that create the character of a deer. A powerful set of survival skills it seems. But now no longer quite enough.

Setting out on its own as dusk creeps over the woodland, the deer comes on a clearing of unnaturally level and hard ground. Suddenly, around a corner and approaching at high speed, comes a noisy contrivance sporting two bright headlights. The young deer does everything that its instincts have taught it to do – in an instant it becomes immobile, sniffing the air furiously,

1

sensing the vibrations and testing its muscles for action – but unsure of where to go. Mesmerized by the lights, the young deer remains rooted to the spot a split second too long, and that young prince of animals, the ultimate descendant of an ages-old line of evolution, is killed instantly as it is hit head-on by a car. The car is probably a write-off, and the driver – if he or she is lucky enough to survive – curses the animal for its 'lack of intelligence' in not getting out of the way.

Like the deer, humans too are the result of an incredibly long saga of evolutionary adaptations that have taken us to the point where we have the intelligence and motor skills to build a car, send an astronaut into outer space, and to carry out phenomenally complicated medical operations using the power of the new nanotechnologies.[1] Because humans have evolved big brains rather than a deer's athletic anatomy, it takes our young far longer to grow up.[2] Unlike the fawn, whose brain was nearly fully formed at birth, human babies are born with incredibly premature brains so that two-thirds of brain growth happens after birth (an evolutionary compromise made necessary by the narrowness of the woman's birth canal resulting from our species learning to stand upright).[3] So most human brain growth is shaped, not simply by instincts in the womb, but by the lessons we draw from real-life experience. Here is the secret of our phenomenal brain: every baby is born with a variety of inherited predispositions that enable it to so internalize such real-life experiences that it is able literally to grow its own brain (in a way that the fawn does not) and so reflect the increasing complexity of the environment in which it finds itself. Thus humans have the capability to adapt, in very quick time, to almost any environment – always provided they keep every one of their mental antennae alert to further environmental change.[4]

Within the past 300 years (a mere split second on our evolutionary time-scale) our ancestors have developed a range of technologies that have enabled our species to spread out across the globe. There are now some twenty times as many of us as there were when the first steam engine was invented in 1728; ten times as many of us as there were in 1824 when the first railway engine enabled a man to go faster than on the back of a horse, and two-and-a-half times as many as there were at the start of the Second World War less than 70 years ago. This vastly inflated population has only been made possible by turning much of the world's population into *specialists*, people who so concentrate on the efficient production of the individual components of a machine or a process, that they have little or no understanding of how any of the pieces actually come together.

Over the past 200 years, fewer young people have been learning about growing up through participating in what were until very recently family farms, businesses or community projects for which they had to learn how every sub-part contributed to the usefulness of the final product. They had to know how things worked, for theirs was a world in which connectivity was obvious – the strength of a chain was well understood to be dependent on its weakest link, just as the speed of a convoy depended on the speed of the slowest ship. Ours is a world of information saturation where the power of computers doubles every eighteen months, and it is estimated that the world produces about five exabytes of new information per year (an exabyte is a billion gigabytes). That's about 37,000 times the amount of information held in the Library of Congress. This brings enormous opportunities: ten years ago who would have thought of 'Googling' an old friend, and five years ago who would have known what a 'wiki' was?

But it has also brought problems. In our search for greater

material rewards, we seem to have decided that there is no longer any reason for young people to learn, as did the apprentices of old, by working alongside older people whose daily livelihood depended on the entire team completing a product that was needed, and was saleable. Instead, and especially in the past 60 years, we have decided that youngsters should spend even longer studying in ever greater detail, and in theory rather than practice, a single aspect of a sub-component, or a sub-discipline, as defined by somebody else. This, we are told, will enable the wonderful productivity of the present technological world to thrive.

In exchange for what was once the satisfaction gained from a job well done, as shipyard workers cheered when the boat they had built together for two or three years finally slipped into the water, people are now paid good money for a job that may have little or no intrinsic satisfaction. All it gives them is a wadge of £20 notes to spend in their free time, but not the satisfaction of a job well done. Too many of us don't even realize how vulnerable this makes us, because we have too readily exchanged wealth today for any sense of personal responsibility for the future. Education for many has come to mean doing what you are told and not asking awkward questions.

Cultural speciation – cultural change requiring people to modify their behaviours and attitudes – proceeds infinitely faster than does *biological speciation*, the development of biological adaptations to changed sets of circumstances. In other words, what we are now expecting from individuals in our so-called advanced culture has far outrun those adaptations inherited from the past which, when properly utilized, streamline the operation of the brain. While the human race is wonderfully empowered by its ancestors, it is certainly constrained as well. It seems that we are endlessly adaptable, but only up to a point. Being driven to live in ways which are utterly uncongenial to our inherited traits simply drives people mad.[5]

In the past 20 or 30 years scientists have learned much about the grain of the brain. We now know that, because of our initial physical vulnerability, we learn a whole raft of skills in the first seven or eight years of our lives through closely imitating the actions of our parents and teachers. Young children's learning is clone-like. It is entirely appropriate that a young fawn should grow up as a mirror of its parents. But for a human child to grow up merely as a clone at a time when the cultural and economic environment is changing so rapidly, would be nothing short of a disaster. In our time the next generation has to be equipped to go where no one has gone before.

To do this we must not forget the past, but at the same time we have to recognize that to twenty-first-century man the past is only a partial clue to the future. The massive structural changes in the adolescent brain that scientists are now discovering through extensive functional MRI scans, apparently shake the internal mechanisms of a teenage brain to its roots. If this is true, and all the signs would suggest that it is, then these have to be essential evolutionary adaptations that ensure the survival of the human race by forcing teenagers to break away from their parents and teachers. 'Get off my back,' adolescents down the ages have pleaded, 'leave me alone. Give me space.' Adolescence is about growing up and no longer thinking like a child. It's about ceasing to be a clone. Sitting still (if only for part of the time!) may be an appropriate learning environment for the pre-pubescent child, but it is largely inappropriate for adolescents whose biological predispositions urge them to find out things for themselves.

And here is the crux of the present advanced world's dilemma. Little more than 100 years ago, American psychologists started to define this self-defining rebelliousness of adolescence as a disease, an aberration, something that had gone wrong, something that meant that teenagers were becoming a threat to themselves. Psychologists and educational bureaucrats alike concluded that something had to be done to prevent teenagers from screwing up. Because that was how they saw it. Adolescence seemed suddenly to be a threat to the careful and comfortable world that teachers of the earlier years had created.[6]

Educational administrators saw only one answer to the problem: put adolescents into school for longer and longer, and give them so much studying to do that they wouldn't have the time or energy to question what an adult society was actually doing to them. And we are still doing this today. So policy-makers, with little background in the neurological processes, expected that, by about the age of 22 or 23, the next generation of young people would have been 'broken in' to the currently defined way of doing things. In this, their thinking resembled that of horse breeders who, until very recently, thought it necessary to break in a young foal after it has run relatively wild for two years. Now horse breeders carefully study the temperament of every foal, and then define unique training programmes that build upon, and extend, what each can do naturally. Human adolescents crave and deserve no less. Deep down there stirs within them the urge to climb the mountains of the mind and see what possibilities lie before them; they are innately Big Picture thinkers, and frequently upset older generations by questioning the compromised lives so many of us lead. That is their nature. It is the apparently unreasonable dreams of adolescence that, years later, drive the progress of what we are proud to call our civilization. It has always been so.

And yet, curiously, educators and politicians over decades have come to see schooling as a way of breaking children into what society defines as growing up, through becoming com-placent pupils dependent on instruction.[7] More recently, society has so outlawed adolescence that most people simply accept the specialized roles that have been created for them, and have but a limited capability to look beyond their restricted world-view to see the ecological, environmental and social crises that are hurtling towards them.

By trying to subvert the natural processes of growing up in order to fit more comfortably into our present economic state, we have created whole generations of young people and adults who are now mesmerized by the bright lights of a way of living that is hurtling, out of control, towards us. Like the young deer, we too are transfixed by the lights which are about to destroy us. Far too many of today's so-called educated people know of no way to find a solution that has not already been prepared for them and described in a textbook. This is because we have effec-tively told young people not to think for themselves, but to follow instructions. This could well be the end of the world which our ancestors laboured to create, and which we have inherited. If it is, it will be our fault for not using the power of our brains to avoid the fate of the dodo.

*   *   *

The argument of this book is that the world crisis that is upon us is the unintended consequence of an education system designed at another time and for another purpose,[8] and now utterly inappropriate to human and planetary needs.[9] To turn the tables in time to avert any or all of the four great crises facing humanity – climate change, terrorism, over-exploitation of resources and sheer mental collapse – we have to start educat-ing people to think responsibly for themselves and to recognize the connections between phenomena that our educated specialists until now seem so incapable of comprehending.[10] In the recognition that adolescence is an opportunity, not a threat, lies society's best assurance of a positive future.

2

The Wonder of Learning

Humans have been using their brains to think for as long as they have been using their stomachs to digest food – both are totally natural processes that we simply take for granted. Just as babies learned to take their mother's milk long before anyone wrote a guide to motherhood, so children were learning to work things out for themselves long before anyone thought of setting up a school. Most of the schools that today's children attend, however, were built when prevailing wisdom assumed that children were born to be taught rather than to learn. Which is why, for so many children, the wonder of learning has been replaced by the tedium of trying to remember what they were taught about something which really didn't interest them very much in the first place.

Making a distinction between learning and teaching is tricky, for, while teaching can stimulate learning, the wrong kind of teaching or the wrong kind of circumstance can too easily destroy a youngster's confidence in learning. The capacity to learn is apparently limitless, but the capacity to be taught depends on who is around to instruct you. This tension is important to understand because popular culture has come to assume that learning is virtually synonymous with schooling and teaching. Learning, it is assumed, is dependent upon sitting still and listening carefully to what you are told so that you can later recall it with total accuracy in an examination. Memory of this kind is important, but learning is so much more than a sophisticated recall system. It is not so much about how effectively a child searches the internet, as it is about how he or she evaluates the accuracy of what they find, and then spots its relevance to what they are trying to work out.[1]

It is the *working out for yourself* bit that is so important. An eminent American biologist,[2] who spent many years living with native peoples in the depths of the jungles of New Guinea, expressed deep concern for the superficiality of Western schooling. He claimed that native peoples impressed him as being on average more intelligent, more alert, more expressive, and more interested in what was going on around them, and more able to respond flexibly to unusual situations, than was the average American or European. If that thought surprises you, you are going to find the ideas set out in this book intriguing. A teacher from India who had worked in England for ten years wrote recently:

> It seems to me that many youngsters in the developing world are, in practical terms, far better educated than their peer groups here in England. In India children growing up really do understand how things fit together. Here in London we teach them about *things*, but back in India they know from their own experience for they have to live their own learning.[3]

That is a most telling phrase: 'Live their own learning.' It's simple, really: learning is a consequence of having to work things out for yourself. Teachers and parents can help children, but only if they realize that they are simply there to help learning happen; it is the learner, the child, who has to do the work. It is through exercising the brain that the brain grows, and learning proceeds.

So, this is our starting point: humans are insatiably curious. It starts early in life with the darting, inquisitive eyes of a young baby apparently surprised at the new world it finds itself in, and asking, 'What's going on out *here*?'[4] Weeks later the baby's first flickering recognition of other people causes parents to gasp in wonder at this little bundle of a personality and in their turn ask, with equal surprise, 'What's going on in *there*?' And so, on through the persistent exploration of the terrible twos, the testing of wills by three-year-olds, and to the continuous search to make sense of what's going on around them, which culminates in that explosion of those wonderful words of sheer delight: 'Ah, now I get it!' Those wonderful 'eureka' moments that we never forget.[5]

Despite many children's apparent indifference to school, coupled with the turmoil of adolescence, humans really were born to learn. We live by our wits, by questioning everything. It's the one thing our species seems better able to do than any other. By asking good questions we make sense of life, and find this exciting and personally fulfilling. The search to make sense is fundamental to our survival, and has been there since the beginning of time. Learning doesn't begin when a child first enters the school gates or end when they leave the classroom; even for the most motivated it can sometimes be the other way around. Why should this be? We have to go back to some first principles to appreciate what is going on.

Humans have been asking profound questions for a very long time. Much of the knowledge that we take for granted started long ago as questions among our distant ancestors.[6] Take the matter of time and space. To our ancestors, with no books to read, no theatres to attend and no films to watch, the sky was their one constant companion, and the sun, moon, planets and stars were as familiar to them as are the stars (interesting word, isn't it!) of today's soap operas. The sky was to them an object of total fascination, holding, they thought, the explanation for everything that happens. Every star was given a story, a character and a sphere of influence. Their movements were studied as carefully as an Enigma code-breaker studied the incoming wartime radio signals for signs of hidden meaning, for irregularities and repeating patterns. The blackness and mystery of space was the nursery for human inquisitiveness, and it was in the study of mathematics – especially algebra and geometry – that so many of the intellectual skills that make up our 'learning toolbox' of today were forged.

Look to your own experience. Some of you might have sought relief from the boredom of an overnight flight and peered out at the star-studded sky through your window. Beautiful the stars may seem, but their positions mean little to most of our generation. If you happened to be crossing the Pacific you might remember hearing that, only 100 or so years ago, young Polynesians still learned to navigate their canoes over thousands of miles of featureless oceans by so understanding the ever-changing relationship of their canoe to certain stars that they would invariably land on the right atoll after perhaps 100 days at sea. You probably marvelled at the skills they had – and you don't think you could ever have – and after a while you reverted to switching on your in-flight entertainment system, and perhaps spent time watching the route map. Every 30 seconds the little symbol for your plane jerked a fraction as it readjusted its position. You started to ponder the marvels that kept your plane in the air, and of the technology involved in global positioning systems (GPS). That technology continuously updates the route map, and keeps planes on exactly predicted courses by monitoring their position and expressing it in degrees, minutes and seconds. Why, in this age of decimalization, you might wonder, do we still hang on to what seems a pretty clumsy way of measuring time and space?

Some of you may also have remembered that it was the ancient Babylonians who, more than 4,000 years ago, tried to do just that as they attempted to explain the movements of the planets.[7] They dismissed decimalization as being imperfect because the number 'ten' can only be divided (as a whole number) into two parts of five. Sixty, they decided, was a far more versatile number, for it could be divided into halves, thirds, quarters, fifths, sixths, tenths, twelfths, fifteenths and twentieths. That is the reason why a circle has 360 degrees, and every degree is divided into 60 minutes, and every minute into 60 seconds, so that when applied to a globe they give an exact location to within less than 100 yards. Today's air traffic controllers don't even question the system, and your pilot is perfectly content to leave his aircraft on automatic control for hour after hour as the technology updates your position with total accuracy, through the application of a 4,000-year-old Babylonian mathematical theory.

If that isn't enough to convince you that what we so often assume to be knowledge started off as somebody else's good questions, then ask yourself why it is that our concept of a month, just as a woman's menstrual cycle, is dependent on the phases of the moon. Why should that be? Once you have pondered this, try to work out how it was that someone long ago decided that there should be 24 hours in a day – why not 25, 50 or even 100? What we trust as knowledge frequently has its roots in profound questions asked across the generations.[8]

How does it come about that we humans, rather than monkeys or your pet dog, ponder such issues and propose such theories? Is it because experience forces us to do this, or is it something very deep in our nature that prompts such questions? Maybe it's a curious mixture of the two? Probably you don't realize, sitting comfortably as you are flying at 35,000 feet, that you are simply rehearsing in your mind the very question that Plato asked Socrates 2,500 years ago: 'Can you tell me, are our behaviours taught, or are they acquired by practice? Or are they neither to be practised nor learnt, but are they something that comes to men by nature or some other way?'[9]

More than 2,000 years later we are still trying to answer such questions. Why is it that humans are so much more inquisitive than other creatures, and how do we take the answers to our question to formulate them into knowledge? We are still not quite sure what we mean by 'nature' when we talk of human nature. What is it about our nature that means we humans are 'born to learn'? We certainly are not as athletic as the antelope; we haven't the strength of a lion or the wings of an eagle, but we do appear to have an amazing array of ways of comprehending what is happening around us. If only we could understand what is the 'nature' of human nature, we would probably get closer to the heart of what it means to be human.

Of all the wise and pithy descriptions that seek to explain the process of learning, it was the sixteen words attributed to Confucius a good thousand years after the Babylonian mathematicians, that do this best:

> Tell me, and I forget;
> Show me, and I remember;
> Let me do, and I understand.

These words are too important to be passed over rapidly. They are important enough to read again, one line carefully after the next. We humans are by nature suspicious of what other people tell us for fear that we're being manipulated to fit into their agendas. Consequently, simply telling a youngster something you think they ought to know – but they don't want to have anything to do with – activates an amazing array of 'crap' detectors in the young brain. All too often, what we tell them just doesn't register. It's *your* answer, not theirs. It's not what they're looking for, so it's ignored. But if you take time out and instead of telling them the answer show youngsters why something is as it is, you'll probably engage their whole attention, so that they may well push you to one side and demand to 'let me do it for myself'.[10] To a parent in a hurry, a teacher or even an enthusiast over coffee after a good dinner, it's only when you climb off your soapbox and let the student, or your dinner companion, take the issue over from you and, literally, *play* with it that they will really come to understand what it is about.

Recently, cognitive scientists have discovered that it is on the effectiveness of the individual's brain to sort out what matters from that which is merely routine or a distraction, that the individual is dependent for survival. There is no short-cutting this process, for you are up against that natural way of learning, that 'grain of the brain'. This is the way nature has made us; simply to remember something is a poor substitute for understanding it; to learn so as to really understand, rather than simply to remember, is what is so critical to the individual's survival from day to day.

*   *   *

The human brain is thought to be the most complex organism in the entire universe. It contains approximately a million million neurons, has 500 trillion synapses (connections between neurons) and sufficient 'wiring', at 70,000 miles, to circle the earth twice. It has more internal connections than all the leaves on all the trees in all the forests on every continent. Seeing stars, it dreams of eternity. Hearing birds, it makes music. Smelling flowers, it is enraptured. Touching tools, it transforms the earth. But deprived of these sensory experiences, the human brain withers and dies. An awesome thought.[11]

The brain learns because that is its prime job.[12] 'Use it or lose it' is the key to its growth.[13] It is our ultimate survival mechanism, constantly taking in fresh information, searching it for any abnormality that doesn't fit comfortably with what it had anticipated, and then deciding what actions to take. In the complex world we humans inhabit, the brain has to operate at many levels simultaneously.[14] It is a sobering thought that none of us would be alive to read this if each and every one of our ancestors had not made enough good decisions to survive long enough to procreate. Those that didn't, simply failed to pass on their genes. The same applies to each of us now. Over vast periods of time the genes we receive from our fathers and mothers incorporated (in ways not yet totally clear) those structures for decision-making that our distant ancestors found most useful. Hard as it may be sometimes to accept, every human has just such a brain.

And we have only recently become aware of all this. Even 40 years ago, in the 'swinging sixties', when the Beatles proclaimed that 'we all live in a yellow submarine', and 'all you need is love', when the oldest of today's teachers were being trained, university courses on education hardly mentioned the brain for the very simple reason that those brain-imaging technologies with which we are now so familiar simply hadn't been invented. Few psychologists had ever seen a brain and, if they had, it would have been a dead one laid out on a slab of marble looking remarkably like three-and-a-half pounds of cold porridge. And just as unappetizing. There was nothing about its physical appearance that would suggest its importance, for the sheer minuteness of its myriad structures meant that they were not only invisible, but virtually incomprehensible. Scientists couldn't even see what they wanted to study. The brain was a black box, a mystery that no one had found the key to open.

But since the invention of PET scans (positron emission tomography) in the 1970s, knowledge of what is involved in the brain has been doubling every seven years. Eighty per cent of what we now know about the brain has been discovered only in the last twenty years. We seem to be on a roller-coaster of a knowledge explosion. It's hard to keep up with or to hold on to all the strands as new ideas come together. One set of findings is of particular significance: in the 350,000 generations (7 million years) that separate us from the Great Apes, our genetic structures only differ from them by less than 2 per cent. If you find this hard to appreciate, then imagine that a single generation is equivalent to a minute. In other words, 350,000 generations are the equivalent to all the minutes in a year that you are awake. Most of us can expect to be familiar with five generations – ourselves, our parents and grandparents, our children and our grandchildren, a span of five minutes which leaves 364 days, 23 hours, 55 minutes to represent the rest of human experience since our ancestors came down from the trees. To get only a 2 per cent difference after all that time would suggest that human evolution proceeds infinitely more slowly than any rate of change due to casual, inaccurate, physical gene copying.

Amazingly, we still look very much like chimpanzees, but our brains have evolved over this comparatively short evolutionary time to give us ten times as many brain cells as they have. It is these cells, and the way they have come to be wired together, that give the human brain a very particular 'grain' which enables each new generation to think for itself and to learn, but in ways which have been shaped by the experience of our ancestors.

We are the pre-eminent learning species, deeply influenced by the instincts and predispositions we inherit from many thousands of generations of forebears.

*   *   *

People have always fascinated me. A lifetime of travelling has given me plenty of opportunities to observe my fellow humans under many kinds of conditions. As a child I loved stories told by old people about their youth, and as a father my professional interest in human learning has merged with my fascination in watching my own children learn and develop. When my youngest son asked me, completely out of the blue, how young children learned to talk I allowed myself a moment to think of the best way of answering an eight-year-old. Impatient with the delay, Tom looked at me disparagingly: 'Daddy, that's a pretty simple question, I bet you're now going to give me a long and complicated answer!' Which is, I suppose, part of the reason for this book – to make complicated ideas relatively simple.

Another reason is my fascination with the nature of adolescence which goes back to 1968 when, as a young geography teacher, I had the opportunity of taking an expedition of seventeen-year-old English boys to spend six weeks living with nomads in the Zagros Mountains of Iran. Intriguing as this was to my students, it was probably I who gained the most from the insight this gave me into the variable nature of human intelligence – my book-learnt students out on the mountainside were as disadvantaged as would have been the experience-learnt nomads in a Manchester classroom. What, I've been asking myself ever since, should be the relationship between theoretical, book-based learning and experiential forms of learning? Between thinking and doing?

When those nomads moved, everyone had something to do, be they five-year-olds rounding up the chickens, seven- and eight-year-olds herding the sheep and goats, or the ten-year-olds who organized the loading of the donkeys. Life depended on collaboration. If any failed in their task, the tribe's well-being was put into jeopardy. Late one evening the tribal chief asked me a very deliberate question: 'We are deeply honoured to have these fine young men visit us. But we are confused. Surely such young men should be at home helping their parents with their work, and learning from them what it means to become a man?' The chief paused and looked appraisingly at his own sons, not simply with paternal pride, but as a businessman looking at his most treasured investment. 'If my sons didn't work with me, if we didn't discuss things together, how could I be sure that I was passing on to them the wisdom of my father, and his father, and his father before him, and all the knowledge that I myself built up in my lifetime?'

Beside a camel-dung fire on that distant mountainside, I tried as best I could to explain the Western model of schooling, deeply immersed as it is in a way of living which these people simply could not comprehend. I wasn't successful. Later, one of the English boys made a comment about adolescence that I shall never forget. 'I heard that question the chief asked you. I've got to know him and his sons well. I know their lifestyle is different to ours, but I would love to have that kind of relationship with my father. You see I feel I hardly know my dad. He works so hard in his office to support me and my sister that we hardly ever talk, and I've no idea what he actually does. He's always tired. It's different for the chief's sons. They have a reason for being around. They seem important to their family and their village. I seem to be a cost to my parents; they don't get very much back from me and I don't understand what makes them tick.' He paused for a long time, and then said, 'Somehow I feel sort of disconnected.'

His words have haunted me ever since. 'Disconnected.' Adolescents are neither overgrown children nor immature adults. Adolescents have a character all their own which, in the long evolution of the human race that scientists are struggling to understand, must have had an evolutionary advantage that increased a young person's chances of survival. Relationships based on friendship, affection and trust, rather than institutions or networks, matter enormously to adolescents as they jockey for position in their social hierarchies, seek mates and form alliances with their peers. We often forget that the reason many older children keep going to school is not out of fear of the teacher or any intrinsic interest in learning, but simply out of loyalty to their friends.

The training I had as a teacher hadn't helped me to understand this. It was only in the late 1950s, just before the oldest of today's teachers were still pupils themselves, that psychology had been shaken out of its hundred-year-long denial of any evolutionary influences on the way people think. Mine was a generation whose understanding about learning theory was based on Pavlov's salivating cats and dogs, correlation tests of cause and effect, and the search to equate a person's reasoning ability to a measurable Intelligence Quotient. To be wrongly assessed in such IQ tests (which happened frequently) was often devastating, and it became clear that young people very quickly came to perform at the level expected of them. Children saw through this more rapidly than did the theoretical psychologists. 'Am I just thick?' asked an obviously intelligent thirteen-year-old in Yokohama a few years ago, 'or am I only good at those things that really excite me?' Intelligence tests reduce the complexity and diversity of human nature to a single number by classifying children simplistically as being gifted, average or unintelligent. Psychologists at the time I was training to be a teacher couldn't make any sense of why a seventeen-year-old should feel 'sort of disconnected'.

*   *   *

So my questions have rumbled on over many years. If humans are born to learn, why does it go so badly wrong for some people? Why are so many youngsters apparently switched off by learning? Do modern lifestyles, in school and out, actually discourage young people from asking questions? Toddlers exhibit an insatiable curiosity – often to the alarm of their parents – yet, within weeks of starting kindergarten a five-year-old's response to its mother's question, 'What did you learn in school today?' was met with a disparaging shrug of the youngster's shoulders and the comment, 'We learned to be quiet and sit still.' Heather tells a similar story that resonates with many people, for she had a mind that worked in an idiosyncratic way, which often got her into trouble. She remembers that, at the age of eight, her class held a discussion about what they wanted to do when they grew up. One boy said, 'I want to be a doctor, then I'll be able to open up Heather's head and look inside to see why she's so stupid!' It took her a while to recover her confidence (with the active encouragement of her parents) and then, alternative thinker as she was (and is), years later she was sufficiently quick on the uptake to ask her professor a question that challenged his statistics. Recognizing that Heather had spotted something he had missed, he offered to pay her as his research assistant, so enabling her not only to cover all her university costs, but actually to make a profit as well!

So what happens to that wanting-to-know instinct? Do schools create an environment that encourages profound questions and independent thinking as children seek to sort out what is for them merely a routine or a distraction? If humans are, by nature, a learning species, do schools build on that potential and work with the grain of the brain, or do they so work against it that they roughen up the surface, and cause deep internal haemorrhaging?

'I understand all that,' one businessman told me, 'but where does that get us? I wasn't brainy enough to do well in school, but somehow when I got out into the marketplace I thrived. Does that mean I'm a late developer and could have done better in school? And if I had been a better pupil, would my brain have evolved in a different way, which might have meant that I wouldn't have done anything like so well in later life?' Which raises a fascinating question: does doing well by the rules of the school possibly limit a person's ability to develop in other areas? 'It was different for me,' commented another, 'for I actually did well in school. I liked the sense of order and well-defined challenges. It was only when I left university that I came unstuck, as out there by myself everything seemed so vague that I lost my focus.'[15]

Success at school does not tell the whole story. Recently I heard a mother pick up the same theme when she said that her daughter was an inveterate hard worker, and indeed worked so hard that it was destroying her sense of excitement in life. The school was apparently delighted with her and was predicting top grades, but the mother was worried that her daughter was so single-minded that one day she would fall flat on her face. 'My son is the total opposite,' she said. 'He hardly ever completes work on time, and scrapes through every exam with the minimum of effort, but I have to admit that he is much happier than his sister. He'll succeed even if he never passes a single exam, but I really do fear for my daughter!'

So how has it come about that we humans are able to ask the big questions of life, about time and space, and about how we learn? These were questions that have been asked in every generation since Plato's conversation with Socrates. Many were the solutions proposed by the philosophers; the brain is like a blank slate waiting for experience to write upon it, said some. It is an empty vessel waiting to be filled, or a candle waiting to be lit, or a statue waiting to be 'released' from a block of marble, reasoned others. More than 2,000 years later we are still trying to find an answer and adding questions of our own. What have we inherited from our ancestors, and how do children learn so very quickly in their first few years? We marvel at the wonder of the learning of a child, or of the sophisticated stories of apparently illiterate tribesmen. Our learning potential is surely one of the greatest wonders of all time.

At conferences I frequently ask participants to reflect on what was their most powerful learning experience, and how this changed the way they think about education. You could try this for yourself. My own story goes back a long way to when I was eight, living in a large, decaying Victorian vicarage in Southsea just after the war. My father employed an old naval stoker, Mr MacFadgen, every Friday evening to carry out running repairs. MacFadgen had served his apprenticeship in the Portsmouth Dockyard as a carpenter in the 1890s, but by the time he was qualified the Navy didn't need any carpenters, and even though he had hands like a surgeon, he spent the next 50 years shovelling coal into the boilers of battleships.

Every Friday after he had finished his jobs he would sit at the bottom of the stairs and we would chat. He had a special way with children. I asked him if he had ever got bored stoking boilers. 'Not at all,' he replied. 'Every cruise I ever went on I took my carving tools with me and bits of old wood, and every port I ever went into I looked for the most beautiful girl I could find and spent the rest of the cruise carving her as a figurehead eight or nine inches tall.' I was mesmerized by his stories. He had been carving for so long that he had four tea-chests full of these beautiful figures. I was excited when he offered to teach me how to sharpen his chisels, and later as he explained how to get the most out of the grain of a piece of wood. 'Having understood all that, all you have to do now is to practise,' he said. 'You whittle away at whatever you want, and every Friday you show me.' For the next three years, Friday evenings were a very special part of my week. MacFadgen told many stories about the ports he had visited, the captains he had known, and the storms he had weathered. He explained the difference between hurricanes and typhoons, and why the monsoon season comes when it does. And he also told me about the politics of the China Seas. Years later I realized that I had been privileged to have been exposed to the ages-old relationship of the apprentice to the crafts master.

At thirteen my life changed dramatically as I was sent away to boarding school. It was a pleasant enough experience in the main but not particularly challenging. There was little woodwork on the curriculum, and I drifted through all my subjects with little enthusiasm and passed them all, with the exception of O-level Latin. In those days you couldn't get to university without that, and I failed the exam three times. The chief difficulty was that my teacher was even more bored with Latin than we were and spent all his time telling us how he had won the war single-handed in his silly little tank in the African desert. I was just about to take the exam for the fourth and final time when the school carpenter, a person so menial that he wasn't allowed into the teacher's room, told me that I had been selected to represent the United Kingdom at an international exhibition of woodcarvers.

My esteem rushed to the top of the chart. Then two or three hours later it started to sink as I realized that nobody in the school, from the headmaster downwards, would show the least interest in a woodcarving result; it wasn't a rugby match, a debating achievement, and it just didn't count. Then I fell to thinking. If I could be one of the best young woodcarvers in the country, why couldn't I pass Latin? As a seventeen-year-old I rationalized that it was because my teacher was in the way. So that afternoon I went and told him that, as I had to pass Latin in six weeks' time, I wouldn't come to any more of his lessons. I would teach myself. In doing this I obviously annoyed the teachers, and frightened myself, and by challenging the entire system my head was now on the block. I couldn't waste a moment. Into my short-term memory over the next six weeks I put virtually the whole of Caesar's Gallic War Books I and II in translation, and provided I could recognize one word in twenty of the Latin, I could remember the rest. For the last three weeks I just spent all the time memorizing my conjugations and declensions. When the results came out six weeks later I was told that I had got 89 per cent, but by that time I had forgotten all the Latin I had ever learned. But I still wood-carve. In the most powerful way possible I learned that learning and schooling are not necessarily synonymous. And that, as I've explained to numerous audiences, is why I do the job I do – to help people develop the confidence to work at their full potential, and achieve things that others might see as exceptional.

Since starting to tell that story several years ago, many are the even more remarkable stories I've heard from other people. One from Canada stands out with particular clarity. It was a late-afternoon lecture in suburban Toronto, and just before it started I was aware of a kindly-looking woman, probably in her mid-fifties, gently helping a considerably older man to a seat in the front row. All the time I was talking I was aware of the older man's eyes following my every movement and listening most attentively. Towards the end of the lecture I could see that his eyes were watering and, as his companion passed him a hand-kerchief to dab his eyes, she looked at me as much as to say 'Go on, don't stop, he's happy, not sad.' The lecture over, I went up to them and shook hands. Her grasp was firm, but his, though positive, was weak with age.

She started to explain. William had been born in Staffordshire and largely brought up by his widowed mother in the early 1930s. Approaching his fourteenth birthday, his headmaster had sent for the boy's mother and strongly recommended that William leave school at the end of term 'as he's never going to make anything out of education'. He should get a job as a ditch digger, the headmaster recommended, as it was a relatively well-paid job but physically so demanding that most people tired out in six to eight years. William was given no chance to express his own opinions, for his mother simply accepted the recommenda-tion, and a month later William started to dig ditches. Knowing that was no way of life for him, he struggled to save every penny he could and then in 1937 simply walked away from home and boarded a ship for Canada. Landing in Montreal, the only job he could get was with a gang of ditch diggers. The gang master, Pierre, was a much older man who, over the next three years, befriended the young William, treating him almost as his own son. But Pierre was obviously ill and failing rapidly, and confided to William that all his life he had been saving money just in case one day he would marry and have children of his own, and would need money for their education. That would not happen now, so he put a proposal to William: when he died, he would leave him all his money on the condition that he used this to train as a teacher. William accepted the offer and, shortly after, Pierre died.

At this point William explained how, by digging ditches during the day, and using Pierre's money to pay for his tutorial fees, he attended evening classes at teachers' college for six years. After qualifying, he got a job teaching on an Indian Reserve where his natural talent and affinity for youngsters experiencing trauma quickly drew him to the attention of the authorities. Within three years he was offered the headship of a large and very difficult inner-city school. For a few minutes his face sprang to life as he told something of the challenges of 40 years before. But he quickly tired. The woman took up the story. Putting her arm gently around William's shoulders she explained that it was he who had appointed her, a newly qualified teacher with no experience whatsoever, to teach in that difficult school. For years William had nurtured and supported a staff of young teachers that became the pride of that part of Toronto. Years later, William had been appointed principal of a teachers' college himself. William looked at me with a smile that seemed to say, 'I'm glad to be able to tell somebody from England that I really was destined for something better than just being a ditch digger!'

Such stories are legion, but sadly we don't often tell them. So now, almost whenever I address conferences, I ask my audience to explain how, from their background, they have come to be where they are now. Many of the stories are remarkable, and not infrequently emotional. Significant numbers of the people who now hold positions of considerable responsibility recall that, as adolescents, they had been truculent, self-opinionated and openly rebellious. It's important to remember these stories for, as one headteacher said recently, 'If only we reminded ourselves more often of where we had come from, we would be more determined as adults to stick by our teenage children and recognize how critically important it is to give them not only our love and support but to create the space which enables them to work things out for themselves.'[16]

These are the ideas that will unfold as you read further into this book. Working on the principle of going from what is simple to that which is more complex, we visit and re-visit issues, rather like peeling successive layers from fruit until we get to the kernel, the essence of what it's all about. Chapter 3 will tell you about the biology of human learning and a process of learning now called Constructivism that enables every individual to construct ever deeper understanding by constantly taking new ideas and relating them to what they already know.

3

Human Nature:
A Brain for All Times

So how is it that we humans are as we are? Intriguingly different to look at, fascinatingly unique in the ways we think, yet all initially shaped by the same basic blueprint. Where do our behaviours come from? Why are adolescents so different from young children? What are the deep structures that shape our behaviours from day to day? How much of human nature comes from past generations, and to what extent are we influenced by our environment?

It was thoughts such as these that intrigued the young Charles Darwin who, as an adolescent in the 1820s, used to go on long, solitary walks through the Shropshire countryside, collecting different kinds of beetles. It was these walks that prompted his thinking about inheritance, and the mechanisms that might bring about change in living organisms. It now goes without saying that Darwin was a remarkable man, but as a schoolboy his headmaster hadn't recognized that, and believed that Darwin was 'somewhat below the average level of intelligence'.[1] Yet it was the musings of this schoolboy which, years later, laid the foundation for his theory of evolution published in 1859. *The Origin of the Species* changed for ever the way we humans think about ourselves, and gave a scientific explanation for how our inherited natures interact in every generation with the dominant culture to produce the extraordinarily diverse panoply of human characteristics.

It was endless and persistent questioning that enabled

Darwin over the years to progress his thinking from why it was that not all plants of the same species grow in the same way, to establishing the general principles of inheritance. Why, within a single family, he asked himself, do some children grow tall, others short; some have green eyes, others blue or brown; or some are alert and imaginative, and others docile? Yet, within all that diversity, the overall shape and form of the species remains remarkably steady from generation to generation.[2] How could this be, Darwin asked himself, and what might there be in our biological make-up that meant that sometimes it starts to change?

After years of painstaking study, Darwin's conclusion was simple: all life, be it of an amoeba, an ant or an elephant, has to be in a state of continuous change – so we humans, like any other species, are in effect a work in progress. All that was necessary to explain such a variety of species would be for an occasional fault to occur, and then reoccur at conception in the transmission of instructions to the next generation. We now refer to these faults as mutations, and the mechanisms for transfer we now understand to be the genes. Which mutations survive would be influenced by the external environment. For example, if a chance climatic change meant that fruit trees grew taller, then the children who were fortunately born tall (through one of those mutations) would have an advantage when retrieving their food, and would be healthier than those children who had to scavenge for food on the ground. Young females in the next generation, looking to maximize the chances of survival for their young, would select as mate the best food provider – the tall one.

'It is not the strongest of the species that survives, nor the most intelligent', wrote Darwin, as he described the essence of biological diversity. 'It is the one most adaptable to change.' Tall people thrive best when the fruit is high on the tree, but another environmental change might give an advantage to a short species, or one that is fleet of foot or can swim or dig holes. Those who can't do this, the tall ones who were originally thriving, steadily lose out in passing on their genes. A new mutation is favoured as mating practices change; women start to favour 'shorties' rather than giants. Over long periods, it is the sum of all these successful mutations that creates a species' specific nature – behaviours which are unique to its own kind.

In theory, that all sounded persuasive, but the vast periods required for it to operate challenged nineteenth-century thinking to its roots. Strange as it may seem to us in the twenty-first century with our ready acceptance of large numbers, for the vast majority of human history the largest unit of time that our ancestors thought about was a person's lifespan, 'three score years and ten'. History was told in terms of human experience, in terms of generations. It was not until the mid-seventeenth century, only some 350 years ago, that a serious attempt was made by theologians and mathematicians to calculate the age of the earth. From the only data available to them, namely the genealogical tables in the book of Genesis, they calculated that the earth had been formed at 4 pm on 22 October 4004 BC In the absence of any other evidence, conventionally educated people accepted this as accurate right up to the time of Darwin.[3] If it had not been for the developing understanding in geology that by then was suggesting the world was as much as 400 million years old, Darwinian theory wouldn't have captured the public's imagination, simply because there couldn't have been enough time for evolution to have happened. Now we, in the twenty-first century, have evidence that the world is more than 4.5 billion years old, which makes it far easier for us to appreciate the reality of genetic mutations and why, to understand the present, we have to go way back into the distant past of our species.

*   *   *

It has only been in the past twenty or so years that research in archaeology, anthropology, paleoanthropology and genetics have come together within an evolutionary framework to give us a much clearer picture of the distant past of our species. Steadily we are coming to appreciate that we humans, together with all our likes and dislikes, our senses and sensitivities, reflect those deep-seated adaptations made by our distant ancestors as they adjusted to ancient environmental problems – adaptions that they passed to us in ways that Darwin explained. Those adaptations still shape the way we think and act. These explain our preferred ways of doing things. It is this variety of adaptations that accounts for the complex twists, turns and convolutions in the grain of our brain. Graphically this gives us a brain with all the texture and resilience of a piece of ancient oak, rather than the unidimensional nature of a piece of pre-formed chipboard – you can do almost anything with the oak but only one thing with the chipboard. Our brains are so special just because they bear the deep imprint of the history of our species, and that more than anything else is what makes them adaptable and open to learning.

From this perspective our growth as thinking, one-day-to-be-conscious beings started some four million years ago when enough of our ape-like ancestors came down from the trees and, balancing precariously on their back legs, started to walk out uncertainly across the savannah.[4] Our ape-like spines have still not quite got used to standing up straight, so the aching back you experienced last night as you leant over your computer is a painful reminder of how long it takes for evolution to adjust to new circumstances. As our ancestors started to explore their new world, they stretched their necks to look forward not downwards, and began to make more extensive use of their brains to deal with a more complex environment. It would take another three-and-a-half million years before the significance of those stretched necks gave us the ability to talk, but the implication of our brains becoming more active meant that they got larger, and that put pressure on the skull to get bigger.[5] Both occurred just at the stage when women, standing upright alongside the men, but only four-fifths of their height, couldn't enlarge their birth canals any further without so weakening their pelvic girdle that it would have made walking impossible.

Here was the evolutionary crunch which, more than any other single factor, has meant that if we humans were not born with an overwhelming instinct to learn – to make sense of ourselves and our surroundings – our species would have disappeared long ago. The explanation goes like this: if being able to stand up and walk gave our distant ancestors an advantage over their tree-living relatives, and if this necessitated having larger and more effective brains, something had to give. We know that other mammals give birth to their young when their brains are at least 95 per cent fully formed so that their young are virtually fully functional from the moment of birth. Human evolution has been forced to compromise so that humans give birth to their babies when their brains are only some 40 per cent fully formed. If we didn't, then pregnancy would last 27 months, and the baby would be too large to get down the birth canal. Whereas the mental development of other mammals is largely within the womb, almost two-thirds of human brain growth results from the interaction of those infant brains, brim-full of evolved predispositions to learn from their cultural environment.

Because women invest nine months of their lives carrying their babies, and then need to spend several more years nurturing them, human females need much support and for far longer than other animals. Here it seems our particular human patterns of sociability, love and bonding started to form. It was this that Darwin believed would explain so much about our 'nature', the deep structures that shape our behaviour from moment to moment. How is it, scientists began enquiring, that through smell and kissing we seek out mates who, with chromosomes sufficiently different from our own, enable us to produce healthy children? How it is that through orgasm a woman is able to test the possible resilience of a partner, and how is it that we have innate techniques for discriminating between honest people and cheats? Sociability is essential to our survival, not just in physical and emotional ways, but as learners we constantly refine our intelligence through testing out our ideas with other people.

Consequently, the way we interact today at a social and cultural level is in many ways the result of organizational skills developed by our distant ancestors out on the savannah of Africa over the course of the last few millions of years. The Sterkfontein Caves to the north of Johannesburg[6] provide fascinating clues to this process. On the cave floor, deep piles of human and animal bones provide archaeologists with a unique cross-section of life over the last 3 million years. For the first half of this time the animal bones are largely intact, but the human bones were all chewed up; we humans were then lower in the food chain than the big cats. A million and a half years ago there was a dramatic switch. It is the human bones that are largely intact, while many of the animal bones show signs of flint knives having cut off the meat. Out on the African savannah more than a million years ago humans passed from being the hunted to being the hunters. Which is why, in simple terms, it is we who go to the zoo to look at the animals, not the animals locking us up in cages so that they can observe us!

So how did this transition happen? It seems that our distant ancestors learned to act collaboratively long before our over-extended necks created in the larynx an organ that enabled us to make structured, controlled sounds at the same time as breathing. No other creature can do this. Consequently the earliest forms of human communication were dependent on a combination of sign language and, most importantly, on empathy – the ability to think ourselves into other people's feelings. Communication that is non-verbal depends on careful detection of visual stimuli, and non-verbal memory has to be dependent on huge processing capacity. Think of how much more memory is used by your computer to process a picture than many pages of text, and you will then appreciate why brains got progressively bigger, and childbirth more problematic, way back in Stone Age times. Probably our hunter/gatherer ancestors emerging from those caves had highly developed forms of visual memory, but thinking in pictures was a cumbersome way of communicating only the most basic of ideas.

How spoken language subsequently emerged is a highly contentious issue, but it probably happened about 100,000 years ago (only in the past week if 10,000 generations are seen as being the equivalent of seven days in our species' year-long evolution from the Great Apes). It must have been linked to some chance mutation within the structure of the brain that made it possible for a few people to find they had something which others didn't, namely the ability to decide what sounds they wanted to make, and then to make them in a way that somebody else could recognize as having a specific meaning (a process that might have its origin literally tens of thousands of years beforehand). All that was then necessary, in Darwinian terms, was for women to favour as mates those men who could devise a way of saying 'I love you' more effectively than in a suggestive grunt, or to say 'Look out, there's a bear behind you' instead of just letting out a panicky scream. If that mutation were to have occurred within a relatively self-contained group then the selective pressures in favour of that mutation would have spread rapidly. By itself, however, that would not have been enough. The brain had then to find ways of processing data (ideas) expressed in terms of symbols, not pictures, and then combine those sounds into what we would recognize as words, and then to create patterns of words (grammar) that could convey complex thinking. We still find that difficult – reading, algebra, foreign languages, or writing this book, are not things which come easily to the Stone Age part of our brain.

There is reason to believe that, rather than developing new neural channels specific to language, the brain, excited (in biological terms) by the benefits to be gained through the exchange of ideas expressed in the more concise forms of words, simply started to hijack those old neural channels earlier developed for visual communication, and adjust them to this new purpose. Which is why in the newspaper you may have read this morning, much of the front page was given over to a photograph. Why was this? As the old adage goes, 'A picture is worth a thousand words,' for, as any politician, parent or teacher knows, we remember fascinating stories (scenarios) far more easily than we can comprehend a careful analytical description of an important phenomenon. It's just how we humans are. And humans love to talk; it is conversation that helps the youngest brains to grow, and the oldest brains to remain agile.[7] As an intensely social, collaborative and inquisitive species, dependent on each other for survival, this sharing of ideas in a relatively small group – about ourselves, about other people, about events past and possible events to come – is the very stuff of our humanity.

With language came the ability to express complex feelings and, as conscious beings, humans became aware of, and responsive to, other people's emotions. At some stage the stories told by our ancient forebears attempted to account for the ultimate mysteries of life, and humans started to envisage God. They created stories that helped them place themselves in the universe. Anthropologists equate the orderly burial of the dead with the development of spiritual awareness. Mystical, symbolic and religious thinking seems to have characterized human thinking everywhere and at all times, as if there were some adaptive advantage to such models of thinking that offered benefits to our ancestors that rationality could not provide. Stories matter quite enormously to humans, and myths are often more significant to human behaviour than 'cold' facts, for, as was said some years ago, 'the lives of nations, as with individuals, are lived largely in the imagination'.[9] We humans have wonderful imaginations.

Today's adolescents, still sensing that they are the night watchmen of Stone Age times, defer sleep until their elders arise with the dawn. Be they at home, in a classroom, or slouching their way through a shopping mall, adolescents have eyes, ears, noses and tongues that equip them with an array of techniques that once helped their ancestors to behave in intelligent ways out on that savannah where their very survival from day to day was dependent on keeping their wits about them. Being inquisitive, asking questions, sorting out what matters most, using their imagination, being collaborative, learning from their elders and exchanging ideas in conversation, are natural to adolescents. It is a truism: 'You can take man out of the Stone Age, but you can't take the Stone Age out of man.'[10] It is this that gives our behaviours the appearance of being travellers from an ancient land. We are empowered by the experience of our ancestors, but constrained as well. That is why, when driven to live in ways that are utterly uncongenial to our inherited traits and instincts, we simply fail to connect and consequently underperform.

*　　*　　*

It was questions being asked by the designers of early computer systems about artificial intelligence that eventually forced psychologists to accept the significance of evolution. Seeking to model within computers the kind of thought processes they suspected might exist in the human brain, cognitive scientists came to appreciate what psychologists had long tried to deny, namely that the brain has numerous inbuilt sets of symbols, operating systems and memory stores out of which it constructs and runs the mental programs that make high-level human thinking possible. This they had to take on trust, for they still lacked the technology to 'see' what they wanted to study. The probable existence of such structures had to mean that genetic processes similar to those that account for the diversity of human physical characteristics must also be responsible for the complex and multi-layered structure of the brain, so enabling it to function in novel and challenging situations.

Slowly, by the early 1980s, it became acceptable to explain the differences in human behaviours in terms of the impact of different environments. Teachers, who had earlier been reassured that the only thing that mattered was the quality of their teaching, were thrown by the suggestion that the child's out-of-school experiences could be as significant as what happened in the classroom. Then, in 1983, work at Harvard proposed replacing the idea of a single, general-purpose intelligence with the theory of Multiple Intelligences,[11] a combination of innate abilities (different ways of making sense of different kinds of situations) that could be observed among people as they multi-tasked their way through the complexity of everyday life. Initially seven separate intelligences or abilities were proposed: to use language to communicate; to calculate and use numbers; to relate spatially and to understand direction; to use rhythm, music and proportion; to use one's body effectively in multiple kinds of ways; to understand yourself, your motives and your instincts and expectations; and to understand similar things in other people. Later an eighth intelligence, naturalistic or spiritual, was added.

Separate though these intelligences may be (you can be very good at one, but useless at another), it is the way they come together that gives us the ability to appreciate what is going on around us so that we can make intelligent and appropriate responses. By the 1990s it was no longer thought fanciful to imagine (though as yet difficult to prove) that these multiple intelligences had their origins deep in our evolutionary history, and that it is through our ability to move effortlessly (if sometimes clumsily) from one intelligence to another that our survival depends from moment to moment.[12] The better our ancestors were able to do this, through a process of genetic mutation and mate selection of these as desirable survival characteristics, so the ability to think around an issue by seeing it from different perspectives (the Stone Age origins of out-of-the-box thinking) became a part of human nature.

While neurologists cannot as yet describe the molecular biology of these separate intelligences, the development of functional MRI in the late 1980s revealed in pictorial form just how complex are the anatomically distinct regions within the brain which constitute such extraordinarily cohesive and integrated whole systems. Through scanning the brains of volunteers given specific tasks to do (like working out mathematical equations, writing letters or composing poetry) it can be seen that several parts of the brain are activated even for the simplest of tasks; the hearing of words takes place in one section of the brain, speech in another, envisaging what the word means in a third part, and generating words in response in an altogether different area.

From this it is clear that while genes provide the chemical blueprints for the complex framework of the brain, it is environmental stimulants that turn some genes on more than others, and so *customize* the individual brain. They work in tandem. It is not nature versus nurture, but nature *via* nurture.[13] How Plato would have relished such findings from molecular biology! One neurologist encapsulated it nicely by describing it as 'activity-dependent development'. The outside world is the brain's food – the richer the diet (experienced by the child through sound, vision, smell, touch and taste), the more rapidly the brain develops. This is particularly true with regard to language development. In study after study around the world it has been shown conclusively that the more dialogue a child is exposed to, and involved in, before the age of five, the more successful, happy and well adjusted that child will be at the age of eighteen.[14] Those (few) children whose genetic predispositions to use language have not been turned on by the age of eight will never be able to talk, which has led to the concept of windows of opportunity during which genetic predispositions for certain tasks have to be turned on, or else lost for ever.

The brain is made up of two broad categories of cells, neurons and glia. Neurons are responsible for processing incoming information, making decisions about how to respond to that information, and controlling the behaviours that follow. Neurons look like bushes or trees, with the branches receiving chemical signals from – and the roots then sending chemical signals to – other neurons by way of chemical neurotransmitters. Serotonin is the brain's impulse modulator, and noradrenalin is the alarm hormone that prepares the body for fight or flight. Billions of neurons bathe one another in chemical messages that influence moment-to-moment changes in brain function, behaviour and experience. It is the responses initiated by the neurotransmitters that govern how one feels at any particular moment – how attentive one is, whether one is deeply satisfied or dissatisfied with life, whether one is anxious or calm. The glia cells play a supportive role, contributing to the blood–brain barrier that limits the passage of chemicals into the brain, helping to facilitate communication between neurons, and forming biological scaffolding that helps hold the numerous sub-units of the brain together.

Drawing much of this research together in the 1990s came the work of Gerald Edelman[15] in San Diego on what quickly became known as Neural Darwinism. Twenty years earlier, building on the work of Niels Jerne and Macfarlane Burnet, Edelman had gained a Nobel Prize for his work on the human immune system in which he had shown that, as a result of chemical interactions in the brain transmitted genetically from generation to generation, the human body is born with a vast number of specific antibodies, each of which has the capacity to recognize and respond to particular types of harmful viruses. The human immune system doesn't just build new responses every time a new threat appears; it simply searches its vast repertoire of defence mechanisms built up in deep evolutionary history until it finds an antibody that is appropriate.

Here is where Edelman is highly significant to the understanding of human learning, for, in 1992 he went on to argue that human learning proceeds in a very similar way. Rather than understanding that our brain is like a computer programmed from outside, he suggested that change in our brain occurs solely through the interaction of internal mental processes with those aspects of the environment that attract its attention. In other words, the drive comes from within the brain, not outside. It is rather like the way organisms respond to the rich, layered ecology of the jungle environment. What happens in the jungle is the result of natural selection. All trees have the innate capacity to reach the sunlight and extract nutrients from the soil; those that do so thrive and reproduce – the others simply die. They are not following specific instructions, but selecting the appropriate options.

Edelman argued that those genetic processes which have evolved over the 350,000 generations since we parted company from the Great Apes, have created a human brain which is fully equipped at birth with the basic sensory and motor components that enable each individual to function successfully in the physical world. An infant brain doesn't have to learn how to recognize specific sounds, and the way a string of words forms a sentence, because such basic neural networks are operational at birth. We don't have to teach a child to walk or talk; we simply provide opportunities for them to access mental processes, predispositions, encased in their brains. As each new challenge presents itself, the brain searches through its enormous repertoire of potential processes for that most suitable for purpose. Not all individuals read these instructions as effectively as others, so not all adaptations are complete or effective.

Thus from a biological perspective learning becomes a delicate but powerful dialogue between genetics and the environment – the experience of our species from the distant past interacts with the experiences we each have during our lifetimes. The whole process is dynamic and continuous. Such a model of our brain is especially intriguing because it suggests that a jungle-like brain might thrive best, not in classrooms designed so that teachers can deliver a specialized segment of a pre-determined curriculum, but by recognizing that however good a class or a school may be, it can never be good enough to give children the width of experience and challenge they need to activate their phenomenal learning capabilities. Our ancestors, after all, came from those jungles, not from something that resembles a shopping mall.

*   *   *

Fortunately for today's anthropologists, there are still a few hunter/gatherer societies in existence in remote parts of the world that can help to explain instinctive behaviours. Geneticists are reasonably certain that the Hadza have lived around the shores of Lake Eyas in Tanzania for at least 70,000 years. Linguists believe that their 'click' language is one of the oldest recorded languages now spoken.[16] There are fewer than 1,000 of the Hadza left, living in groups of between twelve and eighteen people roaming the open grasslands of the savannah. As hunter/gatherers they own nothing; they keep no herds, plant no crops; they live in flimsy grass huts and move on in search of food after only a few days. Life is lived on the fringe; it's tough, but bearable to people who can adapt to its extreme limitations.

Observing such people, it is immediately obvious that storytelling is an absolutely critical part of such a society's existence. Night after night, year after year, the elders tell and retell the stories of the tribe around the campfire. Woe betide any child whose attention wanders, for an otherwise kindly relative will so cuff the child that any further thought of sleep disappears. Once the adult storyteller has completed his tale, one of the children will be required to tell another tale . . . an exact repetition of a story the child would have heard weeks beforehand. Evolutionary psychologists believe that our ancestors have been memorizing such stories for tens of thousands of years. Not only are humans natural learners, it seems that we are natural teachers as well. It was the children who retold stories accurately who not only survived, but probably established a prestige that enabled them to mate more often than the less successful storytellers (that is a thought to meditate on!). Learning a complicated story through constant repetition would drive many an adult crazy, but to a young child, learning through constant repetition is easy and even fun. When today's parent is rebuked for missing out a few words from that favourite bedtime story, you have to wonder at the power of all that evolutionary experience in a young child's brain.

Play is extremely important to the Hadza. Observing their children is like seeing back into the nurseries of prehistoric times. Anthropologists suggest that the more complex the cognitive processes of the species, the greater the importance of playfulness.[17] Without play, children don't go beyond the normal and the predictable. Play is about experimenting in a moderately safe environment. Psychologists define it as a 'state of optimal creative capacity'.[18] It is about imagining alternative possibilities – as Einstein once put it: 'Imagination is more important than knowledge.' Play is about learning how to correct mistakes so that when in future years you find yourself between a rock and a hard place, you are quicker than others to find an alternative route. To observe these hunter/gatherers encouraging their sons to make perfect arrows was to see the finest of pedagogic skills naturally practised by 'unschooled' men who knew that quality learning was about survival. The adult inspired the child, but never overawed her with the depth of his own knowledge. The adult never failed to praise, but never over-praised. The adult constantly urged the child to experiment, to test the flight path of different kinds of arrows, and then to evaluate the results. That is how we humans were learning certainly 60,000 years ago; it is what children today still expect of their parents and teachers . . . but too often don't get.

Those tribesmen taught their sons and daughters to read the natural signs around them with the sophistication that readers of this chapter might expect to apply to a particularly interesting newspaper editorial.[19] Such Stone Age people used many more of their innate senses every day than do those of us whose intellectual skills are measured in terms of the computer programs we use, but whose computers we could never actually make, or repair. Those Stone Age tribesmen sniffed the air, they sensed temperature, they 'read' the sky and the weather, they analysed the movements of birds and animals, and they made fine distinctions between shades of colour that we don't even notice.[20] They had the ability to understand what each other was thinking, often across great distances, something which sophisticated people no longer understand and simply dismiss as being paranormal.

The youngest children create play-worlds of their own. The young girls make toy huts, miniature copies of those their mothers make. They twist bits of straw together to make dolls, and lift occasional embers from the adult's fire for their own hearth. The boys split their time between watching the men make arrows and then practising their own shooting skills, much encouraged by the men. Even the youngest boy seemed able to hold his bow firmly, while boys of only seven or eight could shoot with the classical composure associated with figures of Greek archers on ancient amphora. The bow and the human body seemed to become a single instrument. There was a marked difference between the boys, who were largely silent and concentrating fiercely on their shooting, and the girls who were quietly chattering or singing all the time.

The maps of these Stone Age men are entirely in their heads, for they hunt alone. They find their way effortlessly over vast distances, probably by detecting minute changes in vegetation which, to them, are as obvious as street names and direction signs are to us. The women don't need maps as they work together in such small areas of land that there is never a problem that a question to a colleague cannot solve. Even the structure of the male and female eye reflects these long-evolved predispositions – men have highly focused long-distance sight, while women are far better at seeing the broad picture.

The Hadza, as with other nomads, are a deeply spiritual people. Their every action is seen within a context greater than themselves. 'Every night, when I light my fire with two sticks, I thank my ancestors for the wisdom they have given me so that I can live in this place,'[21] one of the men explained. They have no concept of individual ownership. When pressed, they will say that the land over which they hunt belongs equally to those who came before them, to themselves in the present generation, and to those who are to come. Death does not trouble them, for it is all part of the saga of life. To modern man all this seems irrational, but to them it gives full justification for living, a determination to pass on their way of life to subsequent generations.

Noting a half-hearted attempt to grow what looked like maize on a clearing near one of the huts, I asked the elder what this meant. His face clouded as he explained that some visiting missionaries were trying to persuade some of the Hadza women to become settled agriculturalists. Even though in most years there is insufficient rain to grow crops, the women had been given seeds and spades and encouraged to grow maize. 'This is foolish, for in most years the crops fail,' said the elder, 'but the worst of planting crops is that when people do so and the crops flourish, those who planted them won't share out the harvest with other people. They say it is theirs because they planted it, not because the spirit of their ancestors let it grow. What they don't eat in one year they want to save for a bad harvest. They become selfish and hold it back. It is breaking our way of life. We believe that what people find belongs to everybody. Planting crops makes some people more powerful than others because they can bargain with things that have previously been owned by everyone.'[22]

That was a truly thought-provoking moment. Anthropologists have long speculated that there was a shift from a communal sharing ethic, the root of social conventions for 98 per cent of human history when all our ancestors were hunter/gatherers, to the time some 10,000 years ago when our ancestors started to settle down and stake out their own turf. But there, under the African sun in the twenty-first century, was being explained to me an historic phenomenon as if it were a new concern today. It was these ancient conflicts, the theory of Neural Darwinism explains, that created some of the repertoire of evolved responses which we each call upon daily as we struggle with contemporary dilemmas.

* * *

I well remember returning to England from Africa after one of my visits with the Hadza and attempting to catch up with

papers and journals published while I had been away. Let me
quote a sample of what I found in order to put into context that
conflict between our developing understanding of human
learning, and the social, economic environment in which
children are today growing up. 'Half of the five-year-olds
starting school this term lack speaking and listening skills
needed to cope in the classroom . . . few children are now able to
recite nursery rhymes, or sing songs, and only a tiny minority
are capable of listening and responding to instructions.'[23] Three
other items caught my attention: 'Primary school children too
obese to take part in physical education.'[24] 'More than a third of
seven-year-olds are seriously stressed by compulsory national
tests,'[25] while a third reported that 80 per cent of three-year-olds
in Birmingham[26] had televisions in their bedrooms.

My mind was full of the journey I had recently undertaken.
My conclusion was painful. Today's children in the Western
world, with a genetic blueprint that would enable them to
flourish in a Hadza encampment, seem to be growing up
deprived of the sense of meaning and emotional security which
characterized those ancient primitive societies I had visited. The
children of the nomads are more deeply connected to the reality
of how life works. The Hadza have something that the children
of England are fast losing – they have the love and affection of
their parents, and a community that understands interdependence. If asked to spell the word 'love', for too many it would be
T-I-M-E. In so many ways the Hadza had seemed just like us, or
as like us as we would be if our lives had not got so caught up
with the razzamatazz of modern culture. But in one fundamental way they are totally different from us. They accept life as it is,
while we forever seek to change and mould it to suit our
convenience.

That Hadza man who had criticized the woman for trying to

grow maize was advancing the same argument as would have his ancestor who, living in the same environment, experiencing the same climate and hunting the same animals, did so in exactly the same way as their ancestors had done for hundreds of thousands of years. To ensure that his own children could do the same thing, 'education' under such circumstances meant the orderly transfer of ages-old knowledge to the youngest generation. There was just no need to rock the boat, for the status quo was just fine.

That status quo worked well enough up to some 60,000 years ago, when within a very few generations the hunter/gatherer's predictable world (the African savannah had not changed in millions of years) was shattered by the coming of the Pleistocene Ice Age which covered most of Europe and the African mountains with glaciers, ice sheets and frozen deserts.[27] Climatic change drove our confused ancestors into an ever smaller area of increasingly cold savannah, squeezed between the advancing ice caps and the ocean to the south. Geneticists are now confident that the entire evolutionary experience of our species, encapsulating all the predispositions and adaptations accumulated over the past seven million years, were effectively funnelled down into a population of no more than 10,000 scared and frightened hunter/gatherers.[28] That our species did not become extinct was due entirely to the fact that these few frightened people had access to the same mental processes that you are using as you try to comprehend where this argument is taking us. They could think around the problem through the use of multiple intelligences, and with a well-developed sense of consciousness they could plot abstract strategies of what they might do next. And then suddenly they had to do the unpredictable – take risks, or perish in the attempt. Which apparently was the incentive that created what we now call adolescence – the most recent of the biological adaptations responsible for humans becoming the kind of species that we are. That they succeeded is why you are alive to read this book.

The evidence suggests that some 58,000 years ago (the last two days of the year-long evolutionary story) a tiny proportion of that residual group of frightened people, maybe numbering only 150, literally started to walk out of Africa, and began to colonize the entire world. To do this, the most active and virile of those young people had to stop thinking logically like their fathers, or sensibly like their mothers, and develop the confidence to do the unexpected. They had to become risk takers. What happened is an intriguing story, only now just starting to be understood. Within it lies the clue to understanding today's adolescents, and how it is that their appetite for adventure, their predilection for taking risks, and desire for novelty has actually driven the development of civilization.

That adolescence should be the driving force for the development of civilization sounds totally counter-intuitive, for the experience of so many of today's parents of fourteen- and fifteen-year-old party animals makes it seem at best improbable, at worst simply impossible. Adolescence as a survival mechanism?[29] How could that possibly account for their irrationality, their hot-bloodedness, their reckless behaviour and their emotional instability?

However might this have happened? Imagine for a moment that you were the child of one of the first families fleeing from the devastation of the savannah into the dark, frightening and mysterious forest to escape. You had been born to parents unsure of their new surroundings and anxious to clear a small patch of ground to make a home. Your parents were fearful, for this wasn't the lifestyle they had been prepared for by their own parents. They worried about you, but as you grew older you started to look disparagingly at that lifestyle and shocked them when you said you were going 'to move on'. They tried to frighten you by saying that to do so would be terribly dangerous, for you didn't know what was on the other side of the mountain. 'So what?' you might have replied. 'Sticking around here will get me nowhere. It's boring. I'm off.' Leaving your siblings and troubled parents behind you, you set out. Not all youngsters thinking like that survived, but you did and you got to the other side of the mountain. There you found another successful young rebel. The two of you settled down and quickly forgot about being rebels. You mated and produced children of your own and to your surprise became much like your own parents. Then one day one of your children said, just as you had done to your own parents, 'I'm not sticking around here.' And so it has apparently repeated itself, generation after generation right through to today. 'Give me land, lots of land, don't fence me in,' goes the Cole Porter song. 'Don't fence me in' is the 'evolutionary' plea of the adolescent as each one of them struggles to come to terms with their instincts, and to find out who they are.

Studying the DNA of native peoples today, it is possible to plot the routes our distant ancestors followed as they walked around the world in search of better opportunities.[30] They apparently moved first in a north-easterly direction towards what we now think of as the Indian Ocean, and then north to cross the Red Sea, and on around the coast of Arabia. We even know that their migration averaged three miles a generation. Slow that might have been, but it was enough. Our ancestors reached India some 50,000 years ago and Thailand 10,000 years later. They landed in the Andaman Islands 30,000 years ago, and reached Australia shortly after that. They crossed the Bering Straits into North America between 12,000 and 15,000 years ago, while migration into central and northern Europe was delayed by the last stages of the Ice Age until some 20,000 years ago.[31]

Steadily, through a process of genetic mutation over that 60,000-year period, the blueprint for our species has apparently changed. Earlier in the human story women had selected men who, through the use of multiple intelligences, made thoughtful and successful mates. Now it started to develop further; the men who had absorbed everything that their parents could teach them when young, but had the independence of mind during their teenage years to find their own direction, emerged in their twenties as highly dependable husbands ready for a lifetime of disciplined and routine work. It would seem that the adolescent brain, being 'crazy by design',[32] is the most recent of the evolutionary adaptations that are so vital to our species' survival. That adaptation has built up only over the past 2,500 generations. It seems that it is adolescence that really drives human development by forcing young people in every generation to think beyond their own self-imposed cultural limitations, and exceed their parents' aspirations.

*   *   *

Neuroscience has taught us a lot in the past seven or eight years to corroborate this story as told by archaeologists, anthropologists and geneticists, about the imprint of that experience which still exists like a shadow in the brain of every new-born baby.[33] It goes like this. Scientists have known for years that the infant brain has many more neurons than the adult brain. What determines which neurons survive depends on activity, especially interactivity at a micro level. Circuits that are exercised and used repeatedly grow to become complex and healthy, while circuits that are under-utilized simply wither away.[34] It is this which allows a young child's brain to be sculpted by his or her interactions with the outside world; and it is this which gives our species its superb adaptability. None of the basic systems that manage emotions – the stress-response system, the responsiveness of our neurotransmitters, the neural pathways in which our implicit understanding of how intimate relationships work – are in place at birth. Nor is the vital pre-frontal cortex developed.[35] All these systems develop rapidly in the first two or three years of life, and all are vastly dependent on external stimulants to activate them. From the age of two onwards the child's brain exhibits well-defined developmental phases through to the restless fives, the inquisitive sixes, and the enthusiastic tens. Biochemical developmental adaptations today still reflect the evolution of the human brain to facilitate a hunter/gatherer way of life, enhanced by that of the eternal traveller.

Until very recently scientists considered that this meant that the adult brain was already in place by the age of twelve, and that the turmoil of adolescence could be explained by the growth of the sex hormones that threw the otherwise responsible youngsters off course.[36] However, research findings initiated at the National Institute of Health in the United States in the past five years show that many of the changes that take place in the adolescent brain are of a very different kind. Far from being fully finished, the teenage brain remains a 'teeming ball of possibilities, raw material which is wildly exuberant and waiting to be synaptically shaped'.[37] These changes are so profound that they may rival early childhood as a critical period of development. They don't simply represent the trailing remnants of childhood adaptability or 'plasticity', but are a complete reversal of the processes that had been so successful earlier on in shaping the brain up to the age of about twelve.[38]

Functional MRI scans made during the early stages of adolescence show that many of the neural connections that had been carefully crafted by interactions between the child, its parents and teachers in the first ten or twelve years of life, and which had earlier enabled such children to behave in perfectly predictable ways and to learn very easily through observation, are suddenly fractured. Quite literally between 0.75 per cent and 1.5 per cent of what had once been firmly connected parts of the neural system seemed mysteriously to be torn asunder during each year from about eleven to twenty years of age. Brain scans show many of these dendrites literally floating amidst the white matter of the brain apparently looking to make new connections. 'That's just like my daughter,' said a troubled mother. 'It's as if her internal telephone system is consistently dialling wrong numbers!'[39]

It now seems that it is these processes that force adolescents to create new connections which they will have to rationalize for themselves, and which will replace the connections suggested earlier by their parents and teachers. As this happens, adolescent behaviour becomes unpredictable, unreasonable and careless and constantly questioning and being outlandishly disrespectful of the social order that it had earlier accepted, apparently eagerly.[40] A real pain we think; a stage when youngsters are best tightly corralled for their own safety. Some of the most intriguing changes occur in the pre-frontal lobes (directly behind the forehead), those parts of the brain which play critical roles in memory, impulse control, decision-making, planning and other higher-level cognitive functions. Those frontal lobe circuits that are exercised are therefore strengthened, while others less used are weeded out, so leading to a reduction in the grey matter in the frontal lobes throughout the whole adolescent period.[41] Eventually the adolescent brain emerges leaner and far more efficient.

Of the greatest importance to those nomads in Iran, whom we now understand to be the descendants of people like the Hadza, was the progression of their dependent child to that of autonomous adult. Such small-scale, self-contained communities depended upon the goodwill of their members to ensure cohesion, but such cohesion would have come at too high a cost if youthfulness lasted too long, and there was any undue delay in reaching adulthood. The adaptation that had enabled the young to learn easily in their earliest years through intense emotional connection with older people, had to be balanced to prevent children from becoming mere clones of their parents. In other words, unless those close bonds which had characterized the earliest years were ruptured (forcibly if necessary) the young would not grow to be adaptable to new situations. Those changes in the brain in the adolescent years make it both essential and possible for the young to go off to start lives of their own. Adolescence is a time-limited predisposition. In other words, if the adolescent is prevented (by over-careful parents or too rigid a system of formal schooling or by the restrictions imposed by health and safety regulations) from experimenting and working things out for itself, it will lose the motivation to be innovative or take responsibility itself in adult life.

*　　　*　　　*

This, in brief outline, is how we are, adolescents and adults alike. It is what the past has made us. Every one of us. To the table of the affairs of everyday life we bring all the mannerisms, behaviours and confusion of predispositions – we can be collaborative or competitive; big thinkers or nit-pickers; we can love to distraction, and hate to our (and the planet's) destruction. For better or worse, that is the raw material of the self. But it is not actually what we *are*, for our *very own self* results from our moment-to-moment interaction with the environment, shaped over the centuries by the actions and decisions of our ancestors that still plague the way we think. We are, literally and figuratively, the children of travellers from ancient lands. In twenty-first-century terms our children face the same challenges as did our ancestors' children; our basic biology still empowers them to master both basic skills (those that can be readily taught) and think creatively for themselves (experiential learning).

However, despite the same inherited mental architecture, exposure to life in different cultures turns us into very different people. No indigenous European could survive for long among the sandy, rocky expanses of the Kalahari Desert where the Bushmen have lived for more than 50,000 years by developing a lifestyle so finely attuned to the desert that, away from that desert, they are as useless and vulnerable as any twenty-first-century Londoner would be if he or she were suddenly dropped into the Sahara. Take a baby the day it was born to English-speaking parents in Manchester to be brought up by Swahili-speaking foster parents in South Africa, and by the age of five that child will speak perfect Swahili without a trace of an English accent. Reverse that process and the child from South Africa brought to Manchester the day it was born will speak with a full Mancunian accent, without a trace of its African linguistic origins. The very occasional child, found to be brought up by wolves as if it were one of their own cubs, was only able to make animal grunt-like sounds.

We are who we are not simply because of our biological natures, but from the way in which we interact with our environment. We may think we are beginning to have the brain part worked out, but if we don't understand what has happened to create the world we live in and what is happening around us today, which effectively turns these predispositions on or off, then we will never comprehend why it is that so often we humans fail to live up to our full potential. Nurture is essential to activate our natural predispositions, so nurture and culture become the stuff of Chapters 4, 5 and 6.

4

Nurture and Culture

'Men's natures are alike, it is their habits that carry them far apart,' observed Confucius. And he was right. It's our habits that make us different, not our blood. Habits are our behaviours; first nurtured by our upbringing, subsequently shaped by the values of the society within which we live, they collectively comprise what biologists call nurture. Nature and nurture are the two sides of the coin that make each of us who we are, and that coin has to be kept spinning lest in falling it exposes only part of what we are about. Which would be a disaster, for, without nurture, humans rapidly revert to Stone Age instincts while failing to recognize that the roots of our biological natures rapidly make people dysfunctional. Nurture fine-tunes and personalizes our basic human natures, so creating the wonderful cultural diversity we find around us. This and the next two chapters explain how cultures have made us the people we are.

Cultures take many centuries to build up, but break apart rapidly if the circumstances that created them disappear. That is what happened to the Roman Empire when ordinary Roman citizens became so engrossed in their own pleasure that they couldn't be bothered to protect themselves from the barbarians, and so the empire, having taken centuries to build up, fell apart in 50 years. The Victorians, a tough and entrepreneurial people, spoke of such social change in terms of 'from gutter to gutter'. A poor man is so determined to escape poverty that he drives himself to make a fortune. With that money he provides his own sons with all the trappings of opulence, but gives them none of the self-help attitudes that enabled him to establish his fortune in the first place. That man's son, born into second-generation wealth but with even less personal determination to succeed, ends up in the same gutter that his grandfather escaped from. And, so the moral of the tale goes, the same thing happens to civilizations.

Cultures must not be taken for granted, for they are totally dependent on the successful transmission of their values, ideas and beliefs from one generation to the next. Each of us is who we are today not simply because of our inherited predisposi-tions but because of the culture into which we were born. Cultures are like tapestries made up of threads of many colours that cross and re-cross each other to create the culture we experi-ence around us. Fragile as these may be, they become our tribal realities. That this book is being written not in Spanish but in English, the indigenous language of the people of a small offshore European island, is largely due to the defeat of Philip of Spain's Armada in 1588. The subsequent expansion of English culture, which grew as the British Empire spread to cover a quarter of the earth's surface, was phenomenal. All of which has left its mark on us, be we Americans or Europeans, Australians, South Africans or Canadians.

The English in the early twenty-first century have become a complex people, a veritable bundle of contradictions. We can be both moralistic and judgemental; we tend to give pride of place to theoreticians, and debase the skills of practical people. We have become increasingly self-centred and materialistic, con-cerned more with our well-being today than in our responsibili-ties for the future. We believe education to be important but would prefer others to deal with our own children, leaving us adults with space to do our own thing. Not sure any longer of the roots from which our own culture has grown, we are so unsure of how to explain this to our children that cultural transmission has become increasingly dependent on what schools teach, not on what children learn from their parents and the community around them. Our ancestors of only a generation or so ago would scorn such a simplistic notion, for they knew intuitively from hard experience that quality education was as much a result of good parenting, and the influences of a rich and challenging community life, as ever it was to do with schooling.

So what do today's children make of all this – the ones on whom generations yet unborn will be dependent if the culture that we value is to be transmitted into the future? For many, it seems, not much. 'School sucks,' said a thirteen-year-old English schoolgirl describing herself as Little Miss Attitude. 'Why should we have to do homework? It only makes people angry. We should work hard all day in school (which I don't always do) and when we go home we should be able to live our own lives.'[1]

While adolescents respond well to challenges set by good teachers, they are quickly turned off by teachers whose knowledge is only skin-deep, who stick rigidly to the rules, and make it obvious that they don't actually *like* kids. 'The only reason most people stay in school,' wrote a fifteen-year-old Canadian in 2005, 'is because it's easier to get a well-paid job by getting a degree because school is all about conforming. And that's where it all begins. Focus shifts from teaching and raising an aware, creative, inspired and capable creature, to advancing to the next grade. It's not about the child, it's not about his or her capacity, it's about grades.'[2]

That fifteen-year-old saw what is happening more clearly than many an adult. You will have to decide whether or not you agree with such an assessment by the time you have finished this book.

But before going back to the beginning, as it were, to see where the cultural influences that currently shape English attitudes have come from, we need to pause and look carefully at what is actually happening around us. Are things simply jogging along as they have always done, or is there something abnormal about today's world? Thinking in terms of the Roman Empire all those centuries ago, is our society poised to make a massive jump forward, or might we be just about to fall flat on our faces?

Observe carefully the lifestyles of today's children and ask why it is they often look so beaten. Twice in their adolescent years, mental storm clouds gather in the middle of the summer holidays as youngsters nervously anticipate the arrival of examination results, the new rite of passage. It's not only the teenagers who are nervous, for so much store do politicians and parents place on exam results that the nervousness of headteachers, terrified that a fall of a single decimal point might lower their position in the all-important league tables, allow themselves to compromise on the nature of true education and subject children from the age of five upwards to various forms of annual tests. Parents share the tension by offering their reluctant off-spring anything from a fiver to their own car to 'pull out all the stops and show 'em what you're made of!' The system has become increasingly coercive as pupils are urged to forsake all else and 'never mind the quality, feel the width'.[3] Numbers squeeze out explanations!

Such neurotic focus on grades has diverted society's attention away from what children actually need. The problem is surely far more complex than simply modernizing schools. It is now more than 60 years since the heady days of the mid-1940s when many countries began to introduce free education, pensions for old people, free health care, and the promise that never again would people sink into abject poverty of body, mind or spirit.

Three generations have grown up since then assuming that parents can ignore any long-term responsibility for their children, and that children need feel no responsibility for ageing parents or dependent relatives. Instead, personal responsibility has been transferred in most people's thinking to that anonymous assemblage of agencies known collectively as 'government'. So, rather than attempting ourselves to help our unruly teenagers, we call in professional counsellors; unnerved by the sheer volume of children pouring out of the school gates in the afternoon, we demand there should be more teachers on patrol. Anything, it seems, is preferable to shouldering the responsibility ourselves. We have all become private individuals and guard our privacy relentlessly.

So how is it really going with today's young people, the ones we actually know? Undoubtedly they are better fed, receive better health care and are better housed than at any time in history. Few of them die in childhood. Most infectious diseases have been controlled. Preventative medicines flourish, and many a toddler today could well be fit enough to celebrate the arrival of the twenty-second century with a dance. So far, so good. Yet paradoxically, the wealth of Western nations has brought its own problems, creating an apparent 'affluenza' epidemic.[4] Children eat so much and take so little exercise that vast numbers are predicted to contract diabetes through the early onset of obesity. The family as the basic social unit has collapsed over the past 30 years as Western countries have become ever wealthier.[5] So too have communities, those greater conglomerations of people beyond our front doors, with whom we once used to pass the time of day, and who provided the local context within which the family nestled. The pressures of modern life steal away the time needed to be kind and considerate. Communities traditionally watched out for their own,[6] and represented a collective culture expressed in the stories that parents told their children about where they had come from, why they might be here, and what they hoped to pass on to future generations. Such 'social capital' is a far better predictor of how children will do later in life than are the exam results on which the much-vaunted school league tables are now based.

So, despite our general affluence, it is pretty clear that not all is going well with the children. Increased wealth, rather than increasing the sum of national happiness, has progressively lowered it, and over the past half-century levels of mutual trust have fallen dramatically.[7] Clinical depression has risen rapidly as people fill every moment with frantic activity. The average level of stress now experienced among teenagers in the United States would have had them assigned to a psychiatric clinic in the late 1950s. Society really seems to be out of sorts with itself.

To understand why we are so out of sorts, we should re-examine that explanation given by the Hadza hunter for what happened when his people forsook their nomadic existence, and started to plant crops. Instead of regarding the harvest as something shared equally with everyone, those who planted the crops claimed the harvest for themselves. From that moment, the Hadza hunter explained, men forsook their tribal tradition of supporting each other and became self-centred and greedy as they retained any surplus as a stockpile to trade later when others faced starvation. Extensive and recent research concerning the biological basis of social relationships helps explain this. It seems that every one of the decisions we take subconsciously each day results from an internal conflict between four innate and subconscious brain-based 'drives'. Each of these drives reflects an aspect of behaviour developed in deep evolutionary time which improved our chances of survival.[8] There is the drive to acquire both objects and experiences that improve our status relative to others; there is the drive to bond in long-term relationships of mutual care and commitment; there is the drive to learn and make sense of the world and of ourselves; and there is the drive to defend ourselves, our loved ones, and our resources from harm. Each drive is important of itself, but too much emphasis on one can be disastrous. For example, the perpetual students will get no further than the aggressive trader hell-bent on acquisition if they cannot learn from their mistakes and don't know how to defend themselves. Survival depends on developing a culture of balance. Like an old-fashioned coach and four, the journey is fast and smooth if all four horses pull together, but if one horse is stronger or weaker than the others, the whole team becomes dysfunctional, and the coach probably rolls over and off the road. Undue emphasis placed on one drive makes people, and societies, dysfunctional.[9]

Other research tentatively suggests a biological basis for a hierarchy of preferred interpersonal behaviours, which may lie latent in each of us as possible behaviour strategies.[10] Four levels have been defined. Most basic and straightforward is *Communal Sharing*, that 'share and share alike' behaviour exemplified by the Hadza. Slightly more complex, as it requires some people to acknowledge subservient positions, is *Authority Ranking* where a leader is acknowledged who then imposes his decisions on everyone else – a frequently destablizing relationship that often achieves its results through blood feuds. *Equality Ranking* is a more complex form of behaviour, and requires a high level of mutual trust as people in more settled communities barter – a 'you scratch my back, and I'll scratch yours' kind of relationship. A fourth involves *Market Pricing* which involves bidding and counter-bidding, bluffing and the calling of bluff, best exemplified by the activity of middle-men in complex trading relationships.

Here is where the research has a day-to-day significance for most of us, for these behaviours are apparently layered within young children, starting with communal sharing being well understood by three-year-olds.[11] Children then seem to pass through an authoritarian stage (the bossy five-year-olds), to reciprocal behaviour ('If you are kind to me you can join my club') until, about the age of eight, bartering or swapping is well understood. These behaviours are apparently biologically based, they are innate, and are activated only under certain circumstances. That is why every child needs a rich and diverse set of experiences when they are very young if they are eventually to grow up to become flexible and adaptable adults. Those youngsters lacking such social sophistication may not realize when the rules of the game change in response to different circumstances. They are easily wrong-footed. Tragedies occur daily when two partners to a deal play by different rules. Once a member of the Hadza leaves the security of the homeland and the omnipresent belief in community sharing, he or she is all too easily corrupted by others who see ways of exploiting his or her apparent naivety. Likewise, a young girl in any urban culture who, not yet knowing how to handle her emerging femininity, accepts a relationship she sees as being that of reciprocal friendship, only to find that the man – having bought her affection for a few days – drops her and, as in a market economy, looks for the next bargain.

*   *   *

This goes some of the way to explaining the complexity of who we are – that small group, problem-solving, sense-making species of Chapter 3. Evolution has primed our brains to analyse any situation through a variety of interconnected forms of intelligence, balancing the conflicting drivers of our behaviours, constructing new knowledge, and subconsciously reverting to inherited social patterns of behaviour to achieve our objectives.[12] Behind the blank expression of that person you have just met lies a brain packed with software struggling to give its owner the social edge over you. So beware – it's still a social jungle out there!

Humans have brains of immense biological complexity, awaiting cultural stimulation to create individuals capable of the most extraordinary and unpredictable behaviours. You and I both have brains shaped by these deep evolution experiences, but modified by environmental circumstances to produce a Mozart or a Plato, a Caesar or a Stalin. While the human genome changes incredibly slowly, the better each generation uses its brains, the more thoughtful become the stories passed to the next generation, as they reflect a society's better understanding of the relationship between themselves and the world around them. It is within these cultures that we nurture our children, helping them to see the world as we see it, and to go on and incorporate their new knowledge into the stories they in turn tell their children. Stories are vitally important. They are the bedrock of culture. They breathe the essence of education. And they are always being updated.

So when should an explanation of Britain's culture start? Probably far longer ago than you might have realized. Archaeologists have known for the better part of a century that humans returned to these lands some 12,000 years ago as the ice sheets finally melted. But the archaeologist's research tools of spades, trowels and sieves could tell us little of how these people lived. Guessing that successive waves of immigrants with steadily improving agricultural techniques had frequently moved into these islands, anthropologists had assumed until very recently that as they conquered these lands the new arrivals simply killed off the indigenous population. An almost complete male skeleton found in a cave in the village of Cheddar in 1900 was dated 60 years later through carbon-14 technologies as being 9,000 years old. Historians therefore assumed that this was a relic of an extinct population.[13] But was such an historical hypothesis correct? Evidence of a kind unknown to academic historians is now coming from genetics, as scientists recover significant quantities of mitochondria from ancient DNA.

A little science is needed. Mitochondria is a unique substance found within DNA that does not recombine as it moves from generation to generation, so retaining an exact history of that person's evolutionary past – but only on the female side. Consequently, two closely related people will have almost identical mitochondria, whereas people only distantly related would differ by the number of mutations that have accumulated during the generations that have separated them. In the late 1990s, such a DNA sample was extracted from the Cheddar skeleton, and the mitochondria studied. At the same time DNA was taken from a random sample of 10 per cent of the present population of the village of Cheddar. To everyone's amazement the analysis gave two exact matches, which meant that for 9,000 years the female mitochondria line was unbroken and that for nearly 200 generations the female line for those two villagers had remained in the same geographic location. Historians have had to rethink the nature of ethnic origins, for probably invading armies don't wipe out existing cultures, as to mate with the nubile daughters of a conquered race was – and it is that basic – more fun than to kill them. The rewriting of history has started. The female side of a population, the mothers who tell the stories to children that perpetuate the culture, is remarkably tenacious. Old cultures are more likely to change through the acquisition of new ideas, than being supplanted by other ideas.

We can only guess at those stories from the scant artifacts these people left behind – the mighty stone circles of Stonehenge and Avebury in England, Carnac in Brittany and Callanish in the Outer Hebrides, or with the leylines that link their sacred sites with the alignment of the planets.[14] Nearly 5,000 years ago the ancient Celts wanted to know how the world worked, and they wanted to understand the mind of their god. Their beautiful artwork, expressed in gold and copper jewellery with their distinctive spiralling knot-work designs, symbolize the interconnectiveness of all aspects of life and death, for, to the Druids with their strong belief in an afterlife, death was the beginning of new birth.

Far to the south of the damp, cloudy world of the Celts, around the warm waters and fertile coasts of the Mediterranean, three other cultures – Greek, Roman and Judaic – were evolving rapidly. Over several hundred years these were to be fused into an embryonic European culture that would reach these islands with the Roman invasion in AD 55. The Greeks are now seen as the beginning of nearly everything of which the modern world likes to boast – philosophy, architecture, poetry, drama, music, physical fitness, justice and the concept of democracy – theories and ways of thinking that have remained central to Western thought ever since.[15] They did this while living in a world without watches, calculating machines, compasses, bridges, books or maps, and they lived in houses with no drains, slept in beds with no sheets, read by rush light, and watched lengthy dramatic tragedies standing up. They trained themselves to think straight by constantly questioning accepted knowledge, so becoming particularly interested in education.[16] The Athenians defined the word 'school' as a series of pleasurable activities that took place, not in separate buildings, but alternately in the homes of grammarians who taught writing and arithmetic for one-third of the day; in the homes of artists who taught music and singing for a further third; while the rest of the time was spent in the gymnasium.[17] At the age of fourteen, boys had to leave the villages in which they had grown up and prove themselves as men able to survive on their own, while girls had to return to their mothers to learn about homemaking. The citizens of Sparta were different: they placed a greater emphasis on toughness and rigorous military discipline. The philosopher Plato taught that humans were divided into three groups – the rulers who had gold in their composition, the administrators who had silver, and the farmers who had only iron or bronze.[18]

The Greeks, for all their intellectual brilliance, were to prove no military match for the tough, down-to-earth Romans, whose armies conquered them in 146 BC. Recognizing the value of Greek thought, the Romans assimilated Greek sophistication and then regulated these practices through Roman law and administration. Being set on imperial expansion, the Romans preferred to employ Greek academic slaves to teach their children, rather than educating them within their own homes as had the Greeks. The Romans redefined schools as places of instruction where youngsters learned not from being involved with professionals, but by being taught new ideas in abstract forms. From the start, this was a bad deal for children. Writing of his experiences as a schoolboy in Rome in 325, the man who was later to become known as St Augustine wrote:

> Oh my god, how I suffered. What torments and humiliations I experienced. I was told that because I was a mere boy I had to obey my teachers in everything. I was sent to school. I did not understand what I was taught. I was beaten for my ignorance. I never found out what use my education was supposed to be.[19]

Years later Augustine reflected, as many others have done ever since, that 'I learnt most not from those who taught me, but from those who talked with me.' The Romans prided themselves on their toughness and sense of realism, but were not so much concerned with individual rights as the Athenians, and preferred a baby to die at birth if it showed any signs of weakness. Rather than educating too many daughters, Romans would give unwanted baby girls away at birth to be brought up as future prostitutes.

It was the influence of the Jews which was the most extraordinary – a tribe of desert nomads, frequently driven into exile, doing time as slaves, suffering innumerable defeats, they apparently had everything against them. Survivors from a tough place, the Jews were held together by a rigid discipline and an all-encompassing belief in their being the chosen people of God.[20] They subscribed to an absolute statement of moral values, including respect for life, justice and social responsibility for the weak and the poor. To the Jews, the role of the family was sacrosanct, and honour to father and mother fundamental. It was the 30-year-old Jewish carpenter Jesus Christ who taught that there is a greater strength in being merciful than in being legalistic, that forgiveness is more important than revenge, that life has an eternal significance, and that one's responsibility to one's neighbour is almost as great as one's responsibility to one's god. Jesus was crucified as a Jew, but within only a few years Judaism was being translated by the energetic, intelligent but often bigoted St Paul into a combination of religious belief and the Roman passion for good order, into a new religion – Christianity.

The Romans occupied these islands for nearly 400 years, and called them Britannia. They largely pacified the local tribes, built an extensive road system linking a series of fortified cities, and built many bridges, forts and extensive port works. Roman soldiers and administrators frequently married into the local population, and set up schools where their sons could learn Latin.[21] We even know of the book from which these pupils had to study Latin grammar, written in the fourth century by the Roman grammarian Aelius Donatus. Grammar had to be learned by heart – such as the many parts of speech. It was arranged like a catechism of question and answer: *Question:* How many are the parts of speech? *Answer:* Eight. *Question:* What are they? *Answer:* Noun, pronoun, verb, adverb, participle, conjunction, preposition, interjection. *Question:* What is a noun? *Answer:* A part of speech that has a case, signifying a body or a thing that is proper or common . . . And so it continued just as a lesson might today.[22] Over the years Roman educators put a distinctive structure into everyday speech. With the Emperor Constantine's adoption of Christianity (with much of its Jewish heritage) in 324, the last years of the Roman occupation saw the first tentative fusing of Christianity with Celtic mysticism linking the two religions' belief in an afterlife.

The sudden withdrawal of the Roman army left the British with no political cohesion, making their fertile and well-cultivated land ripe for plunder. So over the next couple of centuries came first Irish raiders, then Danes, Saxons and Vikings, and later Normans. One sixteen-year-old boy seized by Irish slave traders in the Severn estuary in about the year 425 was the son of a Romanized native who had already learned to speak and write in Latin. For years this boy tended sheep as a slave in the Irish midlands before escaping and eventually reaching Rome where he became a priest and, years later, returned to convert the Irish to Christianity. He is known to Irishmen the world over as St Patrick whose birthday – 17 March – they delight to celebrate.

It was the monasteries and isolated hermit cells that Patrick was to found over the next 40 years that was to keep Christianity and a Roman sense of order alive in the gloomiest years of the Dark Ages. Patrick was passionately committed to education and ensured that his monks were rigorous academics and thoughtful in their interpretation of the scriptures. Young monks laboured long hours making copies of classical Latin texts, and just a few of these beautiful manuscripts have survived. The brilliance of their coloured drawings and the intricacies of their calligraphy testify to the fusion of Celtic and Christian traditions. The famous *Book of Kells* is thought to have been written in and around the year 800. We can sense something of the sentiments of these times from the comments these young monks occasionally jotted in the margins.[23] 'Some things (in what I have copied out) are devilish lies, some for the enjoyment of idiots,' scribbled one monk, cursing the poor quality of the ink. Another indulged his fantasies by penning:

> All are keen to know
> who will sleep with blonde Aideen.
> All Aideen herself will own
> is that she will not sleep alone.

Has *anything* changed in the adolescent brain in 1,500 years?

While Patrick and his monks copied out sacred scriptures in their cells perched on the windswept isles of the west, mainland Britain fell into the Dark Ages; the Roman villas fell down, the cities were forsaken, the schools became silent, and the influence of the Druids recovered. A couple of centuries later, back in Rome, military power having collapsed and the influence of the Church having grown considerably, missionaries were sent by the Pope (apparently unaware of the separate, flourishing Christianity among the Celts and the Scots) to convert mainland Druids to Christianity. The missionaries found considerable sympathy for their teaching, overlapping as it did with some of the Celtic beliefs. In a vivid incident recorded in the first history of the English ever written, a nobleman is said to have addressed a hall full of his countrymen. 'It seems to me,' he said summing up the teaching of the missionaries, 'that the life of man is like that of a sparrow which flies in at one end of this well-lit and warm hall from the dark outside. The sparrow is here for a few minutes, but then it will fly out again into the dark night. So the life of man here appeareth for a little season, but what followeth on or what has gone before that surely we know not? Wherefore if this new learning (Christianity) has brought us any better assurity, me thinks it is worthy to be followed.'[24]

Two centuries later it was the remarkable, likeable and extraordinary Alfred, the first and only English king ever to be called 'the Great', who created the idea of England, and the concept of Englishness. Taught by his mother to read, his childhood had been most unusual for its time in that he had visited Rome twice by the age of seven, on foot and partly on horseback, and although he didn't learn Latin until he was twelve, the dream of constructing a nation of well-educated people stayed with him in the darkest days of his struggle to rid his part of England – Mercia – of the pestilential Vikings. These he defeated at the Battle of Bratton on the edge of Salisbury Plain in 878. If Alfred hadn't had a passionate interest in education – he established schools, and trained teachers, trawled Europe for scholars to help him translate the classics into English, and codified the laws – there probably would never have been a language called English. 'The saddest thing about any man is that he be ignorant,' wrote Alfred in one of his many letters to his clergy, 'and the most exciting is that he knows.'[25] Alfred gave the people their identity, and by creating the story of who they were he gave them pride in themselves, so much so that when Edgar became the first man to claim the kingship of all the English in 973, he chose for his double coronation the cities of Bath and Chester, the cities most associated with Imperial Rome. It was Alfred who created the synergy between Christianity, Roman law and the concept of Englishness that was not to wither away until the last twenty years of the twentieth century (see Chapter 8).

So deeply entrenched were Alfred's laws and customs that even the conquest of England by Duke William of Normandy in 1066 did not completely destroy the English language, despite the replacement of all the nobility and bishops by Frenchmen, with French becoming the language of the cultivated elite.[26] The Normans ruled through the delegated authority of the barons and their higher clergy. Mighty castles were quickly built to emulate the White Tower erected to overawe Londoners in 1070. Saxon churches and cathedrals were pulled down, to be replaced by massive Norman cathedrals such as Durham or Winchester, and the sound of choirs of monks singing plainsong was heard throughout the land. Over 9,500 parish churches were built, many of which still stand. Those senior clerics and lawyers needed able assistants, and it was in the households of such men that young boys of promise received an education that would fit them for high office. In the awestruck words of the young boy Henry (who was later to become Bishop of Lincoln): 'When I saw the glory of our Bishop Robert, the handsome knights, noble youths, valuable horses, golden vessels . . . and satin garments, nothing could be more blessed.'[27] Under the Normans, England became a more flamboyant, sophisticated society with a population of approximately 2 million people.

It was in the schools set up by the monasteries that boys whose parents did not need their physical assistance in supporting the family income could learn Latin as young as five. It seems that the pedagogy (how teaching is done) had not changed since the first schools in Rome, for in 1170 a Durham monk, Reginald, noted that the drone of boys learning Latin and the thwack of corporal punishment were everyday sounds around the precincts of the cathedral, while one boy, 'driven by the fear of the blows of a fierce schoolmaster,'[28] resorted to throwing the keys of the schoolroom into the river. Teachers by the nature of their knowledge base in classical literature quickly assumed that mental agility followed from physical intimidation. Frankly, many of those teachers were bullies. Readers of Horace remembered that this famous Roman poet called his teacher 'Whacker' Orbillius,[29] and in the male-only world of monastic schools centuries ago, as in boys-only boarding schools of far more recent years, there was an overt recognition that the ancient Greeks honoured homosexuality, and an excessive 'whacking' environment was fuelled by, or indeed fuelled, pseudo-masochistic practices.

At the age of ten, while the more well-to-do child had already moved to the household of a nobleman, those of a lesser rank might start the formal disciplines of a grammar school (a term first used in 1387 to describe a school that went beyond simply transactional reading and writing to the study of the correct grammatical use of the language) where they worked for between eight and ten hours a day. Children would have earlier learned their alphabet from sheets of large text held up on a piece of wood:

> In (every) place as man may see,
> When a child to school shall set be,
> A book (for) him is brought,
> Nailed on a board of tree (wood),
> That men calleth an A B C
> Prettily wrote.[30]

Learning in the fourteenth century was largely by rote and rhyme, by question and answer, and enforced with the frequent use of the strap or cane. 'Spare the rod and spoil the child' became a catch-phrase already common in the eleventh century. Some schools started to provide boarding facilities, but this was expensive; the weekly boarding fee was the same as the termly fee for tuition – eight pence. In 1382, Winchester College was endowed to provide free boarding education for promising students with possibly a further hundred such schools scattered across the land endowed by local noblemen, such as that established in today's little-known Wotton-under-Edge in Gloucestershire four years earlier.

Just because many children never learned to write, does not mean that they could not read, and it certainly did not mean that they were ignorant. Far from it. In fourteenth-century England most people saw, if not within the day, certainly within the week, all those they needed to communicate with, and so had little incentive to write. But to be able to read was increasingly important, for that enabled ideas developed in one place to spread quickly to others. Six hundred years ago England had many storytellers and reciters of lengthy poems – men like Piers Plowman who, in a ballad written late in the century, described looking across the slopes of the Malvern Hills on a spring holiday and seeing 'a fair field full of folk' (so giving generations of subsequent pupils their first example of alliteration). Then there was Geoffrey Chaucer with his tales of the Canterbury Pilgrims, describing a robust, sometimes coarse and often hypocritical people who ached to live life to the full (Chaucer's famous Wife of Bath had seen off seven husbands; his Sumner 'had a fiery red cherubim's face with narrow eyes but he was as hot and leacherous as a sparrow', or the poor Schoolteacher 'who long ago dedicated himself to logic, but whose horse was as lean as a rake, while he was not right-fat I promise you, and looked kind of hollow and therefore most sober'). Those were English characters of the 1380s, for in the fourteenth century as in the twentieth century it took time for even the best students to master the connection between the spoken and the written word. As today, so in the fourteenth century, schooling and learning were not necessarily synonymous.[31]

Travellers would have been impressed by the country's apparent prosperity, and by the colourful nature of its festivities as well as its beliefs in hobgoblins, witches and fairies. Few yet questioned the biblical teaching that man's present life on earth was simply a preparation for eternity. Men feared that if death caught them unawares there would be no time for forgiveness and – be they king or pauper – it was to the fires of Hell that surely they would be bound. For the English living in today's highly secular society, it is hard to appreciate the quite enormous influence the Church and its teaching had on all aspects of daily life 500 years ago. The Church seemed an impregnable institution, the nearest thing ever seen to a superpower ruled over by a Pope whose spiritual authority was supported by temporal powers comparable in our day to those of the Secretary General of the United Nations, the President of the World Bank, the Chief Executive of the IMF and the financial resources of Microsoft all rolled into one person. To shout that this was heretical was to unleash the same civil powers of repression that an appeal to 'national security' does today.

As every schoolchild knows, it was Henry VIII who screamed that this was heretical – for it was he who first challenged the power of the Church.[32] His dissolution of the monasteries in the 1530s had the unintended consequence of leaving England with an immediate shortage of schools just at the point when expanding commercial interests called for larger numbers of educated young men. Edward VI diverted some of the monies from the suppressed monasteries to create nearly 100 new, free grammar schools,[33] while wealthy merchants early in Elizabeth's reign, no longer able to endow chanteries to say endless Masses for the good of their souls, turned instead to endowing more grammar schools. It was to one of those new free grammar schools, the one in Stratford-upon-Avon, that some fifteen or sixteen generations back (a mere quarter of an hour on that year-long evolutionary clock of human progress) came the young William Shakespeare, possibly, in his words of later years, 'the whining schoolboy, with his satchel, and shining morning face, creeping like a snail unwillingly to school'.[34]

Shakespeare's way of life had more in common with the Hadza, I believe, than we might have with Shakespeare. Think about it; in Shakespeare's time the fastest any man had ever travelled was on the back of a horse, for most travel was at walking speed of two-and-a-half to three miles an hour just as it is today with the Hadza. You think in a different way when you are walking from when driving along in a car – you smell your surroundings, you have time to notice what is going on around you, and you study your companions carefully lest they knife you on a quiet stretch of the road. All food in Shakespeare's day was locally sourced; fruit and vegetables were only available in their season, while dishonest butchers would sell bad meat and short-change you, given half a chance. Books were expensive but, as time was plentiful, if there was something to talk about, you simply talked about it. After 1,500 years, the Renaissance had rekindled men's interest in the kinds of scientific thinking that Aristotle had developed. This was a time to question everything. The inside of a man's body was as unknown to doctors as was the nature of distant continents to cartographers. Yet here also the English were pushing the boundaries, for in 1497 John Cabot and some twenty sailors left Bristol in a boat no bigger than that normally pulled up on an open beach, and crossed the Atlantic and discovered Newfoundland.

Shakespeare's generation in England was the last that, if they had thought about it, could have looked back over past generations and seen how a series of very many small steps in man's co-evolution with the environment accounted for the more comfortable life of succeeding generations.[35] But Shakespeare's generation could hardly have guessed at how much larger those steps were soon to become, and how much faster they would have to be climbed.[36] So look carefully at Shakespeare's time, for that was to be the platform – the half-landing if you like – that was to launch society on a totally new adventure. Consider carefully, as you get into the rest of this and the next chapter, as to whether this wasn't when society was just about to get too big for its natural boots.

As England's population increased to nearly 3 million by the mid-1500s and trade flourished, so merchants became aware of the need for a better educated public. It is thought that there were about 2,000 'Petty' (from the French meaning 'little') schools in England, about one for every five parishes. Surviving records are few, but we know that many of these were located in the porches of churches, or in the back rooms of shops. It was in such places that village children could be taught to read and do basic calculations.[37] Most Petty schools had only a single teacher (hence the alternative name of 'dame' schools), but they were an essential part of how it was that England became the exciting, entrepreneurial, competitive place it was soon to be. The bakers of London in 1619 estimated that it cost sixpence (two and a half new pence) a week to educate each of their children.[38] The Elizabethans were coming to recognize that as children went into what we now call adolescence, they were no longer content simply to be sat down and talked at, yet they weren't skilful enough to earn their own livings, and their exuberance made them terrifyingly vulnerable.[39] A ballad in the previous century had noted:

> But when his friends did comprehend
> His fond and foolish mind
> They sent him up to fair London town
> An apprentice for to bind.[40]

Seventeenth-century Englishmen didn't try to intellectualize adolescence, they simply put the youngsters to work. It was adolescent muscle that did so much of the back-breaking work on the farm, or in the workshop. The skilled cabinet maker or carriage builder relied on his apprentices to turn roughly cut timber into truly squared, smooth and prepared wood ready for the craftsmen to fashion into a marketable commodity. The same held true for the butcher, the baker and the candlestick maker. The apprentice and the master were legally bound to each other – by the 1563 Statute of Artificers (from the word *artefact*, the maker of useful things) every adolescent had either to undertake a seven-year craft apprenticeship, or be indentured as a labourer to a farmer. In a sense 1563 was the first-ever Act of what we might today call a combined department of education and employment.

There was simply no room in those days for youngsters who couldn't do something properly. Both craftsman and apprentice were dependent on each other for their livelihood. There was little slack. Mistakes easily led to devastation. Consequently, school was only the first part of most people's education. Apprenticeship was the period when nearly everybody learned how to earn a living. Apprenticeship was a form of coaching, not a continuation of the teaching the child had experienced in the Petty school. Apprenticeship was about stretching youngsters' powers of reasoning. 'You've got to learn to think like me, then you'll come to appreciate what I'm going to do next,' said the old craftsman. It was about showing how each sub-section of a job came together to create the whole. It was full of intuitive understandings, the things difficult to quantify in a textbook. Apprenticeship was about getting the learner to so understand what the task was all about and eventually to develop such a level of expertise that they knew that they were no longer dependent on simply playing by the rules. Master craftsmen were experts in knowing when to break a normally accepted rule so as to get an even more glorious result. You had to be good to be able to do that.

Shakespeare personifies that wealth of evolved mental architecture that speaks to our deepest emotions. As a child he had to have all his wits about him, every bit as much as did the children of the Hadza, to survive in a way that we, the hurried commuters and consumers that we have become, no longer understand. He was born in 1564 (a year after the Statute of Artificers) in a town of some 2,000 people, to parents who proved excellent role models. His mother was practical, sensitive and quick-witted and taught the young William to read and write, which was fortunate because his father, a successful businessman and land speculator, couldn't actually write. Not that this proved a disadvantage, for he was highly articulate at a time when most people delighted in disputation about religion, the nature of power and authority, the practicalities of trade, and human passions. When William was four, his father was elected Mayor of Stratford.

As inquisitive and energetic as would have been any of our ancestors back on the African savanna, the young Shakespeare also roamed widely through fields and forests so that later in his plays he accurately described no fewer than 60 species of birds, and a remarkable 180 plants. He poached and courted by the light of the moon, and with a lively imagination could see in a thunderstorm the makings of a fictitious and terrible tempest and shipwreck. In the five or six years he spent in school he studied Latin, mastered sentence construction and paraphrasing, and read Aesop's *Fables* as well as Ovid, Seneca and Juvenal. In those days, schooling simply supplemented a youngster's personal experience by creating a disciplined structure for mental development, rather than suffocating a youngster's sense of having to work things out for himself. When, in later years, Shakespeare wrote of adolescents with '*boiled brains*', interested in nothing but 'getting wench with child, wronging the ancientry, stealing, and fighting,'[41] he was probably describing himself.

Once an acknowledged playwright, Shakespeare packed the Globe Theatre day after day because he spoke in the vernacular about issues of a profundity that people who daily experienced the tragedies and rough-and-tumble of life readily appreciated. Shakespeare fed the practical curiosity and excitement of these islanders every bit as much as did those new Protestant theologians who were compelling sixteenth-century Englishmen to search the depths of their souls. As England became more puritan, so education was taken ever more seriously. 'Is there anything more precious, friendly and loveable than a pious, disciplined, obedient and teachable child?'[42] wrote a sanctimonious mid-sixteenth-century reformer imposing his own theological expectations on human nature. By the time Shakespeare died, England had some 450 grammar schools, though most of these consisted of only a single classroom in which boys of all ages were educated by a single teacher. Here was the beginning of that much bigger step that English society was to be the first in Europe to ascend. No one else had gone this way before, so the English had to learn as they went along.

To twenty-first-century readers, perhaps well versed in *The God Delusion*,[43] and maybe *The Dawkins Delusion*[44] as well, my insistence that you won't make sense of how the culture of the English can be understood without reference to the ordinary person's religious faith, may seem strange. But to our ancestors this was their reality, and it shaped everything they did. For 1,000 years the Catholic Church had reassured its followers that all would be well with them in Eternity if they simply followed the Church's rules. The Reformation that occurred just before Shakespeare's birth, had introduced what for simplistic sake I will call the 'harsh' Protestantism taught by Calvin which emphasized predestination – however good you thought you were, you might have already been predestined to go to Hell. This harsh belief system kept its followers forever on tenterhooks, constantly aware that the devil was awaiting around every corner. Much as this might surprise us, they took it very seriously and acted accordingly. Which is why, in setting out for the Promised Land they expected to find in the Americas, they put up with almost indescribable problems. These intrepid farmers-turned-fishermen-turned-deep-sea-sailors, sang their hymns as they crossed the Atlantic in ships no larger than a London double-decker bus. Of the 198 such ships that set out between 1621 and 1640, 197 arrived safely – one of them even recording in the ship's log that they had seen thirteen other ships as they sailed across 'the pond'.[45]

Although possessing the technology to cross that ocean, and a culture inspired by the injunction 'to take dominion over the fish of the sea . . . and over every living thing that moveth upon the earth,'[46] these colonists perished in large numbers through their inability to understand the vagaries of the climate, the nature of the vegetation, but particularly because they suffered from a particular English arrogance. That very English arrogance (which has to be understood in parallel to the influence of Calvin's teaching) was fast coming to overvalue the assumed manners of a gentleman, and the debasing of the practical skills of craftsmen.

That arrogance was in large measure due to one Roger Ascham who, in 1570, published the first book ever written in English on the theory of education. It was to be vastly important, up to and including the 1960s (it is why I had to struggle to learn Latin in the late 1950s). Ascham, former private tutor to Queen Elizabeth, set out three principles. First, he urged the cultivation of what he called 'hard wits' rather than the superficial 'quick wits' of those youngsters whose memories were good, but who couldn't work things out for themselves.[47] 'Because,' he said engagingly, 'I know that those which be commonly the wisest, the best learned, and best men also, when they be old, were never commonly the quickest of wits when they were young.' Second, he then urged teachers to be more gentle with their students, and warned them against what he called 'the butchery of Latine' – go easy on the birch, he was saying, for children who only learn because they are frightened gain nothing. But it was his third precept that was so surprising, and eventually so damaging. 'In the attainment of wisdom,' stated Ascham, 'learning from a book, or from a teacher, is twenty

times as effective as learning from experience.' Sensing that he
might be surprising his readers, he added the trite comment
that it was an unhappy mariner who learned his craft from
many shipwrecks. Consequently Ascham argued that it was
folly for young men to travel to Italy in search of the wisdom of
the ancients, for students would be better off studying books in
a library. Why such a trenchant injunction?

'I was once in Italy myself,' Ascham[48] apologized, 'but I
thanked God that my abode there was but nine days.' This
scholar from damp and temperate England where no men, and
certainly no women, ever took their clothes off in public, was
appalled by the lasciviousness of the statues, the writings and
paintings that archaeologists were starting to recover from the
dust of ancient Rome, and was horrified by the fascination these
held for lecherous sixteenth-century men. 'I saw in that little
time, in one city, more liberty to sin than ever I heard in our
noble city of London in nine years,' concluded Ascham piously
as he defined what he saw as the indisputable role of the school
of the future – schoolteachers would censor what it is that
students study.

*   *   *

By the beginning of the eighteenth century, England was a land
of fertile farms and busy harbours where energy, imagination
and innovation had been bred into the people by centuries of
pushing the boundaries in an island where to do so always
seemed to open further opportunities.[49] Craftsmen and apprentices alike thrived through reciprocal behaviour, empathetic
understanding, collaborative skills and a delight in experimen-
tation. England had developed a robust tradition of making
things well. But these self-sufficient working men and women

were becoming increasingly dismayed at the failure of their Bible-thumping priests to create a more equitable Christ-like society. Such dismayed Puritans seemed caught up in a voyage without a rudder, and 200 set out every week across the seas for America.

John Bunyan caught the mood of this confused people and, with the publication of *The Pilgrim's Progress* in 1678, turned the ordinary Englishman's life from an uncertain journey into an eternal personal pilgrimage.[50] For the next 200 years this was the second most widely read book in the English language. Bunyan literally provided Everyman with a colloquial story, the values of which they could live by, and on which they could model their own lives. Here was to be the 'soft' face of Protestantism. Millions of people subsequently reframed their lives as pilgrims, so regaining the dignity of being 'choice makers' in their own lives. They knew they had filled their own rucksacks with worldly goods, they smelt the stench of the Slough of Despond, and renewed their attempts to reach the House Beautiful, being careful all the time to bypass Vanity Fair and the Valley of the Shadow of Death. Honest men they were, who took life seriously, did the best they could in everything they understood, and laid the foundations for what came to be called the Protestant work ethic.

The English were to maintain these sentiments and entrepreneurial behaviours for a long time. As recently as the early 1700s, only one person in five lived in a town. While London had a massive population of half a million, Norwich, the second-largest city, was only a twentieth of the size.[51] Half of these English urbanites lived in towns of fewer than 2,500 people – little larger than the Ambridge of BBC *Archers'* fame today. These towns were so small that a healthy adult was never more than a ten-minute walk from the fields and woodlands. In this congenial environment the Englishman's way of living was the culmination of the steady co-evolution of man and his surroundings that had gone on, not just for 5,000 or even 50,000 years, but since the beginning of human time. Here was a fine balance between the evolution of the internal mechanisms of the brain – to survive in this equation people had to use on a daily basis the multiple forms of intelligence that we now know reside within each of us – and a manageable, but always challenging, environment. Everything that our imaginative ancestors created had to be made by the sweat of their brow. Life was still on a sufficiently human scale for people to know – at a deeply subconscious level – that everything was connected.[52] They had to act intelligently in all that they did. 'Do not imagine that the knowledge, which I so much recommend to you, is confined to books, pleasing, useful and necessary as that knowledge is,' the Earl of Chesterfield wrote to his son in 1746, 'the knowledge of the world is only to be acquired in the world, and not in a closet. Books alone will never teach it to you; but they will suggest many things to your observation, which might otherwise escape you.'[53]

It was this practical creativity that was the greatest asset England had ever possessed, but in the eighteenth century the English became so busy getting rich that their attitude towards education started to turn strictly utilitarian. The high seriousness of Puritan times had bequeathed to latter generations an intense interest in reading and a desire for self-improvement. In the early 1700s, half the men and a quarter of the women could read and write, yet formal schooling now held little attraction to their children. The young Humphrey Repton was typical of the times in being removed from Norwich Grammar School at the age of twelve because 'my father thought it proper to put a stopper to the vial of classical literature, having determined to make me a rich, rather than a learned man'.[54] Some grammar schools collapsed, never to be heard of again; Winchester College received only ten pupils in 1750, and the number of students going to Oxford and Cambridge fell by nearly a half.[55] Yet in this society where most people were too busy to go to school, innovation knew no limits.

No society in history has ever had to reinvent itself so quickly, or so often, as did England as the eighteenth century began to merge with the nineteenth. Here was the spontaneous expression of a people's energy, dependent not simply on the brilliance of an inventor but on the practical skills of carpenters and blacksmiths, goldsmiths, clockmakers and engineers, in hundreds of towns and thousands of villages ready instantly to turn such designs into new machines. England was full of thinkers who knew how to make their innovations work.[56] There was Thomas Newcomen, a village blacksmith who, in 1712, invented and then made the first steam pump to lift water out of deep mines. Then there was John Harrison, the son of a village carpenter, who over a 40-year period designed and built a clock of such perfect accuracy that it enabled ships' captains to compute their exact longitude, so giving the British Navy the technology to rule the waves. And then William Smith, a former apprentice surveyor who, in the course of building canals, developed such a fascination with the rocks that he exposed that, over a twenty-year period, he forced himself to walk an average of 50 miles every weekend so as to produce, totally single-handedly, the first-ever geological map of England and Wales.

In 1759 the iron masters at the Carron Works outside Glasgow started to forge the new world by smelting iron ore, resulting in the Darby family in Shropshire laying the first-ever iron rails at Coalbrookdale in 1767.[57] Twelve years later they built the world's first iron bridge over the River Severn. Then a Scottish engineer, James Watt, revolutionized Newcomen's steam engine and, by using separate condensers, turned a simple horizontal motion into a rotational force. 'I sell here,' the exuberant engineer Matthew Boulton exclaimed in 1776 as he showed off his new machine, 'what all the world desires to have – power.' By the end of the century the population of England had risen to 6.5 million, while trade had doubled in twenty years and coal production increased 30 per cent in five years. The world had never seen growth or change on this scale before. Men were torn between excitement and sheer horror; writing in *The Prelude* in 1805, Wordsworth said: 'Twas in truth an hour of universal ferment; mildest men were agitated . . . the soil of common life was at that time too hot to tread upon.'

There was a dark, very dark side to all this innovation. In 1771 a former wigmaker by the name of Richard Arkwright built the world's first mechanical textile factory at Cromford in Derbyshire.[58] Within ten years he was employing 5,000 workers and had a capital of more than £200,000, almost equal to the combined expenditure at the time of both the Army and the Navy. The textile industry exemplified what the Industrial Revolution would be all about. Before Arkwright's innovation, the industry consisted of tens of thousands of tiny family businesses, each conducted almost exclusively within the home.[59] Spinning, weaving, cutting and tailoring could all be done within a single family, as indeed could the minding of sheep, and the selling of the final product at the local market. Children by the age of nine or ten knew a lot about the labour that provided their daily bread. They might have been poor, but they had to use their brains effectively on a daily basis if they were to survive.

Industrialization changed every aspect of this equation.[60]

While men of business became phenomenally wealthy in a very short time, the descendants of those countless generations of self-taught farmers, small tradesmen and craftsmen, who made all this innovation actually happen, saw the craft traditions they had inherited from their forebears completely disappear within a couple of generations. Robust individualism was replaced by an unthoughtful, demotivated and unskilled mob of people, ready only for the life of the factory that was then being created. For millions of youngsters over several generations their nature was forgotten, their innate predispositions totally ignored, so depriving them of that nurture which is essential to the brain's natural functioning. This was to be a disaster, for which we are still paying the price. Men who had learned an apprenticeship from their fathers now realized they had neither a craft skill, nor a set of social and moral values to offer their own children. Men lost faith in the value of fatherhood. Adam Smith, the Scottish philosopher who had argued so cogently in *The Wealth of Nations*[61] for the financial benefits to be gained from such industrial processes, had been fearful that, should this happen, then the earlier 'alert intelligence of the craftsmen' would be replaced by factory operatives who would be 'generally as stupid and ignorant as it is possible for a human creature to become'. That is just what happened. Working men lost not only their dignity, but also their sense of purpose. Their informal learning networks collapsed, and literacy levels declined dramatically. Drunkenness increased, matrimony decreased, but the birth rate rose remorselessly.

Here was social melt-down on a scale never before experienced, or anticipated. The Industrial Revolution took England rapidly up a series of steps so high that society started to suffer from vertigo. Elizabethan poor laws had required every parish to levy a rate to defray the cost of maintaining paupers in their own workhouses, but these new industrial cities sprawled across ancient parish boundaries, and the new 'industrial' poor – far from having no work – were so exhausted by the long hours and tedium of factory work that they could neither care for their children, nor afford to feed them. Tender as might have been the consciences of those doing well, the emerging middle classes were nevertheless fearful of interfering with what had earlier been accepted by politicians as the beneficent force of natural laws which, left to themselves, always tended towards balance and stability. Looking across the Channel at the turmoil of the French Revolution, Englishmen were terrified that government intervention in any way might only inflame the situation. It was best, they thought, to do nothing.

So that is what happened. Effectively government did little other than limit to twelve hours a day, six days a week, the time which children below the age of ten could be employed down a mine or in a factory. The Sabbath, however, was sacrosanct; the mills stopped, shops closed and youthful energy released from the horrors and boredom of the factory began to take its revenge. Multitudes of children, it is reported, prowled the streets 'in the shape of wolves and tygers, and honest men feared to leave their homes least they be plundered by children'.[62] This was a threat to social order, obvious to all. Consequently, as the nineteenth century dawned, well-meaning and well-to-do men and women sought to do what Parliament was still unwilling to undertake; they began to establish in the new sprawling industrial cities voluntary Sunday Schools where children could learn to read and discover enough of Christian teaching so that, when they died – which might be soon – they would have, so their sponsors fervently believed, a chance of going to Heaven.

Schools these hardly were; rather they were places of refuge for lost and abandoned children. The idea caught on rapidly. As

Sunday was the day of rest for adults, why couldn't Sunday Schools be set up for all children?[63] Sunday School rapidly became a whole day's activity, including lessons, church services and the provision of what was for many children the only hot meal they received in a week. The movement was a phenomenal success, with three-quarters of a million children attending these schools in the late 1790s, rising to one-and-three-quarter million by 1830, and twice that figure by 1850.[64] The teachers were all volunteers, educated, well-to-do men and women including some of the highest in the land, such as three successive Lord Chancellors. Today some historians look at such people and dismiss them as mere Lord and Lady Bountifuls, but that is to significantly misunderstand the Victorians. They believed that to give of themselves and of their time was better than to pay somebody else to do such an important task on their behalf. (Today in Plains, Georgia, citizens see nothing incongruous in former President of the United States Jimmy Carter teaching Sunday School every week.)

Alert businessmen began to see an opportunity. Impressed by a scheme proposed in 1808 by the Quaker Joseph Lancaster[65] to use pupil-teachers to help provide a cheap, mechanical form of mass schooling, he sought to introduce the monitorial system. These schools consisted of single rooms, 39 feet wide and 106 feet long which accommodated 660 children in 33 rows of 20 desks. One teacher, relying on the services of his monitors, could supposedly teach all 660 children the 'three Rs' at a cost of seven shillings per annum per child. 'Give me twenty-four pupils today, and I'll give you twenty-four teachers tomorrow,' he boasted.[66] To the uninitiated this sounded a bargain too good to be true, but it frightened people as well. 'Giving education to the labouring classes and the poor would, in effect, be prejudicial to their morals and happiness,' claimed members of

Parliament. 'It would teach them to despise their lot in life, instead of making them good servants in agriculture, and other laborious employment to which their rank in society had destined them,' for 'it would render them insolent to their superiors.'[67]

Tentatively over the next 30 years, the churches began to build schools of their own that would operate throughout the week. Twelve hundred were built in the 1820s, and a further 3,000 in the next ten years, all entirely from voluntarily contributions. They were, however, most careful not to give offence to the Victorian belief in the sacredness of the status quo by what they taught, always stating, 'The folly of thinking it unjust that one man should receive more than another for his labour.'[68] Yet this satisfied no one. 'This word-teaching, rote-learning, memory-loading system is still disguised by the name of education, and those who are stored with its greatest lumber [raw and unseasoned timber] are deemed the greatest scholars,'[69] railed William Lovett, the self-educated Cornishman who was to dominate the Chartist movement out of which was to arise socialism, and later in the early twentieth century the British Labour Party. 'Seeing this, need we wonder that scholars have so little practical or useful knowledge – are so superficial in reasoning . . . what is needed . . . is a pedagogy of self-activity, personal discovery and creative understanding. Give a man knowledge and you give him the light to perceive and enjoy beauty, variety, surpassing ingenuity and majestic grandeur, which his mental darkness previously concealed from him.'[70]

Eventually, in 1833, Parliament made a grant of 30,000 pounds to assist the churches in building more schools, but so as not to be thought too enthusiastic about the cause of the education of the poor, Parliament also voted £38,000 for the rebuilding of the Royal Stables at Windsor Castle. But Victorian prejudice against publicly funded education remained enormous, not least towards the teachers. One official commented: 'Little else is required of a teacher other than an aptitude for enforcing discipline, and acquaintance with mechanical details for preservation of order, and that sort of ascendancy in his school which a sergeant major is required to exercise over a batch of new recruits.' Worse was to follow; Lord Macaulay, the detached, intellectual Victorian historian, who disclaimed any interest in science, technology, art or music and proudly admitted his inability to shave himself or to tie his own cravat, described schoolmasters as 'the refuse of all callings, to whom no gentleman would entrust the key of his wine cellar'.

These were the shaky foundations on which British primary education were to be built – education seen as charity, and a way of keeping children off the streets so that parents could work ever-longer hours. What, then, of the possible origins of secondary education, and whatever happened to apprenticeship? These are the concerns of Chapters 5 and 6.

5

Hands-on Apprentices to Hands-off Pupils

The Industrial Revolution was the most fundamental transformation of life in the history of the world, and for a brief time this coincided with the history of the British Isles. An entire world economy was built up and around what happened here, giving these small islands a global influence and power never before seen anywhere. For nearly a century it appeared as if Britain were the world's only workshop, its only massive importer and exporter, its only carrier, its only imperialist, and its only foreign investor. All this came at a great cost, for it reshaped the British in ways with which, 200 years later, we are still not comfortable.[1] Neither are those other countries whose developments in the nineteenth century were so shaped by being part of the British Empire, or through the influence of the English language. Most people today are unclear about the origins of their culture, and as such are confused about what they see as a desirable future.

The theme 'hands-on apprentices to hands-off pupils' runs as strongly, and as devastatingly, through educational policy in the United States, Canada, Australia, India, New Zealand and the former African colonies as it does in England in the early years of the twenty-first century. The roots of so many of the problems that beset today's education systems are to be found in this chapter. While English readers looking to understand fully the nature of the problems in their land need to take careful stock of the whole of this chapter, Canadians, for example, may ponder that it was the British North America Act of 1867 (written at the same time, and with the same attitudes, that Forster was preparing 'The Education of the Poor Act' in 1870) that probably explains much of the tensions in Canadian education to this day between the federal and the provincial jurisdictions. While Australians, as well as Canadians, will see the explanation for their sometimes separate Catholic, Protestant and public school boards, all English-speaking countries can see the spreading influence of the elite independent boarding schools serving only those who could afford their fees.

The Industrial Revolution, first in England and then in many other countries, progressively turned vast numbers of formerly self-employed men into 'proletarians', workers who had no other means of support than the money they were paid for a job. No longer had workers to think for themselves, they just followed orders. Most work became a highly regulated, monotonous and routine activity over which workers exercised no control and in which they had little interest. Instead of working within their homes, employment was now to be in factories in large, anonymous cities – cities that denied the kinds of integrated, inter-dependent communities from which their ancestors had come. Most destabilizing of all, the Industrial Revolution set up a conflict between the natural relationship of man to his work (a balance that evolved over a million years so as to create the human ingenuity that had given birth to the Industrial Revolution), and the economic rationality of the capitalist present.

England's reservoir of thoughtful, innovative people was drastically reduced during the early stages of the Industrial Revolution, so that the next generation of children inherited a vastly depreciated sense of a community, as well as ways of living in which people no longer learned as they worked. Some Englishmen had much more money in their pockets, but the quality of life of the majority had been vastly undermined, and those most broken by the experience were assigned to the workhouses, their children forcibly taken from them. It took Oliver Twist just six words, 'Please sir, I want some more,' to expose the callous world of those workhouses in 1837, the year Victoria became Queen. Desperate with hunger and reckless with misery, Oliver's request was simplicity itself, yet it called forth brutal treatment from Mr Bumble the beadle and his view that such insolence meant 'I've never been more convinced of anything in my life, than I am that that boy will come to be hung.'[2] With such stories Dickens began to prick Victorian social complacency.

The English, however, prefer good-news stories to facing harsh realities, so it was the invention in 1857 of that fictitious schoolboy, Tom Brown, that was to prove extraordinarily influential in transforming secondary education, and class-based social attitudes, in England and across the emerging Empire. Thomas Hughes, the author of *Tom Brown's Schooldays*,[3] entered Rugby School as a twelve-year-old boarder six years after the soon-to-be-enormously-famous Dr Arnold was appointed headmaster. The book was compelling reading for young adolescents dreaming of getting away from the constraints of home, with its stories about Flashman, the school bully, pillow fights and of young Tom's pugnacious defence of Little Arthur. More important still, Victorian parents saw in such an education a way for their sons to ascend still further up the social ladder which they themselves had tentatively started to climb years before. And that was largely what Victorian England was all about, gaining social prestige.

The Rugby School that Arnold created was like nothing that had existed before, anywhere. Arnold recognized that the

Industrial Revolution would produce increasing numbers of self-made men who had no wish to see their sons go through the same grubby apprenticeships that had made them wealthy.[4] Arnold offered the emerging wealthy middle classes an education that would take their children off their hands for eight months of the year and introduce them only to children like themselves. By ensuring a deep commitment to Christian values, fused with the teachings of ancient Greece and Rome, he would turn them into 'gentlemen', the ultimate social aspiration of Victorian self-made men. He did this, not by creating a nineteenth-century version of the glass, steel and concrete 'schools of the future' that twenty-first-century men imagine to be a sign of quality, but by building a bridge back to the hallowed walls, the cloistered quadrangles and the classical curriculum that men persuaded themselves had been the values of pre-industrial times. Arnold put character firmly at the heart of elite public school education, and made Rugby School probably the most famous, and the most copied, school in the world.

To understand how Arnold identified the 'unique selling points' for his own times, we should remind ourselves of the educational world that he burst upon. For decades, Englishmen had been losing interest in the ancient grammar schools that had offered free education to local children of ability. Well-to-do parents looked for broader opportunities where their youngsters' energy and gumption could be well applied. Some, like the Revd Edmund Nelson, arranged for his eleven-year-old son Horatio to join the Navy as a mid-shipman in 1769.[5] Others preferred to send their sons to private commercial establishments, some of which taught foreign languages, geography and accountancy. Such schools might seem to be an appropriate response to the market forces that Arnold had identified, but most of them disappeared within a few years simply because they lacked the one thing that mattered to the Victorians – social cachet, the mark of belonging to the upper classes.

It was potential social cachet that Arnold saw in the ancient buildings of Rugby School. With extraordinary energy he took the rough and tumble of a largely unreformed Georgian boarding school and infused it with a fresh sense of purpose. 'What we must look for in this school,' he told the pupils, 'is firstly religious and moral principles, secondly gentlemanly conduct, and thirdly intellectual ability.'[6] Manliness to Arnold meant the ability to conquer moral weakness – not just physical prowess on the games field, which didn't interest him greatly, but the mental and spiritual determination to find responsible self-fulfilment. Arnold was determined to convert the emerging middle classes to his vision of an England and an Empire led by Christian gentlemen. When he was appointed to Rugby, it had an income of £6,000 from its ancient endowments, an enormous sum and enough, the citizens of Rugby argued, to produce a free, quality education for 500 boys. (Twelve pounds a boy compared with 35 pence a year charged at a monitorial school.) With remarkable, but remorseless, sleight-of-hand, Arnold totally overthrew the town's ambitions and progressively filled Rugby with fee-paying pupils drawn from a distance and made possible by the rapidly expanding rail network.

Progressively Arnold defined the Victorian public school as an elite, fee-paying, boarding school (with no connection to its local community) exclusively for the sons of emerging gentlemen, and possessing a passionate commitment to Christian beliefs and ethics. He reinvigorated the classical curriculum of Roger Ascham and virtually banned the teaching of science, writing in his diary, 'Rather than have [science] the principal thing in my son's mind, I would gladly have him think that the sun went around the earth, and that stars were so many bangles in the bright firmament.'[7] Quite right too, probably thought many a self-made man seeking entry for his son to the ranks of the gentry, for science reminded him too forcefully of the mechanical things which had enabled him to make his fortune in the first place. But this was to be a devilishly narrow education for young men who, within twenty years, would be reading Darwin's thoughts on evolution.

The egalitarian expectations of the founders of Elizabethan grammar schools, who believed that good education should be available to all regardless of income, and whose schools had earlier educated Shakespeare, Milton and Wordsworth, were now to be hijacked and become available only to those who could pay. Within a few years it became 'a fact beyond dispute [that] Englishmen of the upper-class send their children away from home to be educated . . . and the reason . . . is not the teaching [but that the boarding school is] a better place for a boy to grow up in than the home'.[8] One of the most enthusiastic of Arnold's followers was to claim that to admit tradesmen's sons would have resulted in the sons of gentlemen shaking hands with school fellows behind the counter, 'so creating a confusion of classes that wealthy parents would have found most distasteful'.[9] And that was exactly what the emerging Victorian upper-middle classes did not want to happen. To the socially ambitious, the way Arnold had defined the public school was the ideal mechanism to create, and subsequently to perpetuate, class divisions. The Victorian public schools became immensely popular to those who could afford to buy into the system. Within a mere twenty years those ancient grammar schools were to be transformed and filled almost entirely with boarders, so that the opportunity for local boys of ability but limited finance were reduced dramatically. But 'public', in a way that suggests they were open to everyone, they certainly never were, and were never intended to be.

*   *   *

The Victorian public schools were a glorious distraction in the eyes of those self-made men who now saw themselves as some of the most powerful people in the land.[10] But they were a disastrous distraction nevertheless, for to donate money for a school library, a fine new Gothic chapel, even to provide schools and chapels in Africa, diverted these powerful men's attentions and energies from the social horrors to be found in their own backyards. Only 80 miles north of Rugby, Manchester's population had increased tenfold in 70 years, with cotton output increasing in the new cotton mills by 39 per cent in the second decade of the century and 47 per cent in the third. Trade boomed, fortunes were made but wages went up by only 5 per cent. The grandchildren and great-grandchildren of the displaced craftsmen of the pre-industrial era worked extraordinarily long hours for a barely living wage to create the profits that the emerging middle classes then used, among other things, to build their enormous country estates and their mock gothic mansions, and to send their sons to the public schools.

A visiting Frenchman shuddered as he beheld the belching smokestacks and the crowded and stinking slums of the newly built industrial cities, for 'civilized man is turned back almost into a savage,'[11] he noted in his diary. In industrial cities there was literally nothing for children to do – no parks to play in, no schools to attend, initially no churches in which to gain a sense of purpose, no apprenticeships to train in, and no older people with time to talk to them. Instead there was just the grinding boredom of life in the factory. An American visitor in 1845 wrote that 'every day I live I thank heaven that I'm not a poor man with a family in England'.[12] Adam Smith's worst fears were being born out just at the moment when the public schools emerged triumphantly as idyllic places for rich children to attend. Far from the Puritan dream in the seventeenth century of a society of interdependent men and women, nineteenth-century England was fast becoming instead 'two nations, between whom there is no intercourse, no sympathy; who are as ignorant of each other's habits, thoughts and feelings as if they were dwellers in different zones, or inhabitants of different planets. You speak', wrote Disraeli soon to become Prime Minister, 'of the Rich and the Poor.'[13]

More than halfway through that century, which had seen more wealth created than ever before anywhere in the world, 40 per cent of children still had no school to attend, and most of those who were in school left before the age of eleven. Parliamentarians, still convinced by arguments that nothing should be done which might encourage the poor to have large families, believed that however rich or poor a person might be, each was responsible for his or her own destiny. It was not Parliament's duty to intervene. Consequently the well-to-do remained utterly opposed to any form of national education provision for fear that this might upset the social order. Lest it should be thought that a Commission set up 'to enquire into the present state of popular education in England and to consider what measures, if any, are required for the extension of sound and cheap elementary education to all classes of people,'[14] might result in government becoming more involved, an official hastened to reassure the Commons, 'We do not profess to give these children an education that will raise them above their station and business in life,[15] but to give them an education that will fit them for just that purpose.' The early Victorians were determined to maintain their social standing whatever the cost.

To justify receiving a government grant, pupils in every school were to be quizzed each year by an inspector in four subjects. For each child who failed to grasp a subject adequately, that grant would be cut by a quarter. 'I cannot promise the House that this scheme will be an economical one,' said the Minister, 'and I can't promise it will be an efficient one, but I can promise that it shall be one or the other.'[16] The cleverness of the comment was greeted with a round of nervous applause. Charles Dickens saw such 'payment by results' for what it was, a mechanical treadmill that killed the imagination, and forever dulled the mind. In his fictitious Mr Gradgrind, Dickens portrayed such a teacher as 'a man of realities . . . a kind of cannon loaded to the muzzle with facts, and prepared to blow them out at one discharge . . . he and some hundred and forty other schoolmasters had been turned out at the same time, in the same factory, on the same principles, like so many pianoforte legs'.[17] While Parliamentarians didn't want to become involved in the minutiae of running schools, they were steadily coming to accept that something had to be done to release that natural talent of children which earlier generations had shown was so abundant among the people.

Samuel Smiles was a man who knew just what needed to be done. *Self-Help*,[18] which this enigmatic figure – one-time doctor, sometime journalist and always a moralist – published in 1859, sold a quarter of a million copies. It stirred men to action and stiffened their sinews. It was eminently quotable:

Daily experience shows that it is energetic individualism that produces the most powerful effects upon the life and action of others and readily constitutes the best practical education. Schools, academies and colleges, give but the

merest beginnings of culture in comparison with it. Far
more influential is the life-education daily given in our
homes, in the streets, behind counters, in workshops, at the
loom and the plow, in counting houses and manufactories,
and in the busy haunts of men.[19]

Smiles was a kind of economic re-embodiment of the spirit of
John Bunyan. 'The spirit of self-help is the root of all growth
and a man can achieve almost anything by the exercise of his
own free powers of action and self-denial.'[20] His phrases stick in
the mind with the tenacity of a scriptural text. 'You are what
you make yourself to be; help from without is often enfeebling,
but help from within invigorates.' *Self-Help* was about resilience, the determination that the more you can do for yourself,[21] the more in control of your future you believe yourself
to be. *Self-Help* defined what the Victorians thought of themselves.

The mid-Victorians not only thought differently from their
grandparents who had first created England's industrial wealth,
they thought very differently from us, especially about religion,[22] democracy and social order. Well-read as many of them
were from their boarding school education in the writings of
Plato, Aristotle, Sophocles, Virgil and the rest, they saw it as
perfectly natural that their God-given status as the elite gave
them the authority to reform all aspects of national life. By
putting a highly Protestant theology together with the Greek
concept of social order and Roman discipline, these Victorians
became a highly paternalistic, order-conscious, self-directed and
ever more class-structured society. In social terms, what Arnold
had done at Rugby was as influential in shaping Victorian
society as what Arkwright had done 60 years before with his
textile mill at Cromford. Victorian England was a fusion of

these two revolutions, one economic and the other – based on a totally new type of school – social.

Delighting in the fact that Britain was by far and away the richest country in the world with her trade exceeding the combined trade of France, Germany, the United States and Italy, the mid-Victorians convinced themselves that this was the way it would be for ever – a truly 'British world'.[23] Yet England's lacklustre performance in the Crimean War (1853–56) had shown that education had to be taken far more seriously, for a modern state required fit, healthy as well as literate men. The *laissez-faire* attitudes of the first part of the century were giving way to a determination to create a national system of education that would both keep the masses under control, while also fitting them for an industrial economy. But of even greater importance to eminent Victorians was the need for more able administrators to lead their expanding empire. So while the churches remained concerned to extend elementary education to all those who still had no school to attend, Parliament gave top priority to the education of the sons of the upper classes.

A Commission was established in 1862 to investigate the oldest public schools (The Nine Great Schools).[24] While criticizing many of their archaic administrative procedures, the Commissioners happily concluded that due to the education that the country's leaders had received as boys in these 'great' schools, the English people should be indebted to these schools for the qualities on which Englishmen prided themselves most: 'Their capacity to govern others and control themselves, their aptitude for combining freedom with order, their public spirit and their vigorous manliness of character.'[25] These schools, they argued, were responsible for 'moulding the character of the English gentleman'. Here were accolades indeed for the revolution that Dr Arnold had earlier brought about, but then the

Commissioners went on to berate the schools for virtually ignoring modern languages and science teaching, so placing 'the upper classes in a state of inferiority to the middle and lower classes'. Despite such harsh criticism, the Commissioners concluded that what the country needed above all else was a massive expansion of public schools to increase the country's leadership capability.

Consequently a further Commission was set up to investigate the other 3,000 or so endowed schools established in earlier times in many towns and villages to be found across the country.[26] What those Commissioners quickly discovered was so appalling that their report could not be glossed over. Only a quarter of these schools even attempted to offer an education higher than that necessary for the manual classes. In other words, three-quarters of the schools did little more than had the 'dame' schools of a century or more before. Only 218 had a kind of grammar school curriculum, and of these 101 made no attempt to prepare boys for university.[27] So, little more than six generations ago, in a country whose population was fast approaching 11 million, with an empire soon to include a quarter of the world's population, that left just 100 schools which accepted a responsibility to prepare boys for university.

In a final twist, on average half of those schools sent only a single pupil to university each year. Indeed, one north country grammar school founded in 1524, and now a reasonably well-known public school, had conditions so bad that the commissioners despaired 'at putting it into any class at all. In its present state it simply clutters the ground.'[28] The Commissioners then went on to evaluate the elementary schools set up by the churches over the previous 50 years. From their enquiries they concluded that approximately one-third of the money needed for these schools came from the churches, one-third from government grants, while the parents paid the remaining third (between two and four pennies a week). Preoccupied with the priority to be given to more public schools for the elite, the Commissioners then reached the extraordinary conclusion that it was a waste of endowment funds for these any longer to be employed in the education of the poor. The poor, they concluded, were almost able to look after themselves.

To the consternation of local people in town and country alike, the Commissioners recommended the closure of all charity schools, and the confiscation of their funds. In future even the poorest child would have to pay for what previously had been free. 'To put a fee on for education where one has not existed before will, when anybody writing about it in three hundred years hence, be quoted as a mark of the barbarities of our age,' stated an apoplectic governor of a Birmingham school.[29] The Commissioners were totally unmoved. They looked most favourably at some well-placed but undersubscribed old grammar schools and started to transfer to them the funds that had previously been bequeathed for the education of all children, regardless of their parents' wealth. Quickly those old grammar schools favoured by the Commissioners began to emulate the kind of boarding school that Arnold had built at Rugby. That, argued the Commissioners, was what mid-Victorian England most needed – not charity schools for the poor, but subsidized elite boarding education for the middle classes.

*   *   *

It was over the winter of 1869/70 that two separate events occurred which initiated so many of the tensions that still run with such devastation through the English educational system more than a century later. The first was the establishment of what was called at the time 'a sort of club' of public school head-masters. The second was the passing of the 1870 Education Act (called in its drafting stage 'The Education of the Poor Act') dealing exclusively with elementary education.

In the meantime, plans were being formulated by W. E. Forster who, with a new Liberal government pledged to reform education, had assumed Parliamentary responsibility for educa-tion.[30] Forster inherited two problems. First, he had to deal with his party's enthusiasm to use the confiscated endowment funds to establish a national examination system, and a national certi-fication system for teachers. This was a radical departure from earlier Victorian thinking for, at a time when most Englishmen still thought that education (whether you had it or ignored it) was a personal responsibility, these proposals incensed many of the old Tories and, by intruding on their assumed autonomy, these plans infuriated the public schools. Second, while the churches wanted an enlarged grant to expand a specifically Christian form of elementary schooling, an increasingly influ-ential secular lobby wanted education freed from all such control by the Church. Forster was a sincere and honest man, but his party was in difficulty, and he was forced to compromise at every point.

The public school headmasters saw in Forster's support for a national examination system a threat to the freedom they saw as theirs to define a curriculum for the elite totally separate from the elementary curriculum for the working classes. The head-masters bridled at the support which they feared Forster was about to give enthusiastic scientists, and they were especially contemptuous of Forster's proposal for a certification system for teachers. It is important to understand what happened, for these headmasters, who were the guardians of the sons of the upper classes, were to do everything in their extensive power to limit the education of the lower classes. 'How ridiculous it will seem in years to come,' wrote one of them as he denigrated the work of the Commissioners, 'appointing a lot of squires and a stray lord or two to gather promiscuous evidence on an intricate professional question, and sum up, and pronounce infallible judgment on it.'[31] It would be hard to be much more dismissive than that.

So over that Christmas period those headmasters, small in number but immensely influential, defied Forster to go any further with plans that might in any way equate public schools and their pupils as being co-equals with the staff and pupils of lesser schools. So influential had their 'old boys' network' become that Forster was obliged to back down, and all plans for a national system of examination and teachers' certification were lost for more than 30 years. The power of this self-appointed group of autocrats to develop the education of the upper-middle-class elite totally separate from any national system was confirmed by default. It was to be a devastating setback for the education of ordinary Englishmen.[32]

Bruised by this confrontation, Forster turned to the elementary schools where he found even greater problems. It is hard nowadays to appreciate just why our Victorian ancestors were so convinced that personal charity was a better use of their money than taxation applied by a third party, but Forster perfectly understood the contemporary Victorian's need to be personally involved. So while the National Education League, an organization much backed by business leaders in the cities, urged the setting up of a national system of education funded through a local tax on householders, the majority of Parliamentarians remained bitterly opposed to anything that took the control of schools out of the hands of the Establishment. Forster trod very carefully and compromised again. He reassured Parliament that, 'if we are to hold our position among the nations of the world, we'll have to make up for the smallness of our numbers by increasing the intellectual force of the individual'. That sounded just fine, until he unpacked his solution: 'Our object is to complete the present voluntary system, to fill up the gaps, sparing the public money where it can be done without, procuring as much as we can with the assistance of parents, and welcoming the co-operation of those benevolent men who desire to assist their neighbours.'[33] Here was no grand, revolutionary plan. Forster looked to retain the philanthropic traditions of Victorian society and combine these with the levying of a direct rate to be applied where the churches had not been able to build schools themselves.

The 1870 Act required every borough to identify where there were gaps in the current provision of schools.[34] Forster then made significant grants to the churches for them to establish more schools. Where this was not done by the end of that year, arrangements were made to establish locally elected school boards. The possibility of non-church-controlled education quickly caught the attention of secular reformists. Here was a problem that Forster had failed to see, and which was to increase with every passing year. In comparison with many of the church schools that were 70 or more years old, these board schools were modern, larger, often better built, properly equipped, and able to pay their teachers higher salaries. Compulsory taxation, the churches were forced to admit, was a more assured way of raising money than passing around a collection plate. Yet the principle of such taxation was vehemently attacked by many: 'You can't break the laws of nature,' argued one of the public school headmasters, 'which have made the work and powers of men vary in value. This is what I mean when I ask, why should I maintain my neighbour's illegitimate child? I mean by illegitimate every child brought into the world who demands more than his parents can give him, or to whom the government makes a present of money. The school boards are promising to be an excellent example of public robbery.'[35]

Only irresponsible people, thought mid-Victorian Tories, would leave it to government to educate their own children. The Liberals, however, were starting to realize that so great had the gap become between what the rich could afford to spend on their children's education, and what the poor could hardly afford, that without government action this would eventually undermine the country's ability to compete with better educated societies. Here was the beginning of the clash between two competing political positions; is education primarily for the good of the individual (the position of the Tories), or was it to be a general good that would serve society as a whole?

The 1870 Education Act was the first of the six 'turning points' in education that have created the England of today, the others being 1902, 1944, 1965, 1988 and 2003. The 1870 Act, by opening up the possibility of non-church-controlled education, quickly caught the attention of secular reformists, and cities like London, Birmingham, Leeds, Newcastle and Bristol were quick to establish local Boards of Education. Disraeli again caught the mood of the times: 'Upon the education of the people of this country, the fate of this country depends.'[36] Taking control of their fate by establishing their own school boards released amazing energy, especially in the rapidly growing industrial areas. There was a rush to build new board schools, often of red brick and towering over the local urban landscapes like factories. Soon these became commonplace. A school for infants in Birmingham had 600 children within a year, and 900 nearly a year later.[37] There were indeed big gaps to fill, and there were certainly increasing numbers of children to educate.

Queen Victoria set the pace with nine children of her own (none of whom of course ever attended a state school), while married women between the ages of 20 and 40 bore a child roughly every three years, so giving an average of six children in a family. Victorian reformers were beginning to argue that, because children were brought into the world through no will of their own, they had the right to be fed, clothed, sheltered and, to some degree, educated. The issue, as yet unresolved, was whose responsibility should all this be? Meanwhile, in all but the better-off families, children were expected to undertake extensive daily chores, and eventually to contribute to the family income as soon as they were old enough to be useful. Working-class life was tough, but still rich in experiences showing children how to survive. Rural families still lived in a kind of pre-industrial age: 'Father used to say, I shan't leave you much money, but I will teach you every job around the home and in the garden, and you will always be able to get work.'[38] Yet for the affluent, the age of retail therapy was already dawning: 'We go to purchase something we want; but when we get to the shop there are so many more things that we never thought of until they presented their obtrusive fascination,' remarked a Lady Jeune in London in 1897.[39]

As the century wore on, the adolescent grandsons of those early Victorian entrepreneurs dreamed of the opportunities the Empire provided to prove their worth. Mix their public school education and evangelical zeal to spread the Christian gospel, with the entrepreneurial fervour of those other men escaping from the working classes, and there was the energy to create a 'greater Britain beyond the seas'.[40] With fortunes to be made, and no exams standing in the way, an average of 100,000 men and women a year migrated overseas. Like no other generation before or since, each saw that they had a destiny – if they were bold enough to seize it – which meant they need not go down a Welsh coal mine, work in a Lancashire cotton mill, herd cattle in Devon, or grow corn in Tipperary. And as they colonized new lands, they repeated the same mistakes as were being made in the mother country – the wealthy created and endowed one kind of school for their own children, such as Upper Canada College in 1829, St Peter's College in Adelaide, South Australia, in 1847, Sydney Grammar School in 1854, Wesley College in Melbourne in 1868, Auckland Grammar School in New Zealand in 1869 and St Swithin's in Johannesburg in 1870 – while setting up school boards to provide schooling for those whose parents could not afford to educate their own children, with monies raised through taxes levied on the entire population.

It was among the growing industrial areas that enthusiasm for the board schools was at its highest.[41] Here people were starting to want more out of education than elementary schools had earlier provided. Because the new school boards were frequently small, sometimes with fewer than five schools, ratepayers could see what they were getting for their money, and the locally elected trustees often worked tirelessly to foster a strong sense of local community. Education was increasingly catching ordinary people's imagination, and excitement was in the air. In many board schools twelve- and thirteen-year-olds could now study subjects such as English literature and elementary science, algebra, history and book-keeping, with some even taking up Latin. More and more children began to stay on beyond the age of fourteen. Then evening classes were provided for older members of the community to study subjects that had not been available to them when they were young.

For the ordinary people of England the board schools of the 1890s were almost too good to be true. If youngsters wanted to stay on longer, and had already reached Grade Six, then the schools were enthusiastic to add more subjects, thereby requiring the trustees to make still bigger demands on taxpayers. Because education was largely a local affair where the obvious benefits could be seen, this was not regarded as a major imposition. Some school boards in Yorkshire even established what became known as 'higher-grade' classes in which youngsters of between fourteen and eighteen could be trained as teachers. Here were the possible beginnings of the all-through school dreamed of by Milton 250 years before. Having been blocked from all routes through to secondary education up until then, it seemed, at long last, as if the working classes now had a real chance.

It was not to be. The grammar schools became increasingly envious of these higher-grade elementary schools, for they saw in their pupils of thirteen and above the very youngsters that they were failing to attract to their own institutions. Those technical and mechanical institutions which had specialized in industrial training for 30 and more years looked on with horror at what they saw as a dilution of standards when technical education was taught by elementary schoolteachers. Meanwhile the church schools became increasingly jealous of what could be achieved by raising money through the rates. The elite public schools stood back and looked at this proliferation of technical and scientific education with disdain, and concluded complacently that technical education was none of their concern.

Chaos ensued. By the late 1890s nearly 2,500 school boards had been established, educating nearly half of the country's children, with the other half being under the control of some 15,000 church schools each with a separate set of school governors. It was pandemonium. While Forster had been right in claiming that there had been big gaps to fill, his solution had created still greater confusion. The haphazard administration of these two separate systems brought the schools of England virtually to their knees in 1899.[42] No one was in charge. Parliament was struggling to maintain at arm's length a national system of education with no clear idea of what it wanted to achieve.

*   *   *

Just occasionally history really is shaped by an individual, and that is what was about to happen. The full story of the seven years from 1898 reads like an old-fashioned whodunnit. At its simplest the story goes like this. In 1898 a new junior clerk was appointed to the Office of Education to be responsible for statistics – one Robert Morant, a former pupil of Winchester who had earlier spent several gap years tutoring the sons of the King of Siam. Morant was the ultimate authoritarian.[43] He believed that the education he had received at Winchester was the best in the world. He had a strictly hierarchical view of society and was extremely dismissive of ordinary people. He thoroughly disapproved of the school board as a threat to the class assumptions that he believed should shape social policy, and he was particularly contemptuous of attempts to introduce science into the curriculum.

None of this would have mattered had not this most junior of civil servants also been a workaholic, with very little actual work to do, and in a department that really didn't know its own mind. To fill in his time Morant began sifting through piles of old files, and discovered that there had never been any formal parliamentary approval for school boards to raise taxes for any form of schooling which went beyond the 'three Rs', or beyond the age of fourteen. Incredible as it may seem to us, various pieces of ambiguous legislation had simply been heaped one on top of another over the course of the previous 30 years, with no one apparently understanding what had, and had not, been approved. Quickly the significance of this hit Morant; individual school board members, in setting taxes that could now be shown to be illegal, had unwittingly made themselves personally responsible for repaying such monies to government. Here was political dynamite. Morant surreptitiously slipped parts of this information to the government's official auditor, who confirmed that the school boards had indeed acted illegally, and that meant that individual school board members (some 25,000 across the country) would be personally responsible for paying back large sums of money.

Many influential and powerful local people, who all the time had thought they had been acting in the public interest, faced imminent bankruptcy and lost all stomach for any further advocacy of state-provided education. Worse still, their sense of commitment to the common good and their willingness to work with government, which up till then had been unflinching, was devastated. A whole swathe of respectable, middle-class people rapidly withdrew from public life. This was to prove a fatal breakdown in trust, because without the involvement of such people, education became terribly susceptible to central government control. There was chaos, and politicians were in a quandary. Heads rolled, and the prime minister, in a move unprecedented before or since, promoted Morant to be in charge of the entire Office of Education.

In the preceding months Parliament had debated the possibility of encouraging the development of higher-grade elementary schools to the age of sixteen, giving an all-through education just as is now done with spectacular results in much of Scandinavia. This was the solution fervently preferred by those living in the cities. The alternative was to set up separate elementary and secondary schools which would involve the creation of new *provided* grammar schools. Morant turned to those he knew and understood best for advice – the headmasters of the most prestigious public schools. They consistently stressed the need for a sharp distinction between secondary and elementary schools. Why? To such men the influence of the Greek philosophers was immensely strong; children below the age of ten didn't matter very much. They saw elementary schools as a form of social control, and very little, if anything, about intellectual gravitas. What mattered were good secondary schools, uncontaminated by younger pupils.

With this advice Morant set out the bare bones of the 1902 Act, the second of the turning points that have shaped England's education system. They amounted to this: the three separate agencies concerned with education were combined into a single office of Education and Science, which Morant would head up.[44] The Act then limited elementary education to pupils below the age of fourteen, so cancelling all teaching of science and technology in the higher-grade classes. The Act abolished the school boards and passed their financial responsibilities to the newly created county councils which in future would allocate money to education out of a general fund that also covered roads, sewers, libraries, cemeteries and public amenities. To the fury of the secularists, government would contribute to the cost of the ageing church schools built 100 years before. Morant's solution suited the administrators, and by limiting the involvement of local people, consolidated the role of central government.

The passing of the Act involved some of the most heated and vehement debates ever heard in the House of Commons. Herbert Asquith, himself later to be Prime Minister, argued passionately in favour of the further extension of the upper elementary school for all children from the ages of five to sixteen, and warned Parliament that if it voted against this 'You'll put an end to the existence of the best, most fruitful and the most beneficial educational agencies that ever existed in this country.'[45] Asquith and his colleagues lost, and Morant won. More than 40 years later, when the third of these crises, that of 1944, was again causing fierce debate in Parliament, Winston Churchill 'shuddered' as he remembered the bitterness of the 1902 debate.

The 1902 Act left the public schools virtually free to go their own way. Having defined all former board schools as now being 'elementary', and limited to those below the age of fourteen, England was left with a tiny rump of mainly small, often rural, grammar schools out of which to create a national secondary system. Within six years Morant created 245 new provided grammar schools with 150,000 places. An impressive achievement, but actually catering for significantly smaller numbers of pupils than had earlier been accommodated in the higher-grade elementary schools. No wonder people were bitter and felt let down. These grammar schools were to follow a strictly classical curriculum with little science, and even less technology, uniforms had to be worn, and rugby was given precedence over football. Pupils were taught to think and act as if they were associate, though always inferior, members of a public school, always feeling superior to their colleagues for whom there were now no places to be found after elementary school. The use of the public schools as a yardstick by which all aspects of secondary education were later to be judged, still casts deep shadows across twenty-first-century educational thought.[46] And that grammar school culture would reflect Winchester and Eton, not Manchester, Newcastle or Birmingham.

*   *   *

That is a lot of history to digest. If you are one of the many who see the past as another country where they do things differently,[47] then there really is no need to dig through the dusty pages of Victorian controversies. But much closer to reality is the statement, 'Those who cannot remember the past are condemned to repeat it.' Without knowing where our attitudes towards education have come from, we have no foundation on which to build for the future. This chapter has closed with reference to Winston Churchill, a man whom some readers will remember personally, and vast numbers will have seen on TV, so with Chapter 6 we are about to move into modern times, and Chapters 7 and 8 into the contemporary world. Depending on your age, and when this history starts to become part of your own personal story, you will be discovering why it is that education policy and processes are not the simple issues you once thought they should be.

6

Lest We Fail to Learn from Our Mistakes

In the first years of the twentieth century, America replaced England as the world's richest, and soon to be most influential nation, whose ever-expanding new universities would influence educational policies in other parts of the world. Away from the champagne and lively house parties of the early twentieth century, England was having to face up to the implications of its well-entrenched social arrogance. Englishmen didn't like doing this. In 1901 the Prince of Wales told an astonished conference at the Guildhall that England had 'to wake up commercially and stop being so complacent,'[1] and an economist added, 'We can ill afford to teach foreigners, and not learn from them in return.'[2]

That complacency took a hard knock when in 1901 war broke out in South Africa over the ownership of the Transvaal gold-fields. A mere 80,000 Boer farmers held down, and very nearly overthrew, a British Army of almost half a million men. For three years the result was in the balance. Adolescents, craving excitement, raced to enlist in the Army. Emblems of soldiers and sailors appeared on everything from matchboxes to hatboxes. Eton became the first of many public schools to introduce an Officer Training Corps into the curriculum. Khaki uniform and burnished brass became symbols of manhood for the sons of the wealthy, proudly displayed in march-pasts and at speech days.

England was changing as the influence of the Church declined and the power of the press increased. Back in 1870 the sub-manager of a fancy goods store had seen a commercial opportunity in the millions of young people emerging from that economy schooling which had taught youngsters to decipher print without thinking overmuch about what it said. Such readers wanted a modicum of news and plenty of titillating scandal, expressed easily in short words and short paragraphs, all recounted in story form. He called his paper *Tit-Bits*, and it was such a success that in 1885 he took on an assistant, a 25-year-old Irishman who then, several years later, went on to launch a rival paper, the *Daily Mail*, which had a circulation of half a million within three years, while *The Times*, the newspaper of the educated establishment, had less than a tenth of that number. Such simplistic journalism was to have disastrous consequences for, in the build up to 1914, the British public were more influenced by the newspaper proprietors than by their elected politicians. When Germany announced in 1909 that it would build four more battleships, the British press, led by the *Daily Mail*, clamoured, 'We want eight, and we won't wait,' which quickly became a music hall refrain.[3]

The scene was being set for a European war largely caused by colonial jealousy, and fanned by the popular press. The arms race that built up in 1913–14 had all the attraction of a game of Monopoly to overgrown schoolboys. Adolescents in their hundreds of thousands grabbed their rifles and, with the impetuosity caused by their 'crazy' dendrites and supported by heavy artillery, rushed carelessly onto the battlefield in August 1914. One later recalled the enthusiasm of his public school chum to the news of the outbreak of war: 'Glorious, glorious! A war is just what we need. It will wake us up from our sleeping. There's a real chance now of sweeping away the old traditions. I wish I could go and fight, and if I could go, by God, I would have my shot at the bloody Germans.'[4] Which, presumably, was also the attitude of German adolescents who, under the influence of a similar Prussian form of education, rushed enthusiastically into a war that should never have happened.

Here was the build-up to what would be the third of the six educational turning points, that of 1944. The First World War did nothing to solve the problems of the world's earliest industrial nation as it started to pass into mature old age. Between the two wars the children of the masses continued to go to free day-schools until the age of thirteen and then left to earn their own living, unless they belonged to the small minority who won scholarships to the grammar schools. Meanwhile the children of the privileged went to expensive preparatory schools and at the age of thirteen went on to increasingly expensive public schools. All the while both the public schools and the new provided grammar schools remained tenaciously wedded to the classical curriculum reinvented by Dr Arnold. Why? Was it really Latin and Greek that created the intellect that shaped England's leaders? Might not some other aspect of that rich cocktail of public school life be responsible? Was it simply in the boys' genes, or because, from their earliest years, they were told that they were the best, and came to believe it?

In 1903 the American Edward Thorndike published research which showed that 'habits of mind' were shaped by much more than the discipline and practice of a single subject. Basing his work on conditioned responses in animals, Thorndike formulated two laws: one showed how an association of ideas led to an automatic response, and the other how punishments and rewards could be used to strengthen a preferred (desired by the teacher) response. The degree of transfer between one learning task and another was dependent, Thorndike demonstrated, on the essential similarity between two situations.[5] Students who had learned one foreign language well were in a good position to learn a second easily, but whether or not they became good district officers in Africa was more dependent on their survival skills learned in the rough and tumble of the school playing fields, or in the back streets of an industrial town. If you grew up being told you would one day be an officer, chances were that you would: but if you came to see yourself simply as a manual worker, then manual worker you would most likely become. The public schools ignored this research for 60 years and continued to use the Classics as a convenient way of controlling their social intake.[6] But for those shaping a socialist agenda, such research was heaven sent, for here was the evidence they needed that to improve opportunities for the working classes, massive social change was needed as well as better schools.

So much more complex does this account of conflicting ideas about education and social structures become in the twentieth century that the style of this and subsequent chapters changes to incorporate summary statements which, while probably reading less like a piece of interesting prose, should help the reader to retain control of the overall picture as more actors appear on the stage.

Edward Thorndike was the first of five Americans who were soon to be highly influential in shaping education in the English-speaking world. The second was Frederick Winslow Taylor, the young engineer who, by using a stopwatch to time every action of workers at the Mid Vale Steel Works in Pennsylvania in the 1880s, showed that manual labour could be accurately analysed and quantified. Every task, every movement, Taylor argued, should be defined in advance by an expert who would use his scientific insights to tell each worker exactly what to do, and how to do it. By following instructions exactly, productivity grew rapidly, but the workers' sense of ownership and pride in their craft skills largely disappeared.[7] To compensate for the boredom of such repetitive activities, Taylor argued that higher wages should replace job satisfaction. 'The primary, if not the only, goal of human labour and thought is efficiency; that technical calculation is in all respects superior to human judgment . . . the affairs of citizens are best guided and conducted by experts,' said Taylor.[8] Taylor did more than anyone else to destroy the craftsman's attitude towards work, and denigrate the significance of the individual. Shortly the President of the highly influential Carnegie Association for the Advancement of Teaching proclaimed, 'It is more and more necessary that every human being should become an effective economic unit. What is needed is an education system that is carefully adapted to the needs of the economy. A system that sorts people efficiently into various positions that need to be filled in the stratified occupational structure.'[9] Education was to be geared to the needs of the state, not the individual.

A third American, the psychologist John B. Watson, denied that evolution had any part to play in understanding the function of the human brain. He agreed with Thorndike and Frederick Winslow Taylor that what mattered was the precise quantification of inputs (that which was taught) and outputs (that which could be measured). The management of external motivation, and the construction of a closed environment, were the essence of the Behaviourist model of learning. 'Give me a dozen healthy infants, well-formed, and my own specified world to bring them up in, and I'll guarantee to take any one at random and train him to become any type of specialist – doctor, lawyer, artist, merchant chief – regardless of his talent, penchants, tendency, ability, vocation and the race of his ancestors.' Here was the 'perfect system',[10] argued Watson, to equip millions of young people for a straightforward life as producers and consumers in a modern society. Learning should henceforth become something schools did to you, and quality instruction was seen as more important than encouraging students to think things out for themselves. Children's minds were putty to be shaped by well-trained teachers. The shadow of this thinking still remains and has deadened the imagination of millions of children in many countries.

In Europe, the French psychologist Alfred Binet sought to separate the influence of inherited factors from those acquired from the environment by developing a test for intelligence based on vocabulary, comprehension and verbal relationships.[11] That was far too subjective for the English psychologist Cyril Burt who built up a totally different explanation. Through the study of identical twins, Burt sought to compare the relative contribution of genetics and environmental factors (nature or nurture?) to intellectual functioning, and claimed that approximately 80 per cent of intelligence is determined by genetic factors. From this, Burt concluded that the social divisions in mid-twentieth-century England were entirely natural, and had resulted from evolutionary processes operating over long periods of time. Burt therefore recommended in 1941 tailoring different kinds of education to youngsters of different intellectual capabilities, and argued that a single intelligence test administered at the age of eleven would accurately predict future intellectual performance. Those tests were nothing like as predictive as Burt claimed, and several generations were to be scarred by the mistake.[12]

The fourth American to have great influence was Granville S. Hall, President of the American Psychological Association. In 1904 Hall published his lifelong study entitled *Adolescence*. Hall observed that, as America and England had become increasingly mechanized, so men had become too busy getting rich to have any continued interest in supporting apprenticeship. Once a youngster was strong enough to join the workforce, his learning was over – there were no more questions to be asked, and nothing else to find out. As a result, factories were filling up with exhausted but totally unfulfilled adolescents. 'Youth is awakening to a new world, and understands neither it, nor itself,'[13] explained Hall in horror as he looked at an 'urbanised hothouse life that tends to ripen everything before its time. Increasingly urban life with its temptations, sedentary occupations and passive stimuli, had come to dominate just when an active life was most needed,' he explained. 'If the vulnerability of adolescents were to be ignored,' he went on, 'the result would be a disaster both for the individual, and for society at large.'[14] Englishmen too recognized that the collapse of apprenticeship meant that 'the devil finds work for idle hands to do'.

The uncontrolled behaviour of adolescents in 1898 had led to the use of the word 'hooligans'. Baden-Powell's Boy Scouts and Girl Guides partly filled this vacuum from 1907.[15] In the early years of the century, hundreds and thousands of men and women felt so concerned that adolescents were getting a raw deal that across the country they formed numerous youth clubs, and established football teams every Sunday morning after church to keep youngsters off the streets in places like Manchester, London, Liverpool and elsewhere.[16] A century later, when few remembered the Sunday services, the whole world appeared to follow the fortunes of teams such as Manchester United, Fulham, Bolton Wanderers, Charlton Athletic, Rangers and Everton. Literally armies of volunteers staffed such activities, making it possible for 80 per cent of all five- to fourteen-year-olds to attend Sunday School in the years immediately before the First World War, while an enquiry made in 1960 showed that three out of every five men had earlier belonged to uniformed organizations when they were young.[17]

The fifth American was John Dewey, Professor at various times of Philosophy, Psychology and Pedagogy in the newly established universities of Minnesota, Michigan, Chicago, and then later at Columbia and New York. Dewey strides like an intellectual colossus across two centuries. Born in 1859, his early life was spent in rural Vermont, and later he immersed himself in all the social issues as America's agricultural economy gave way to the industrial world, and then literally to the atomic age. Issues of democracy and community suffuse all Dewey's writing. 'Schools will be at their most successful when they saturate children with the spirit of service and interdependence,' wrote Dewey. 'Give youngsters an appreciation of their culture and technological knowledge, and empower them with the skills of learning and effective self-direction.'[18] Dewey feared that the scientific management of people demeaned the very essence of our humanity. If employers were to treat people as if they were automatons, then human nature would dry up and people lose all sense of being responsible for their own lives, wrote Dewey, and community itself would become a nebulous concept, and democracy itself inevitably would be weakened. You can't bring up children to be intelligent, Dewey argued, in a world that is not intelligible to them. To which we might add in the early twenty-first century that streets which are unsafe for children to play in are as much a measure of failed educational policy as are burnt-out teachers or decaying classrooms.

Sir Richard Livingstone, later Vice Chancellor of Oxford, was England's philosopher appropriate to his time, but he lacked the public platform that John Dewey had achieved on the other side of the Atlantic. 'Why are we an uneducated nation, and how can we become an educated one?' Livingstone asked. 'For we have compulsory education, magnificent schools, an impressive army of teachers, and an enormous educational budget.'[19] Yet, despite all that, it seemed that 'the chief uses of our present education system are to enable a minority to proceed to further education, and the rest to read the cheap press. To cease education at fourteen is as unnatural as to die at fourteen. The one is physical death, the other intellectual death. The vast majority of the population, having been shown a glimpse of the Promised Land, are then left outside.' The majority of the English had been treated as if they were to have no leisure, or as if it didn't matter how they used what leisure they had. 'Our problem,' argued the Vice Chancellor, as he harped back to the loss of apprenticeship, 'is that we all ignore a vital educational principle, namely that the study of subjects of which you have some first-hand knowledge is far easier, far more meaningful, than studying the theory of a subject of which you have no practical experience.'[20] We had moved too far from the hands-on apprentice to the hands-off pupil, explained Livingstone.

Livingstone's analysis of the situation was shrewd. Many school subjects are like pre-digested food, complete in themselves. Mathematics, algebra, chemistry, physics and some aspects of language can be studied almost in isolation from real-life experiences, and for them schooling alone is sufficient. But other subjects such as literature, history, religion, philosophy, economics and politics can only be taught to a limited extent in school, for they await the young learner's personal experience of life to turn them into meaningful knowledge. In one of his most memorable phrases, Livingstone wrote, 'If a school sends out children with the desire for knowledge and some idea of how to acquire and use it, it will have done its work. Too many leave school with the appetite killed and the mind loaded with undigested lumps of information. If a school is unable to teach its pupils to work things out for themselves, they will be unable to teach them anything else of value.'[21]

Livingstone's solution in 1941 is well worth revisiting in the early twenty-first century, for however good schooling might become in the future, he argued, adolescents need a rich array of non-school-based experiences if they are to grow their minds in ways that will enable them to internalize what is studied in the classroom. So Livingstone proposed that full-time schooling should cease at the age of fourteen and for the next three years every youngster would be required to earn their own living for three days a week. They should then spend the other two days studying, in some form of continuous education, those subjects that most relate to human life – namely philosophy, literature and history. Like Milton and Dewey, Livingstone knew that democracy was as dependent upon well-educated farmers, shopkeepers, craftsmen and factory workers, as it was on intellectuals and politicians understanding the reality of everyday life.[22] By the age of seventeen, youngsters would have such a range of learning experiences that they would know themselves well enough to decide just what form of further education would best suit them.

*   *   *

In 1939 Englishmen did not rush off enthusiastically to war as had their fathers 25 years earlier, and it was abundantly obvious to the politicians that when the war was over (and hopefully won) returning servicemen would demand more genuine opportunities than had been available to their fathers' generation. Churchill, while being a great war leader, had little personal interest or commitment to social reconstruction but he recognized that plans had to be put in hand to provide universal schooling up to the age of fifteen. In 1941, days after the bombing of the House of Commons, Churchill appointed R. A.

Butler as Minister of Education. 'I'm too old, now, to think you can improve people's natures,' the lugubrious Churchill told Butler. 'Everyone must learn to defend himself. You must make all the young cadets into powder monkeys, and relieve the pressure on gun sites. I should not object if you could introduce a note of patriotism into the schools.'[23]

Butler himself had reservations about his own boarding school experience and later in life he questioned the appropriateness of examinations when taken so young as being of any realistic use in assessing future potential. He wrote in his autobiography: 'The advantage of day-school education . . . is that children are half the time in the world; the great need of a public school is to look outward, not into its monastic inner self.'[24] He quoted his older cousin who had been killed in the war as saying, 'The penalty of belonging to a public school is that one plays before a looking-glass all the time and has to think about the impression one is making. As public schools are run on the worn-out fallacy that there can't be progress without competition, games as well as everything else degenerate into a means of giving free play to the lower instincts of men.'[25] Churchill, however, had no such qualms, and had a strong nostalgic attachment to his old school, Harrow. 'I think it would be a great mistake,' he said, 'to stir up the public schools question at this time.' Instead he urged Butler 'to add industrial and technical training' to the curriculum, 'so enabling men not required for the army to take their places promptly in the munitions industry or radio work, and that would be most useful'.[26]

The scene was being set for the 1944 Education Act, the third of the turning points in education that have shaped today's schools. Butler was an able politician, with two former headmasters of Harrow among his ancestors, as well as being the son of the Master of a Cambridge College and having a mother who had strong imperial connections with India. Very much the patrician, Butler was really a late Victorian in his attitudes. He has long been seen as the architect of the 1944 Education Act that finally gave England the fully national system of education it so badly needed. Or did he? And was this most polished politician, who never quite became Prime Minister, as astute as has been thought? He faced daunting issues: the appalling shortage of secondary school places, the need to reduce class sizes which were sometimes over 50 in the elementary schools, the deteriorating condition of church schools, and an acute shortage of teachers.

Temperamentally, Butler was in favour of Livingstone's ideas, as he was as ambivalent as many of his contemporaries about the possible value of a public school education in a post-war Britain. His Permanent Secretary, however, had no such reservations. Sir Maurice Holmes[27] was a former classical scholar and an archetypal civil servant in the mould of Robert Morant. He believed that he should control his Ministers through whatever puppet strings he could pull. He provided Butler with copious briefings on the research of Thorndike, the ideas of Frederick Winslow Taylor, on Watson's theory of behaviourism, on G. S. Hall's theory of adolescence, while he tolerated Cyril Burt personally lobbying Butler on the issue of intelligence tests. Butler largely ignored most of this thinking but listened carefully to Holmes when he urged him to think, as the ancient Greeks had, in terms of secondary schools for three different types of youngsters.

A committee under the chairmanship of Sir Cyril Norwood, yet another classical scholar who was also headmaster of Harrow, described the characteristics of young people in ways that could lead to them being divided into 'certain rough groupings'. First, there were those who 'can grasp an argument and follow a piece of connected reasoning'; second, those 'whose interest and abilities lie markedly in the field of applied science or applied art'; and third, those who are 'interested only in the moment, and incapable of a long series of connected steps, to whom abstraction means little'.[28] Butler had hedged himself about with Establishment figures. He took no notice of Livingstone, and accepted the validity of intelligence tests, and the appropriateness of eleven as the age of transfer. Seeking inspiration for post-war education in England, he turned back to the segregated social policies advocated by Plato 2,500 years before. Obeying Churchill's instructions not to reopen the public school issue, Butler simply accepted that such schools were of no immediate concern to Parliament, even when approached by several of the public schools in 1941 seeking state scholarship as a way of shoring up their own rapidly-collapsing financial base. The public schools were to be every bit as independent in post-war Britain as they had been before, and probably as class-segregated.[29]

So in March 1944, Parliament enacted Butler's Education Act, the third of the turning points in English education. Three months before the Allied armies landed in France, Butler had done what a good Minister was expected to do; he had built a coalition of political support that gave his Department's proposal an easy ride. The school-leaving age would be raised to fifteen at some point 'soon',[30] and thereafter to sixteen. Butler never gave serious thought to creating the all-through schools that had been argued for so forcefully in 1902 as well as by Milton in the 1650s. Because there was so much uncertainty about when the school leaving age could be raised to fifteen, Butler agreed that three years should be lopped off the old elementary school curriculum to make eleven, not fourteen, the age of transfer, so giving all pupils a minimum of four years of secondary education, even though it had reduced most significantly the role of primary education. Secondary education was then to be split into three different strands, entry to which would depend on the results of intelligence tests and the 'Eleven Plus' examination: an examination taken by all children approaching their eleventh birthday which combined questions of general intelligence with questions of general knowledge, together with mathematical and literary assessment.[31]

Churchill lost the 1945 election, and for the second time Britain was to have a socialist government. Into Butler's shoes stepped the diminutive and fiery Ellen Wilkinson.[32] She had to turn some very old elementary schools into new primary schools for children below the age of eleven, and work with the discredited deal earlier made with teachers whereby, in exchange for not raising their salaries, the school holidays had been lengthened from ten to fourteen weeks. What was even more difficult, she had to deliver a form of secondary education that was not of her devising, and at a time when post-war resources were incredibly scarce. It was in the early planning for the Modern school, the schools that were expected to take those pupils 'to whom abstraction means little,' that Wilkinson came closest to creating the kind of progressive learning environment anticipated by Dewey. Modern schools were encouraged by Labour politicians to create within their walls an image of an idealized home, a haven from the pressure of society – a place far removed from the deadening routine of industrial work into which it was feared such children would all too soon be forced. Behind the Modern school stood the ghost of the lost pre-industrial age village[33] for, in this confusion of philosophies, Labour's idealism sought both to protect the child from the ravages of capitalism, while at the same time to try to build that meritocracy of talent that would be able to rise rapidly through the grammar schools.

Neither party was fully committed to making the selective system work. From the start, a third more money was allocated to the building of new grammar schools than was allocated to Modern schools. Eight years later the capital cost of Modern schools was cut by a further quarter.[34] Take a walk around schools built at that time and you will notice startling differences. Even in 1965, twenty years after the tripartite system had been introduced, four-fifths of Modern school buildings were deemed inadequate, a third of them had no science laboratory, a half no gymnasium and a quarter no library, but the grammar schools on the other hand were all fully equipped.[35] The impact of the Eleven Plus was frequently devastating, and what was even more unacceptable was that one child in seven could be shown, after a year, to have been misplaced, and that became a national scandal. Parents were instantly suspicious and spent much money on extra tuition to make sure that their children were well groomed to out-wit the testers. Public antagonism grew even more vociferous as it was noted how quickly youngsters slipped into performing simply at the level expected of them. To understand England today is to remember that very many of the grandparents of today's so-called 'difficult' pupils had themselves been discarded by these earlier tests. It wasn't their fault; it was a result of a system that was flawed from the start.

*   *   *

It is here that we move into the beginnings of remembered experiences. It is important to remind ourselves how different England and Western countries were in the years immediately after the Second World War. A snapshot of that world is to be found in the editorial of a monthly magazine that spoke about practical ideas to the general public in the late 1940s of ways that could make both ends meet. It was the summer of 1948, a time when the country was recovering from the problems of post-war reconstruction and a particularly savage winter that had seen the coldest temperatures for more than 100 years. There was little fuel for tractors, and even less food for horses, and so the English did what they most liked to do – reverted to their own simple devices. Called out of retirement to save the harvest were old farmers who were asked to get out and sharpen their sickles and scythes.

> They must have loved it, in spite of the ache of bodies growing old, because to be able to do well and neatly any piece of skilled work stirs a man's pride and satisfies something deep down in his nature as nothing else does. In the modern world this need is too often left unfulfilled, and not only unfulfilled, but often is so over-laid with an easier type of pleasure that a man may hardly be aware of its existence. If he feels restless and discontented, he tells himself that he needs more money, more opportunities, more leisure, more anything, rather than face the hard fact that only in one's own ability to do a job well can one hope to find any sort of contentment.[36]

That was written long before my co-author Heather's time (and the times of most of our readers) but I can just remember it down on my grandfather's farm in Devon as the last fleeting glimpse of a world that had virtually disappeared. The Allies might have developed the technology for the atom bomb, but many people still enjoyed the satisfaction of harvesting crops in the way their ancestors had done thousands of years before.[37] As a child growing up in that time, I and my contemporaries were nevertheless better clothed and better fed, were heavier, taller and reached puberty earlier than children in pre-war days. Our mothers understood all about keeping regular[38] bedtimes for their children, routine eating hours, and keeping their child's bowel movements regular. This was still a make-and-mend society where boys learned from their fathers how to repair boots, change washers, and were expected to know how to skin a rabbit, clear a blocked-up drain and how to detect ordinary tricks of crooked thinking. There were only a million television sets in 1953 and so families really did play endless board and card games together. They also read a lot and, as the economy improved, many youngsters found jobs on market stalls on a Saturday, delivered newspapers, cleaned cars or ran errands.

In those idealistic days college lecturers likened education to a three-legged stool which, unlike an ordinary four-legged chair, could find balance however uneven the floor.[39] The legs, they said, represented the home, the school and the community – emotional growth, intellectual growth and inspirational ideas. If any leg were too short or too long, the stool couldn't balance. Be careful, people then said, don't let schools in the future take over the roles which are the natural responsibilities of home or community. 'Always remember,' a Chief Education Officer sagely told parents, 'children are children first; they are only school-children second. They are much more influenced by the conduct of their parents, than by their teachers. If you wish to help your child you should do this not by leaning heavily on his or her homework but by respecting your child's efforts to find truth, and sympathize with his difficulties; in other words, it means going on with your own education.'[40]

Over the years that followed it was the unfairness of the Eleven Plus Exam, every bit as much as it was the idea of selection itself, that was frequently devastating. One Headmaster in the 1950s recalled how a father told him about his own son:

'We always thought, his mother and I, that he was a bright laddie. I have a shed, and in my spare time I do a lot of carpentry. He used to come in and help me, and then he started making things for himself. He made a bookcase, and he bought a blueprint and rigged up a wireless set for himself. Pretty good reception, too. We bought encyclopaedias from a traveller who came to the house and we encouraged him to read them, and he did. He used to spend a lot of time in winter evenings reading about science.' The father stopped, and then after a pause he added almost apologetically, 'Oh well. Maybe we built our hopes too high.' He smiled wistfully. 'You always think your own bairns are pretty good. Better than they are really, I suppose.'[41]

That headmaster disclaiming any religious affiliations said that when he heard one of the new psychologists describe a boy as 'IQ 79', he would always side with the religious man who thought of him instead as 'a child of God, full of infinite possibilities'. Parents who watched the miracle of birth and growth were briefly informed by schools, on the basis of a single number, that the miracle was over. Their children were just ordinary, below-average IQ. The magic had fled, and the wonder gone out of life.

After twenty years the faults of the 1944 Education Act were so glaring that they could no longer be ignored. It wasn't that many of the aims hadn't been eminently worthy; the formation of moral and ethical standards, intelligent use of leisure, and the social skills needed to support family and community ('Families can't be built upon half-baked personalities')[42] were all highly desirable. It was simply that the opportunity to develop those skills were mightily constrained by the kind of school a child attended.[43] If it was the grammar school, then the academic curriculum severely limited the development of social skills, while if it was the Modern school the near impossibility of pursuing academic study to any depth deprived most young-sters of the chance of progressing much beyond the lifestyle of their father.[44]

So, with no trumpets sounding, no groups of rival MPs haranguing each other, no powerful statement from a Perma-nent Secretary or Minister, and without any significant parlia-mentary debate, the Department of Education issued what was called Circular 10/65, and sent it to every local authority. Bland as that sounds, it was as monumental in its significance as the Acts of 1870, 1902 and 1944. Again in its deference to local sensitivities, it was as gentle as had been Forster in his unwill-ingness to upset the 'benevolent interest' of the status quo. What it said was this:

> The government are aware that the complete elimination of selection and separatism in secondary education will take time to achieve. They do not seek to impose destructive or precipitous change on existing schools; they recognize that the evolution of separate schools into a comprehensive system must be a constructive process carried through care-fully by LEAs in consultation with all those concerned.[45]

The context for the comprehensive school

Before looking at how Circular 10/65 was to be implemented, it is necessary to take a further look at immediate post-war England to understand why it was that the introduction of community-based comprehensive secondary schools – a system that had worked moderately well in America and Canada – was virtually doomed from the start because of England's lack of a common social identity. The English 60 years ago were much as they had been hundreds of years before – almost exclusively white, English-speaking, self-assured and accustomed to exploring other peoples' lands rather than accepting strangers into their own. They had forgotten that they themselves were essentially a polyglot nation with a gene pool enriched long ago by Celts, Romans, Danes, Saxons and Vikings. For the past two centuries the English had been so preoccupied with defining the niceties of class distinctions that they seemed to have lost any agreed understanding of who 'they' might be. Herein lies the roots of so many of England's contemporary problems – without a sense of civil society, of true mutual responsibility one for the other, it is almost impossible to form a sustainable vision for the future.

All this happened very rapidly. It started with the arrival of 500 Jamaicans in 1948[46] on the *SS Windrush* to meet a labour shortage in post-war British factories, and for the first time the English had to recognize foreigners living in their own street. They didn't like it. Not knowing how to treat such immigrants, they regarded them rather like guests in a large country house – immigrants were there at the invitation of the host and were expected to behave as good guests normally do, simply fitting in (and one day going back home) and playing cricket and buying English goods. The smallness of their numbers didn't initially threaten the English way of life, based as it was on a set of common, if unspoken, values which simply left Englishmen to go quietly on in their own idiosyncratic ways, untroubled by intrusive laws. That complacency was to take two knocks, one internal and the other external, that would utterly change English society before the end of the century.[47] The first of these knocks came when the post-war generation started to challenge the relationship of law to morality. The voice of the Victorian liberal philosopher John Stuart Mill[48] was heard again: 'The only purpose for which power can be rightfully exercised over any member of a civilized community, against his will, is to prevent harm to others. His own good, either physical or moral, is not a sufficient warrant.' In other words, just because something was deemed immoral (by a Christian code), it should not necessarily be illegal. Others, meanwhile, thought very differently: 'Without shared ideas on politics, morals and ethics, no society can exist. If men and women try to create a society in which there was no fundamental agreement about good and evil, they will fail . . . for society is not something that is kept together physically; it is held by the invisible bonds of common thought.'⁴⁹

With the decriminalization of homosexuality, the repeal of censorship and abortion laws, and the easing of the law on divorce, the average English man or woman, never having thought of themselves as abstract thinkers, now found themselves confused by having to work out the niceties of moral distinctions, invariably appearing not as black or white, but shades of indeterminate grey. All kinds of social, religious and class tensions surfaced, many of which had been suppressed for generations since Victorian times. Lack of confidence in who you think you are, and what you stand for, quickly generates anxiety, and possibly xenophobia, because those who don't respect themselves find it hard to confer respect on others. In post-war England, men and women began to disown their inherited culture. Intellectuals, championing what they saw had been the unfair treatment of the working classes and foreign nationals, quickly came to assume that any faction backed by Britain was automatically wrong. This was John Osborne's world of *Look Back in Anger*. A degree of self-hate began to become part of British attitudes. In addition, the more the moral consensus disappeared, the more moral conversation died.[50] In the name of freedom it seemed that freedom of opinion itself was defeated, for political correctness left arguments polarized as thoughtful discussion was replaced by soundbites.

That loss of a social, philosophic and moral togetherness, so necessary for civil society, was to be catastrophic as the country faced its second knock – large-scale immigration. By the late 1950s some 200,000 West Indian immigrants had arrived in England – too numerous to pretend any longer that the country-house analogy would survive.[51] These were followed by Maltese, Cypriots, Hungarians and Czechs, and then by tens of thousands of Kenyans and Ugandans, highly energetic entrepreneurs with a strong sense of social cohesion fleeing from repressive regimes in Africa. A new metaphor, that of a large hotel – a place of many rooms within which all were able to do their own thing – permeated public debate. But hotels are primarily for tourists. They are places where guests can watch what goes on outside, but have no shared common identity with the local community. Hotels are no substitute for homes, and it is homes that people want. So when the Sikh communities campaigned to maintain the social customs of the Punjab, while living amidst the textile towns of the north of England, many called for large-scale immigration to be stopped lest it result in much bloodshed. Meanwhile intellectuals, modernizers and Christians alike hurriedly repudiated such demands and persisted in their belief that tolerance and good neighbourliness would eventually resolve all these tensions.[52]

It could never be as simple as that, for no amount of good neighbourliness by individuals could compensate for the inherent attitude of the English, built up over 200 years of colonialization, that they were the ones who had to change the foreigners, not be changed themselves. Lacking a moral consensus, reasoned argument was largely replaced by fear of political correctness so undermining civil society just at the time when it was most needed. Subsequent government legislation has been torn between two conflicting expectations – on the one hand a passionate and proud tradition of being a country that offers asylum to political refugees, and, on the other hand, a strong belief that national identity could not accommodate too many ethnic diversities. Immigration has changed Britain more than any other single social event over the past 60 years. We don't talk about the same things or in the same way any more. And despite all the emotional energy that well-meaning immigrants and English men and women have put into trying to make multiculturalism work, we seem to have become a rawer, less tolerant, and ever more fragmented society with no real sense of who 'we' are.

Fortunately, civil unrest comparable to that suffered in the southern states of America that Enoch Powell had foreseen 30 years before has not come about.[53] What has changed has been the nature of what it means to be English, but that has been achieved by a further reduction in any conscious agreement as to what being English actually means. Increasing numbers of people, indigenous English, or nationalized English of foreign origins, sought personal satisfaction in forms of hyper-individualism which wrought havoc on civil society. Such confused and muddled people were incapable of envisaging the kind of world for which they ought to be preparing their children – hence the subsequent dilemma for the comprehensive school: there was no sense of a moral imperative for all children to be educated together. It has to be an ages-old truth that, if you don't know where you've come from, and are unclear as to where you actually are now, you will never be able to reach your destination – you simply drift. Which seems to be what so much of England has been doing for the better part of a couple of generations.

Which meant that with the implementation of the fourth of our turning points, Circular 10/65, the tripartite system unravelled and endless political and social tensions erupted. For comprehensive schools to have any chance of fulfilling their potential, they needed to cater for all the children of the community, of all social classes and of all intellectual abilities. If a selective school, be it grammar or independent, were to cream off the brighter children, then the overall culture of the comprehensive would come to resemble that of a Modern school. The English might have been ready for this in 1944 when the enthusiasm at the end of the war to create a more equitable society manifested itself in all aspects of the welfare state, but now – twenty years on – those egalitarian expectations had evaporated with the failure of the new Modern school to build up any form of parity with the grammar schools.[54] People were losing faith in schools. Not that comprehensive schools would have had a smooth passage twenty years earlier because, even then, class tensions still ran deep. The thought that a miner's son might sit next to the doctor's daughter, however academically compatible they might be (as they did in Wales and Scotland) was inconceivable. English men and women might have voted for the Socialists, but when Harold Wilson confused the public by claiming that 'comprehensive schools are grammar schools for everyone,'[55] he didn't really fool anybody. The English had come to accept class divisions as a natural part of life; be you a road sweeper, a foot soldier, a captain of industry, a general, doctor or the practitioner of an alternative lifestyle, you were more committed to the company of those who thought like you, than you were to accepting a diversity of lifestyles. 'U' and 'non-U' (us, or non-us) was the catchphrase of the time.[56]

Put simply, the concept of a comprehensive school sought to undo the damage wrought by intelligence tests and to improve the opportunity for those children coming from deprived backgrounds. Comprehensives sought to capitalize on the sense of local community and to bind formal and informal learning opportunities together. In doing so, they tried to unpick much of the 1944 and 1902 Education Acts. What they left intact, however, was that other aspect of 1944 – the division of education at the age of eleven. Now, in 1965, plans were already afoot to raise the school-leaving age to sixteen (1973), so making ever more obvious the impossible situation of primary education to provide quality basic education, having had three years lopped off its curriculum by Butler. While this tended to keep the size of primary schools quite small, the more the school-leaving age was raised, then the larger the comprehensives became, and the more disruptive frustrated adolescents became (who would have rather been a hundred miles away). So headteachers were tempted to invent more subjects and give greater choice, in the false expectation that even the most disruptive pupils would eventually find something to interest them. Which led to the schools getting still bigger again.

I remember it all so clearly; called the 'ROSLA rabble' (Raising Of School-Leaving Age – awful acronym!), these youngsters were bored out of their minds. On a spring morning in 1974 I recall a class of fifteen-year-old boys enviously staring out of the window at their mates of the year before already earning good money on a neighbouring building site. Nothing the teachers could say could ever counter the influence of their fathers, one of whom had said to me the previous evening, 'What the bloody hell's the value of that to my boy? He should be out learning the rough and tumble of life, not sitting getting bored with geography. What good will that ever do him?' That father was one of hundreds of thousands who were convinced that a new form of schooling was increasingly replacing the hands-on apprentice with the hands-off pupil, and that, he was quick to explain, was 'a bloody awful idea'.

Circular 10/65, in the breadth of its proposals, could have been more beneficial for young people than had the Acts of 1870, 1902 and 1944 put together. But it wasn't. Grand proposals require great sponsors, and both parties were at best equivocal in their support for comprehensive schools. No great champions emerged. Some of the most strident supporters of egalitarian comprehensive education in their youth became, years later, just as ardent in their support of their rights to send their own children to grammar schools, or to public schools. The choice represented a bitter pill for many to swallow, and now, more than 40 years later, the issue is still unresolved.

7

Adolescents Left Out

In order to understand why adolescents have been so misunderstood and left out of our calculations in recent years, we need to look at the common origins of British and American thinking about social structures and education. Soundbites, so beloved of politicians, all too often confuse our understanding of complex problems. When George W. Bush described to the American people his educational programme in the year 2000 as being *No Child Left Behind*, he anticipated Tony Blair's *Every Child Matters* legislation of 2003. They hoped that by acknowledging the public's deep concern that large numbers of children were getting a raw deal, it would somehow be assumed that their policies would correct this. Would that it were that easy, for, as both men surely realized, the solution to such problems lay every bit as much in the hearts and minds of their people as in legislation.

English and American cultures have a symbiotic relationship, each feeding off the other in slightly erratic ways, that goes back centuries. One of the first things the English settlers did was to set up the Boston Latin School as a replica of an English grammar school, while in 1643 Massachusetts issued an edict requiring every settlement, once it had 50 households, to provide a school for all its children. This worked well. The one-room schoolhouse, so beloved of American folk memory, gave the American colonists almost universal literacy by the end of the seventeenth century. Yet from the mid-nineteenth century it seems that literacy levels in that land have fallen badly. A recent analysis of the educational level needed to understand the language and syntax of men hoping to be elected presidents of the United States, showed that Abraham Lincoln, out on the campaign trail in 1858, spoke at an 11.2 grade level (meaning that he assumed his audience could understand at the level of an educated eighteen-year-old). Education in that vibrant community schoolhouse was working well. In the 1960s Richard Nixon and John Kennedy both spoke at tenth grade levels, but by the year 2000 George W. Bush won the election by speaking at a 6.7 grade level. Al Gore lost when speaking at a 7.9 grade level.[1]

Was this simply because the reading level of the people had fallen, or was it because people today feel so confused by the quantity of available information, that they have fallen out of the habit of making up their own minds about big issues? Whatever it is, by following the KISS rule ('Keep it simple, stupid') political analysis all too easily becomes superficial. It is a real problem for our times. In Britain in October 2007 Sir Menzies (Ming) Campbell was forced into a sudden resignation as leader of the Liberal Democrats because of the relentless pressure of 24/7 journalism that turned 'his measured old-fashioned decency into a liability'.[2] Soundbite politics frequently leaves the root cause of problems untreated.

America experienced the Industrial Revolution later than England, but from the 1820s her ports were inundated with the poor and demoralized refugees escaping from European cities.[3] These presented such a threat to the social cohesion of the new republic that schools became the prime agent for making good Americans out of young immigrants of diverse cultures. As America became mechanized in the mid-nineteenth century, many anticipated Taylor's ideas about scientific management and looked to schools to prepare young Americans for the discipline of a factory life. Others like John Dewey, epitomizing the idealism of the Founding Fathers, were appalled, and feared that such utilitarian education would quickly undermine the proper functioning of democracy. Following the Great Depression in the 1920s and early 1930s, President Roosevelt, partly responding to psychologists' concern that adolescence was an aberration from which youngsters had to be saved, but even more concerned to create work for millions of unemployed adults, approved legislation which effectively prevented adolescents below the age of eighteen from entering full-time employment. Immediately this created several million jobs for adults, as well as requiring the training of half a million more teachers.

So the American High School was born in reaction to adult unemployment rather than any deep-seated conviction that what adolescents needed was more time in school. Such an arrangement jogged along largely unnoticed (as it did also in England) until the late 1970s when the emergence of the new industrial economies of the Far East effectively destroyed the viability of much American manufacturing industry. As millions of adult Americans were put out of work, the inadequacies of the high school curriculum they had experienced in their youth became all too obvious.[4] Such workers lacked any sense of responsibility for themselves, had no idea how to learn new skills, and believed that their union would always guarantee their wages. They had no idea of how to work things out for themselves. 'Why should they?' I was told in Pittsburgh in the early 1980s, 'because for several generations the backdoor of the school faced the front door of the factory, and it didn't need many qualifications to cross over.'[5]

America panicked. 'The Excellency Report' of 1983 graphically described the mediocre performance of its high schools by concluding dramatically: 'If an enemy had done this, we would have declared it to be an act of war.'[6] Which stirred up a hornet's nest of recriminations, just as it had done earlier in 1976 when the British Prime Minister, responding to the growing sense of confusion in education, had invited the public to investigate 'the Secret Garden of the Curriculum'.[7] Both England and America had created large secondary schools without thinking through what they were expected to achieve. A comment by a much respected American stands out vividly: 'To blame schools for the rising tide of mediocrity is to confuse symptoms with disease. Schools can rise no higher than the expectations of the communities that surround them.'[8] What children think, and do, is progressively influenced as they get older by the values and assumptions they absorb, largely subconsciously, from the people among whom they live. The research is pretty conclusive: schools can, in the short term, improve a child's performance and behaviour, but once that intervention ceases, the child quickly reverts to what influences him or her most – namely the values, ideas and aspirations of family, peer group and community.[9]

*   *   *

Believing as I do in that metaphor of the 1960s which likened education to a three-legged stool, able to provide balance however rough the circumstances, then sense can only be made of politicians' ambitions for schooling if we know what is happening to the child's life at home and in the community. It is only when, and if, these three parts come together in an equal partnership that a complete education becomes possible.

The expectations and aspirations of a nation reflect deep-seated assumptions that have built up over long periods of time. They are expressed in the stories and traditions which these people honour, and which come to define who they think themselves to be, and help explain their behaviours. To the English it was the fusion of the practical, self-help and entrepreneurial skills of the late eighteenth century, with the evangelical zeal of the Victorians to spread a very English form of civilization around the world, which converged in the 1930s (through a movement best described as Christian socialism)[10] to lay the foundations for a Welfare State – an idealized society providing free education and health care, unemployment pay, and pensions for the old out of taxes paid by everyone. Introduced in the immediate post-war years, the Welfare State, of which the 1944 Education Act was the linchpin, was ham-strung from the start by insufficient money, and by the hidden undercurrents in British society dating from Victorian times that social class distinctions (all too visible in the slums of the inner cities) were all part of the 'natural' order of things.

These hidden tensions have made the English confused and illogical. They willingly voted for the Welfare State in as far as it removed the threat of large medical bills, and provided something of a pension for an elderly relative for whom they might otherwise have had to care. But the well-to-do were nothing like as convinced that their own children should sit cheek-by-jowl, even in a grammar school, with the children of the working classes. From the very moment in 1945 that secondary education became free and available to all, there was a significant and sudden increase in applications to the public schools by parents who, no longer having to pay for their children to attend grammar schools, decided that the only way open to them to maintain their social exclusiveness was to go private.[11] That says a lot about the English, even 60 years ago. Twenty years later, having failed to find any acceptable way of deciding who should be offered a place at a grammar school, politicians became ever more uncertain both as to what secondary education should involve, and how it should be delivered.

Circular 10/65 was to be the fourth of the educational turning points that have shaped today's system of schooling. That Circular effectively gave local authorities permission to experiment with various solutions to secondary education. Comprehensive schools were conceived by ardent educationalists as beautiful dreams, but were most often delivered in confusion. The fault was essentially one of lack of vision, but it was also partly historic for, in implementing the 1944 proposals, the planners had assumed that most middle-class children would go to grammar schools, and so the best-equipped schools were in the better residential areas and the worst in areas of least privilege (and the greatest need), in which places were to be found the Modern schools which would educate 70 per cent of the population. So as the economy faltered in the 1970s just as elaborate reorganization schemes were being started, a comprehensive school based on a former grammar school in a good residential area seemed an altogether different animal from one based on an old secondary modern in a decaying urban area.

Here was the real cause of the bitter disputes that were to emerge in the 1980s between Conservative and Labour-controlled authorities, both of which had earlier supported the removal of the Eleven Plus; well-placed schools wanted to hold on to their advantages and get on undisturbed by government, but those schools dealing with a disproportionate range of problems needed strong LEAs which would 'skew' resources away from the privileged schools so as to establish something of a more level playing field. Conservatives backed the former (in many cases as a way of maintaining the grammar school ethos) while Labour was pledged to the level playing field. Readers in the United States, Canada, Australia and elsewhere may remember similar tensions.

To understand how the idealism of the post-war years could have withered, we have to look at how the aspirations of the British people had changed. First, it was a spiritual issue, for in the early 1970s, just when these problems were surfacing, came the point when a dwindling proportion of people (whose idealism and sense of civic responsibility had created the Welfare State), who really did believe that their reward for a life of selfless dedication would be in the Hereafter, fell to a point where their influence on other people became almost negligible.[12] Suddenly (and it was suddenly) it became totally acceptable for anyone to be openly materialistic, ambitious and self-promoting. A *Times* leader of April 1971[13] claimed that 'there are probably still more people in Britain who will give total effort for reasons of idealism than for reasons of gain'. But it wasn't to last much longer. Curiously it was Margaret Thatcher, daughter of a Methodist lay preacher and one-time Sunday School teacher herself, who subtly shifted the focus away from the Parable of the Good Samaritan[14] to the Parable of the Talents[15] by famously proclaiming that the Good Samaritan could only be 'good' because earlier he had been successful enough to have money to give away. The Welfare State, and education in particular, was shortly to be prised from its philosophic roots – more people wanted more opportunities to be entrepreneurial, with fewer restraints on their personal activities.

And it is here that the fault-line between the indigenous English and the 'new' English (who, in the 2001 Census, amounted to 4.7 million people) is most fraught. While many of the recent immigrants have contributed much by way of social capital to their new home, the experience of other

immigrants has not been good. It seems that the thing many of
them fear most as a result of living among the English is not that
they will have a Christian heritage imposed on them; rather
that, as their children leave the supportive culture of their
homes in the morning, they will catch a spiritual chill and a
cultural vacuousness from the native English children they sit
with in class. Dealing with such issues is never easy. Years ago I
heard a man skilled in these affairs say, 'You can never be a true
internationalist unless you have first been a nationalist.'[16] It was
a phrase that intrigued me. For years subsequently I have tried
to say to myself, and to anyone who will listen, 'You will never
understand another person's religion unless you understand
your own position on spiritual matters.' And the English, as a
result of that first cultural knock, are as unsure of the nature of
their spirituality and as nervous of talking about it as any
teenager listening to their parents talking about sex – both the
teenager, and the Englishman, have still to grow up. Society is
doomed to fall apart if we don't understand each other's deepest
motives, aspirations and fears. To reconcile the 'hows' of life
with the 'whys' of life becomes an ever more critical matter; as
an eminent biologist said at the State of the World Forum in
San Francisco: 'The future sanity of the world depends on the
coming together of two great disciplines that haven't spoken for
more than a hundred years – biology and theology.'[17] It takes a
thoughtful person to work this out.

Two incidents illustrate this. With all the razzamatazz that
surrounded the Millennium celebrations in London in the year
2000, it was only at the very last moment that it was agreed that
these should include a short Christian prayer.[18] Why? Apparently for fear of those politically correct bureaucrats advising on
national policy that this would offend non-Christians. That was
surely absurd, for without accepting that 1 January 2001 was a

birthday, there was nothing to celebrate. It was just another date, another year. Be you Christian, Muslim, Hindu, Sikh or totally otherwise-minded, there is no way you can understand British culture without appreciating the key significance of Christianity over the centuries. If we can't understand each other's cultures – the black spots as well as the achievements – communities are doomed to fall apart, for ignorance can never bind people together as well as knowledge can, and only then can we begin to understand how one day we might all be able to live together.

The second incident that illustrates the full enormity of the muddle we seem to have got ourselves into involved a teacher from London in 2007. Taking advantage of the many nationalities sitting in her class, she asked several pupils to define the nature of the cultures that they came from. The class listened intently as their friends gave lively accounts of what life was like in their country of birth. Then it came to the turn of an English girl. Shrugging her shoulders, she mumbled, 'I've nothing to say, I don't come from anywhere interesting, from nowhere special.'[19] That girl lived within walking distance of Shakespeare's Globe Theatre, a bus ride of the Museum of London, the Houses of Parliament, St Paul's Cathedral, Buckingham Palace, the Science Museum, the National Gallery and the theatres of the West End. Her ignorance is not simply a failure on the part of formal education, but a far bigger failure on the part of civil society to involve her, and presumably her family, within an active relationship to their community where each knew that they mattered and where life was full of interesting possibilities.

Another fundamental shift in people's behaviour started in the mid 1960s with the widespread availability of the contraceptive pill. Probably nothing separates us more from the world of our ancestors than that we should ever think to question 'Why have children?' While the immediate pleasure derived from sex may compensate for the danger and pain of childbirth, individual pleasure has, ultimately, to be balanced with the overall needs of society to maintain, but not exceed, its natural capacity. In the West, our attitude towards family and children had earlier been conditioned by those religions that came out of the desert with their rigorous and unbending ethical codes – a child had to be the total responsibility of its father. Again, the modern soundbite is too deceptively simple – is sex 'recreation or procreation'? The relationship between sex, marriage and the raising and lifelong nurturing of children is complex, yet, as expressed by a seventeen-year-old Canadian boy, gloriously simple: 'Parents have children so as to help them [the parents] to grow up.'[20] And here is the problem that seems to be getting worse; increasing numbers of today's adolescents suffer from the fact that their parents just haven't grown up themselves, and so have nothing to say to their children about how they could become effective parents themselves.

In the inter-war years, and increasingly in the 1950s, the influence of Freudian psychology dominated social policy-making. This taught that civilization all too easily becomes an oppressive force that thwarts man's basic urges by transmuting them into dangerous psychopathological behaviours. As a means of extending national happiness, socio-biology encouraged the belief that freedom to do your own thing should become the ultimate aim of policy, a philosophical position apparently bolstered by evolutionary biology's belief that all behaviour is driven by 'selfish genes'. But by 1995, evolutionary psychologists were moving away from selfish genes alone as the drivers of human behaviour and were exploring again the role of group selection as an explanation of altruism. They were suggesting that a larger threat to individual mental well-being was the way modern society 'thwarts civility'.[21] There is a kinder, gentler side to human nature, and it seems that this was increasingly a victim of repression. The problem with modern life, increasingly, is that too little of our social contact is 'social' in the natural intimate sense of the word; less that we are *over-socialized* than that we are *under-socialized*.

In recent years, suddenly, it seems socio-biology is turning the clock back to something that Darwin said in his second book *The Descent of Man* in 1871: 'Although a high standard of morality gives a slight or no advantage to each individual man and his children over the other men of the same tribe . . . an advancement in the standard of morality would certainly give an immense advantage to *one tribe over another*.' Group selection is now seen to be every bit as significant as individual, selfish choices (the maiden aunt, the unmarried priest are not furthering their own genes but through altruistic behaviour they benefit the genes of the entire group, be it family or tribe). In 2007 evolutionary psychologists could summarize this as 'selfishness beats altruism within groups; altruistic groups beat selfish groups every time'.[22] Looking back over history, virtually all the great empires arose in areas where major ethnic groups came into close contact with each other and invariably the successful empires were the ones which had a high level of co-operative behaviour. As with empires, so with individuals and families. People who pull together, pull through; those who can't co-operate, disintegrate. As Benjamin Franklin said, as he paused before signing the Declaration of Independence in 1776: 'We must all hang together, or, most assuredly, we shall all hang separately.' The world of the early twenty-first century so over-emphasizes the satisfaction of the individual that we forget it is only through altruistic, collaborative behaviour that societies thrive.

Then, third, was the enthusiasm in the mid-1980s for England to cease being a country that made things, and become instead an economy based on service industries. Thirty years ago people still took pride in what their communities made. But the processes of that industrial productivity were largely moribund, and the difficulties were as severe at management level as they were with the unions. Margaret Thatcher looked back at the battering which her predecessors Heath, Wilson and Callaghan had received from this industrial turmoil and resolved to rid herself of industrial England and, in a single leap, move into a new England that would become ever more adept at selling things. She was splendidly successful. But not every youngster is temperamentally suited to selling, analysing data, or simply being a link in an efficient production network where you never see the end product, or meet a customer. Which is why the switch to a service economy has radically changed our assumptions about ourselves, for it quickly stripped out of city, town and country opportunities for adolescents to learn through doing something, and consequently apprenticeships have all but disappeared. In terms of our inherited natures, this is having disturbing consequences, for satisfaction in a job well done has been replaced by the motivation to earn more money,[23] and that is undermining many of the values that had once made England so successful, and the English people content.

Fourth, there has been the impact of cheap petrol. Humans have always needed to move around, to collect, to trade, to share ideas, to fall in love, and to defend themselves. Perhaps more than any other land, Britain is covered in a dense network of footpaths, bridleways, drove roads and meandering country lanes made by our ancestors as they sought the safest, easiest way to walk from A to B. Until half a century ago, communities

were still largely what they had been since our Stone Age ancestors found that a cluster of caves was more congenial to our
species' survival than separate bolt holes – places where people
came together to make a living, full of noisy, argumentative
groups of people who understood the need for mutual support.
Cheap transport changed all that. First it was the railways that
made travel no longer dependent on muscle power, but by the
1950s people started to forsake the railways and took to the car.
One statistic tells all. In 1970, 70 per cent of nine-year-olds
either walked to school or went on their bikes. By 1995 that
figure was down to 17 per cent. Placing the country's faith in
cars rather than trains, 4,000 miles of railway lines were closed
in the mid-1960s but, despite short-term petrol rationing
during the oil crisis of 1973, nothing seemed to dim the Englishman's belief that the future lay in building new roads rather
than in improving the railways.[24] Inevitably we have gradually
given up walking. Not only are we becoming obese, we are
losing the opportunity to think naturally when our bodies and
minds are not in tune with everything that is going on around
us. Now there are about 21 million licensed cars on British
roads, even though half of all journeys made are for less than
three miles. It is this which has squeezed the life and colour out
of communities.

All four of these issues – the justification for greed; sex,
marriage and rearing of children; the move to a service economy;
and the collapse of communities – are changing what we think
about ourselves. By the mid-1980s we were not the same people
as we had been when the Welfare State had been set up – more
preoccupied with our own well-being, less secure in our personal
relationships, less willing to pay taxes that through redistribution
of wealth would benefit everyone, and uncertain as to the nature
of our work. Each of the legs of that three-legged stool was

becoming ever more unsure of itself. And it was democracy that was suffering; the exercise of the rights of informed, wise, robust and practical everyday people who, invariably it seems, know better than the politicians about what really connects to what, which keeps a nation steady on its course. The ballot box only works if the voters are wise enough to know what is going on around them, and for that we need to be more than processors of statistics, more than motorists, and much more than consumers – we need to be good, responsible citizens and good neighbours.

It is adolescents who are suffering most; too young to drive to meet their friends; unable to find places to hang out without being seen as a threat to social order; with few weekend jobs to take up, and often living in fractured families with no appropriate adult role to follow, they see themselves, and are seen by adults, as a 'tribe apart'.[25] I recently heard a young Canadian rebuke an audience of adults: 'You should know us better than to simply look at us in a drugstore as if we were all shoplifters.'[26] The modern world has turned adolescence from a time of purposeful learning to grow up, into a sedentary period of passing the time in the expectation that you might just become a celebrity on TV. It is very, very different from the world that many of us adults grew up in years ago, and it's not particularly nice.

*   *   *

These changing aspirations of the British people were reflected in two particular aspects of public life: a decrease in confidence in the structures of government in general, and the failure at local levels to define a vision for secondary education. Following the half-hearted directive of 10/65, the education system was simply running out of steam. By the late 1970s there was an appalling lack of leadership, both in terms of the knowledge of elected members, and professionally in terms of headteachers and Chief Education Officers, both of whom allowed themselves to become preoccupied with maintaining the status quo rather than planning boldly for a better system. People exhausted themselves with turf wars, the writing of papers, attending endless conferences, and arguments about matters of trivia. Bureaucrats flourished, but nothing actually changed, and no bold visions were articulated. Creative people were frustrated at every turn, and vast numbers of them left the profession. It was a depressing time in which to be around.

With the election of Margaret Thatcher as Prime Minister in 1979, the Conservatives entered into an eighteen-year battle with local government about the expenditure of monies raised from national taxes but administered locally. Chief Education Officers were, to Margaret Thatcher, the personification of all that was reckless in local council spending, and she never accepted, with her particular hard-nosed conservatism, that to educate children in the old, decaying, inner-city areas needed additional resources. So she chose Kenneth Baker[27] to use an education bill to bring local authorities to the heel of Westminster. Baker saw himself as both an insightful intellectual (he published a book of his own poetry, and openly let it be known that he hoped to succeed Margaret Thatcher), and the voice of modern industry striving to move Britain into a new age. He aligned himself with the new technological, free-market Establishment. He was prepared to go far further in his reforms than Thatcher had anticipated. He was too quick to accept the argument that if British youngsters were not sufficiently entrepreneurial, this was the fault, not of the secondary school, but the shameful result of experiential teaching in the primary school. It was the primary schools which were failing the nation by not preparing their pupils well enough for the transfer to secondary education.

To make sense of what was to become the fifth of the educational turning points, the Education Act of 1988, it is necessary to understand the tensions that had developed between primary and secondary teachers over the previous twenty years. The problem of secondary education went back to the decision of 1902 to block the extension of elementary education (and its methodology) upwards beyond the age of fourteen. From 1902 onwards the influence of the public school curriculum, with its emphasis on selectivity and on the teaching of separate subjects, dominated secondary education. Such assumptions were anathema to the elementary teachers, and their dismay had intensified when the 1944 Act further reduced the influence of 'teaching pupils rather than subjects' by stopping primary education three years earlier, at the age of eleven. Coincidently, in the years after the war, many well-educated women, still barred from most of the professions, sought employment in primary schools, and with their sensitive and intelligent approach to children's experiential learning, progressively demonstrated the validity of what cognitive scientists were starting to describe as 'making thinking visible'.[28] The tragedy was that when such alert, inquisitive and engaged pupils entered secondary school, they found it boring and undemanding; secondary teachers were so unnerved by such questioning pupils that they came to see in the experiential pedagogy of the primary school a challenge to their conventional subject-based authority.

Had those secondary teachers (and, I suggest, the Ministers) read the Report 'Language for Life' chaired by Lord Bullock and commissioned by an earlier government in 1975 into the nature of spoken and written English, they would have found the clue as to what was needed. 'If children are to develop the speaking and listening skills in the use of the English language, then every lesson has, in effect, to become a lesson in English, and every essay, be it in history, biology or economics, should be marked for its correct use of language as well as its subject content,' noted Bullock.[29] To primary teachers this was what they had always believed, so to them it was pure common sense to use subject-specific material to develop basic skills. But to their secondary colleagues the suggestion went down like a lead balloon, for they didn't accept that the teaching of basic skills was any concern of theirs. 'Outrageous!' was the cry in many a secondary school staffroom, 'I have studied history [it could have been physics or mathematics] for years at university. Now I'm expected to add to my workload by also becoming an English teacher! Ridiculous!' Government never implemented the Report. It was far too challenging of the pedagogic status quo. A key opportunity was lost.

A year or so later, a Report on mathematics[30] said virtually the same thing. Consequently both Reports hardly ruffled the secondary sector for the very simple reason that they knew not where to put them – they had no mechanism to deal with an educational issue that was not easily allocated to a single department. Compounding the tension, the next year Her Majesty's Inspectorate responded with an insightful Paper that built on the thinking of Bullock by setting out a future curriculum in terms of 'Areas of Experience – such as the ascetic, the creative, the social, the political and the spiritual.'[31] This was just what the primary teachers wanted, but again the cynical voice of the secondary teacher chanted, 'So where do I now teach kids chemistry in that lot – is it alongside an ethical discussion of nuclear energy, the nature of the universe or the beauty of a nuclear power station, or what?'[32]

*   *   *

These two issues – the attack on local government and the reform of education – finally converged to create the 1988 Educational Reform Act, the fifth of the educational crises since 1870 that have shaped the present system of schooling. The Act was described by the press as a 'gothic monstrosity of legislation,'[33] while Ministers claimed that it 'would inject a new vitality into educational policy . . . and create a new framework which will raise standards, extend choice and produce a better-educated Britain'.[34] But Baker was in a hurry. Because he never questioned the appropriateness of transfer at the age of eleven, he never stopped to think deeply about the conflicting 'models of learning' that were involved, so consequently secondary schools were set to get ever larger and more complex. A compulsory National Curriculum was created, and new arrangements for the local financial management of schools reduced the power of the local authority. City Technology Colleges were established as a new form of state-funded school administered directly from Westminster so as to make a reality of the Conservative government's commitment to extended choice. At the same time all schools were made directly responsible to central government.

As every teacher knows, the planning of a curriculum is notoriously difficult. Before 1988 it was an annual battleground between the expectations of the different subject areas, and a school's commitment to the all-round development of the individual child. Inevitably the curriculum was a compromise, for there was no absolute right way of doing it. Butler had been right 40 years before to see in this continuous struggle the opportunity for headteachers to keep their staff constantly involved in thinking about the work they were doing, and assessing the value of one alternative over another. When a neighbouring school came up with a slightly different curriculum from yours, it didn't mean that either of you were wrong – far from it. Each of you had fine-tuned what was happening in your school to the nature of the community inside school and beyond the school gates. Under insightful, wise and dedicated headteachers this kept staff on their toes; under good and dedicated Chief Education Officers, headteachers were extended and refreshed by the overall strategy for their part of the country. Working well, the whole system was galvanized by constructive tension, but where a sense of overall direction was lost, the whole system faltered – good ideas withered on the vine, inertia predominated, and there was a dearth of men and women willing to go beyond management to leadership. Educationalists were about to have the agenda taken over by the politicians.

If the starting point for the National Curriculum had been 'Areas of Experiences' as suggested by Her Majesty's Inspectorate (first set up in 1850), then the curriculum might have emerged more as a coherent whole. But the starting point was expressed in terms of subjects, each of which wanted so much content that it was like squeezing a quart into a pint pot. The National Curriculum as eventually constructed defined English, mathematics and science as core subjects. In reality it was pretty similar to what Morant had advocated for the grammar schools in 1902. But now there were to be national attainment targets based on SATs at the age of seven, eleven, fourteen and sixteen which would later lead to defining the four key stages of schooling. Every subject would have clearly defined objectives and measurable outcomes for each year that could be broken down to agreed programmes of work by the week. Every child, regardless of his or her own personal dispositions and possible inadequacies, would follow the same syllabus.

By giving more power and financial autonomy to schools, the Act reduced the ability of local education authorities to address the needs of different parts of their areas, but made every school subject to micromanagement from Whitehall. This effectively paved the way for the eventual takeover of the entire educational system by Westminster within the next fifteen or so years. But far from being the best national curriculum that could ever be devised, as was proclaimed by government, it was so flawed and so unworkable that in the years to come it had to be revised time and time again. So bitter were the arguments that the former Chairman of the Post Office was called in as a mediator to overhaul the entire curriculum.[35] 'This was because,' apologized a government Minister at the time, 'the early architects of the whole system built into it too much bureaucracy, and too much convolution.'[36] After six years of vicious fighting and demands made on teachers to undertake programmes that would shortly be abolished, the curriculum virtually ended up where it had been six years before in those schools that had carefully thought through these issues. In the meantime the stuffing had been knocked out of what good teaching was all about because the Minister made the cardinal mistake of any inexperienced teacher – he had punished the whole class rather than isolating the culprits. If you put the whole class into detention, you simply show that you can't cope.

Within less than twelve months, Baker had been pushed sideways and never became Thatcher's successor. Yet his approach to heavy-handedly beating up the profession was continued in late 1991 when his successor appointed three men to undertake a three-month enquiry into primary school teaching methods. Nicknamed 'the three wise men', their rapidly produced report was, as one of them said bitterly afterwards, 'hijacked' and 'misinterpreted' by the Minister to justify an all-out attack on experiential learning techniques and urged instead a return to whole-class teaching. This, together with the replacement of Her

Majesty's Inspectorate the following year by the Office for Standards in Education (Ofsted), reflected Conservative ideology that insisted that assessment was – in the jargon – 'summative', that is, it should be used to make objective comparisons between different groups of people, results and rates of progress. While not denying that this was one use of assessment, primary teachers had seen that the most valuable aspect of this was 'diagnostic' – something rather like a doctor reading a set of blood pressure results to assess whether a patient needs treatment, and, if so, of what kind; it is never used to compare groups of patients. In replacing HMI by Ofsted, the new inspectors were trained to be just that – inspectors, working to a closely defined set of criteria that simply recorded a mass of objective data about a school, a pupil, a subject area, and interpreted this through a points score that rapidly led to the creation of league tables. What the politicians wanted was data, and data that would enable them to show that the policies they were applying were actually working.

By the early 1990s it wasn't only the educational world in turmoil; outside school everything seemed to be changing – in Tiananmen Square the tanks had crushed the students, while in Germany the Berlin Wall was being torn down. People were starting to talk about perestroika and globalization, both of which would quickly add further twists to our national expectations and aspirations. 'Who are you?' I was asked in Estonia just after the Russians had left. 'When we helped to tear down the Berlin Wall we did so because we wanted to be free to make decisions for ourselves. But you thought we did this because we wished to replace Communism with Capitalism. Now it looks as if we are replacing one tyranny with another. Surely you in the West are about more than just money?'

*   *   *

We now come to three more factors that have fundamentally shifted our assumptions over the last fifteen years. Information technology in the 1990s was rapidly changing the way people thought and, in the minds of many, starting to confuse information with what an educated person was all about. Lest I seem to be suffering from technophobia, let me explain that I was an early enthusiast for computers in education, and was responsible for putting in what became England's first-ever fully computerized classroom in 1979 with a terminal for every pupil. The aim was simple, and rooted very much in the practice of schooling. I'm a bad speller who early in life recognized that I could fool my teachers if they couldn't read my handwriting. Many were my Bs that they couldn't distinguish from my Ds, and the As from my Es. The strategy served me well through university, but because I hated the tedium of rewriting an essay for which I had already gained seven out of ten, I hardly bothered to take notice of the teacher's suggestion. Consequently I never really improved, I just jogged along at 70 per cent. Years later, as headmaster, my secretary presented me with a draft of a letter I had recently dictated and showed me how we could improve this through the use of a word processor. That intrigued me. What might happen, I asked myself and my teachers, if every child in every subject could use a word processor for every essay they ever wrote? Then a teacher (of any subject) could require a pupil to provide (with all the ease made possible by the word processor) a revised essay which should incorporate all the teacher's suggestions. I, and others who thought like Lord Bullock, saw that this could lead to a dramatic improvement in pupils' literacy skills, and reinforce the professionalism that older students should seek for their work.

Quite simply I had seen the technology as a means to an end, certainly not an end in itself. In the fifteen years that have followed, it seems to have gone exactly the other way. To simplify the teacher's task (and especially to make the marking of children's exams much easier) subject content has progressively been modified to make it conform to the way in which pupils' learning can be fitted around the binary processes of a computer. For an examiner to read through a pupil's answer carefully and then award a mark is now seen as too subjective. Better, it is thought, for the examiner to offer pupils a choice of, say, six alternative solutions and simply require the student to tick that which he or she thinks is most appropriate. Rather than opening up more interesting possibilities, education has become more and more about giving the right answer. Administrators meanwhile suffer from a surfeit of confusing statistics.

Schools no longer feel like the best of them used to feel. Thirty-year-old Maria is typical: trained between 1994 and 1998 to deliver the National Curriculum, she resigned after six years' teaching, feeling bitterly disappointed. 'A robot could teach in today's educational climate. The job is formulaic – introduction, learning objectives, key vocabulary, main activity, plenary, assessment, targets. Deliver these things and you're a successful teacher. There is no requirement for teachers or children to be able to question, create, analyse or discover. The school system has become a machine churning out clones of individuals,'[37] she said.

Information technology has now merged with technologies of communication, putting each of us in touch with the world 24/7 – but also placing each of us 'on call' 24/7. This has created globalization, the second of these last three factors that shape current schooling. Successful economies are no longer those based on physical resources, but on the creation and application of knowledge. Classical economic theory (that of Adam Smith) argued that when wheat prices rose, consumers bought less and equilibrium was restored at a lower level of demand, a kind of negative feedback like a thermostat. In the new global economy it is knowledge about alternative capacity or processes that has become infinitely more important than conventional constraints of supply and demand – the metaphor has shifted from a thermostat to an avalanche. Too expensive to print this book in England? Well, search the web for spare capacity elsewhere, conclude a deal over the internet, electronically transmit production-ready text, and let printing start tomorrow in China, and let the local publishing company go hang. Globalization stimulates about one billion dollars more trade every hour of the day, and it's governed by a single rule: 'Do unto others what you would prefer they didn't do to you.' The impact of this on how we think about the world and other people is profound: 'If you believe that the world is a vast larder, each item with a price, then you simply plunder it.'[38] Think of your supermarket on a Saturday afternoon, and then work out why all the local corner shops have closed down and ask yourself where have all the adolescents gone who used to spend much of Saturday on their bicycles delivering groceries? How have we come to accept such an economic model without questioning what might be its long-term implications?

Third, consider the implications of something that might seem only trivial – the lifting of restrictions on Sunday Trading in 1995. Humans are not the only species that need regular rests – indeed it seems that the more complex species' cognitive processes, the more rest it needs. Brains get even more fatigued than muscles. Baboons spend 20 per cent of their waking hours gently caressing their partners as they pick out any fleas in the crevices of their fur.[39] Our Stone Age ancestors apparently spent only 18 per cent of their waking hours hunting and preparing their food – they spent an enormous amount of time apparently telling stories around the fireside. The more relaxed people are, the more inclined they are to smile and laugh – two activities that are especially good for our health. We still need the rhythm of regular and proper holidays as well, for 'all rest and no play makes Jack a dull boy'. The Commandment that 'six days shalt thou labour and do all that thou has to do', holds the Jewish people together to this day. To a secular world it seems that the injunction to worship God so contaminates the concept of Sunday as a day of rest, that free-thinking peoples want to dismiss this as an unnecessary hangover from an outdated religion. Which is nonsense; even the Russian communists at the height of their power didn't go that far. So just how did we turn every day of the week into a work day? Is this really a liberalization policy? Was it because we thought it would be good for our health, or is it – an uncomfortable thought – that so many people are removed from what our instincts may tell us are our preferred ways of doing things (getting satisfaction from work which we have done well, that rest becomes its own wonderful reward) that we have instead become mall rats, only happy when we are coveting something?[40]

*   *   *

The Labour Party that came to power in 1997 would not have been recognized by those who earlier created the Welfare State in the 1940s, and who sought to replace selective schools with comprehensives in the 1960s. Tony Blair entered Downing Street claiming that he had only three items on his agenda – Education, Education, Education.[41] It took a while for people to understand that this was an extension, not a retraction, of previous Conservative policies. New Labour's belief in the superiority of business management led to strategies in which 'management by objectives' permeated all aspects of schooling.

Those who knew Blair well realized that he had an unshakable faith in what has become known as *performability*.[42] As an economic rationalist, Blair believed that it was possible, and certainly desirable, to measure every kind of performance, be it of a pupil or waiting times in hospitals. In this Blair was a latter-day version of Frederick Winslow Taylor (now with access to the extraordinary processing power of electronic communication) and so convinced of the system that if it didn't produce the results he wanted, it was simply because the measurement techniques needed further refinement.

Before the election, Blair had reassured the public that he would push ahead even faster than the Conservatives with the reform of primary education, and made the raising of standards in literacy and numeracy an absolute priority. Again, readers in other lands will immediately note similarities with policies in their own countries. Blair set the ambitious target of moving from 63 per cent of eleven-year-olds reading at their age level to 80 per cent by the year 2002, with similar expected improvements in mathematics. Government then set up a new Standards and Effectiveness Unit to oversee a structured Literacy and Numeracy Hour in every primary school, all of which would be on top of what was already being required from the National Curriculum. This was to be supported by an even heavier testing regime. The load became unbearable, while the message from the Department could not have been clearer. In 2001 the Minister stated, 'The work of the Department of Education and Employment fits with the new economic imperative of supply-side investment for national prosperity.'[43] To this end the regime of endless testing was bent to demonstrate to an ever more anxious public that it really was safe to assume that schools could do it all. Describing how a 'nose to the grindstone' approach to education inhibits the proper growth of children's minds, it was noted in 2002 that the generation then leaving school had been publicly tested in each of their twelve years of schooling. And what, parents and political commentators continuously asked, were the tests for? 'If you are forever doing formal tests and waiting for someone to give you marks, then you never learn the skills for assessing yourself and measuring your own knowledge and ability against genuine, outside challenges. The constant neurotic focus on grades stops teachers from encouraging connections and fostering creative flexibility.'[44]

And it was here that government shot itself in the foot. By so misunderstanding the nature of learning, it set itself unreasonable targets so as to pacify the media's thirst for stories of extremes. Government was either on course to fail or to further antagonize the teachers by putting the blame on them. Whereas in the mid-1980s most sixteen-year-olds had gone into their GCE (General Certificate of Education) exams in almost total ignorance of what the examiners might ask, now their teachers knew exactly how the examiners would mark the pupils' scripts, and it became all too easy to drill pupils in ways that enabled them to hit all the key phrases, words, ideas and facts their teachers knew would satisfy the examiners. 'At GCSE our children go into the exam incredibly well prepared,' a teacher explained, 'but by God are they bored by school.' And so the population at large came to convince itself that the standards set by the examiners were falling, and that children should take even more subjects. With that ever-increasing pressure to improve the performance of schools, England was forgetting that for children to grow up properly, there was much more to education than sitting in classrooms.

*   *   *

The horrible death in London of an eight-year-old[45] in the year 2000, and the subsequent enquiry which attributed this to failure at twelve different levels within the social/medical support services, was a direct challenge to Blair's belief in 'performability'. Government responded with a massive agenda entitled *Every Child Matters* that was to be the ultimate in joined-up thinking. Defining five outcomes for children as: being healthy, staying safe, enjoyment and achievement, making a positive contribution, and economic well-being, the Act legislated to set up what are euphemistically called Full-service Extended Schools, and nicknamed by the media as wraparound schools, these were to be opened before normal school hours to provide breakfast, and to remain open hours after lessons finished to provide after-school clubs, childcare and social support systems throughout the year. Here with the Act of 2003 was to be the sixth of those educational turning points that have shaped schooling since 1870.

Seeking to justify this contentious proposal, government reminded teachers of the importance of working closely with parents. It cited English research which showed that parental engagement can account for up to 12 per cent of the difference between the performance of different pupils, consciously ignoring OECD who put this figure two-and-a-half times higher at 29 per cent (which, if taken notice of, would have caused ministers to make it easier for more families to have breakfast at home). Why didn't they state it the other way round? To have done so would have meant reminding parents of their responsibilities, and that is something which politicians are fearful of doing in case it upsets people's perceived rights. Despite the apparent language, government still does not want to attribute to families the significance which they merit. The Prime Minister, in his passionate foreword to the report, opened by saying: 'For most parents our children are everything to us: our hopes, our ambitions, our futures . . . but sadly some children's lives are dreadfully different. Instead of the joy, warmth and security of normal family life, these children's lives are filled with fear (often) from the people closest to them.'[46]

That same autumn, teachers reported that they had never experienced such an ill-prepared generation of five-year-olds: half of them lacked the speaking and listening skills needed to cope in a classroom, and many could neither clean their teeth, tie their shoe laces, nor hold a knife and fork, and they had little understanding of how to socialize. The Prime Minister was out of touch, and an increasing proportion of parents seemed not to care. Only some 10 per cent of children sat down to more than one family meal a week, about 50 per cent of marriages were ending in divorce, 40 per cent of children were being born to single mothers, and 7 per cent of children experienced their fathers being in prison at some stage during their school years. Still the pressure on families built up, as the demand to feed an ever more buoyant economy (applauded by the same Prime Minister) knew no limits.

Having established consumerism as the driving force in the economy, government was now having to pick up the broken social pieces before they in turn upset the economic cart. Until the 1980s, a teacher's role had been defined as being *in loco parentis* – to act in place of a parent – but the Conservatives started to change that so that the language eventually used by Labour in *Every Child Matters* was subtly different. The responsibilities had been reversed. It is teachers who are now urged, as a way of improving school examination results, to work with parents. But don't the children belong to the parents, not the state? If something has gone wrong, which it manifestly had, was it not the parents (ordinary people like you and me) who had to be strengthened to do our job properly, and not have our responsibilities taken from us and reallocated as jobs to professionals? In a detailed critique, the Conservatives claimed that such policies would result in 'nationalizing the upbringing of children' for 'in the guise of a caring, child-centred administration, this government is effecting a radical change in the balance of authority between parents, children and the state'.[47]

Every Child Matters raises profound questions about the role of teachers. This is emotional territory, for teachers, like everyone else, come in all shapes and sizes, and they have their good days and their bad. Some age before their time, others go on regardless. Strangely, there are now more trained teachers who are not teaching than those who are. With just over 400,000 full-time equivalent teachers, there are 42,000 in training at any one time, which suggests an average professional life expectancy of only ten years. This is strange, for older readers well remember a different kind of teacher. We remember the eccentrics whose enthusiasm for sport, medieval art or music exceeded their subject passions. We were fascinated by those who talked to us, and we never knew what would happen in each lesson. We were brought up to be interested in everything, to be broadly educated and multifaceted. Never in their wildest dreams would those teachers of years gone by have anticipated the 'workforce reform' called for in *Every Child Matters*. Government resolved that all the agencies involved with children should from now on each have specific targets, and be put under the unified control of a Director of Children's Services. Many Directors of Education would now occupy a second-tier post, with the local education authorities stripped of most of their powers. This was *performability* in action.

Having so misunderstood the multi-dimensional nature of

children's needs, schools have been left by government with little opportunity to consider the actual, broad, learning needs of children. Schools are increasingly defined by politicians as mechanisms to meet the ambiguous specifications of the National Curriculum, and the teacher has inevitably been replaced by an instructor, the person who delivers to a model designed by a committee of experts. New teachers may be more focused on the classroom than their predecessors, but they are less aware of the multitude of tasks that make up a teacher's job; they are less keen to run extra-curricular activities and less imaginative about lesson planning. In their training there is precious little consideration given to how children learn, to the philosophic questions that have to be answered in every generation as to why we think as we do, while the starting point for the history of education is taken as 1988 (approximately page 140 of this 220-page book!). The idea that there might be better ways to teach things that lie outside these programmes is heresy to most newly qualified teachers.

*   *   *

Rather than guiding principles or strong personal leadership in the first part of the twenty-first century, there has been a sequence of ministers and senior civil servants each acting according to their own understanding of where things were when they took over – that is why they only looked back over the affairs of the past few months, and had no sense of their historical context. They became extraordinarily short term in their thinking. What happened at a policy level over the past 30 or 40 years could be seen as something of a family squabble between Ministers of Education (husbands) and Permanent Secretaries (wives), with the local education authorities as a large number of offspring. The rougher the arguments, the more frequent the divorces, the more shaky becomes the family home; and the more confused, neurotic and worried become the children. There has been a dramatic speed-up in these changes over the last few years. In the past 40 years, there have been twenty Ministers of Education, and six in the past ten years – three of whom have held office for less than eighteen months. With nine Permanent Secretaries in the past 37 years, there have been five since 1993. That's a high turnover that doesn't allow for concerted long-term planning. Just to confuse matters, the family name has changed four times. Until 1992 it was the Department of Education and Science, and then it became the Department for Education and Employment. In 2001 it became the Department for Education and Skills. In 2007 its family name became hyphenated as the family split into the Department for Children, Schools and Families, and the Department of Innovations, Universities and Skills.

Something else has happened, something sinister to the future of democracy. There has been an ever-increasing number of what, in terms of a family, could only be called illicit relationships, backstairs influence by mistresses, people wielding enormous influence, but having been neither elected by the populace nor trained through the Civil Service. Large numbers of special advisers have been appointed, ranging from men like the Chairman of the City Technology Trust, which was transformed into the Specialised Schools Trust administering hundreds of millions of pounds, or the Prime Minister's appointees to the Downing Street Policy Unit, or the heads of think-tanks with direct links through to Downing Street. All this has resulted in the bog-standard, democratically elected Member of Parliament left with little to do other than voting from time to time as directed by the party whips. It makes a mockery of democracy. That has to be really worrying, and is not a lesson any of us would wish our children to learn.

As for government partnerships financing local expenditure as decided by local people, these have been replaced by ring-fenced grants designed by Westminster, only to be applied to a pre-determined prescription. As for fraternal relationship between schools, forget it; school budgets depend upon pupil numbers, and everyone else's pupils are fair game if it's extra income you need. Local authorities have lost virtually all their responsibilities, constantly over-ruled if the combination of government's wish to strike a deal with a sponsor could mean the provision of a glossy new glass, steel and concrete erection – an academy – even if the existing schools are under-subscribed.

Weighed down by all this, by the mountains of paperwork they create, and by being held accountable to numerous external agencies,[48] are the headteachers – an endangered species, as few are now willing to take up such a thankless task, even though, as Frederick Winslow Taylor would have recommended, they are now paid more than ever before. And below them are all the millions of youngsters for whom it was supposed to be about. No wonder that when a future Wordsworth, feeling the sun on his back and the fresh breeze on his face, asks to go out to play, the terrified teacher slams the door in his face saying, 'That is not in my approved lesson plan, nor is there time to complete a risk-assessment form.'

*   *   *

In February 2007, UNICEF produced a report on the well-being of children in the 21 richest countries in the world. They based their findings on 40 indicators, which they then used to define six specific categories. British children, despite living in the world's fifth richest country, came bottom for the quality of family relationships, sex, drink and drugs, and for overall happiness. Less than half of British youngsters found their peers 'kind and helpful', more than a fifth rated their physical and mental health as poor, and considered themselves to be the least contented in the Western world. Britain has the second-largest number of children growing up with only one parent, and shared the dubious distinction with the United States of having the largest number of children growing up in households with a family income less than half the national average. British children were much more likely to have been involved in a fight in the previous twelve months than other nationalities, and more likely to have been bullied. Coming twelfth for health and safety, and seventeenth for education, British children were – by the UNICEF statistics – in overall bottom position, just below the Americans. Which takes us right back to the opening paragraphs of this chapter. While Britain and America were at the bottom of the table, the other English-speaking countries, Ireland (9th) and Canada (12th) weren't doing too well either. What's up with English-speaking peoples?

An embarrassed British government responded by quoting, with all the statistics it made sure it had at its disposal, that the various initiatives it had taken since 1997 were lifting 240 children a day on average out of poverty, and expected to remove child poverty by 2020.[49]

It was in the nature of this response that the British really showed the weakness of their position. It goes back to Blair's belief in 'performability', and the conviction that government controls all the action. So many of the factors that account for these appallingly low levels of child well-being are not specifically the result of government action or inaction. They are the result of something much deeper, more organic than that. They are the result of the individual decisions made every day by millions of separate individuals, far too many of whom make their decisions simply on what matters most to them at the moment. And, as damning as it is to say this, far too many adults rate their own short-term well-being as more important than the long-term well-being of children. In terms of our expectations and aspirations, the British and the Americans are not the people they once were.

Young people, especially adolescents, are caught up in the vortex of this whirling mass of conflicting expectations and aspirations. The most stunning change for adolescents today is actually their aloneness – it may not seem like that when you listen to their excited chattering, but beyond their own peer group there is less inter-generational connection now than there has ever been. They talk endlessly to one another, but to the rest of society they remain that tribe apart. This is not because they necessarily come from parents who don't care, or from schools that don't care, or from communities that don't want to value them, but rather because there hasn't been time for adults to lead them through the process of growing up. Youngsters of today are growing up in a world in which the values of mutuality and reciprocity that were once an integral part of British life have been overwhelmed by a shoulder-shrugging individualism that excuses most adults, and society as a whole, from what we used to think of as the responsibility to respect, nurture and support youngsters as they gradually edge into adulthood.[50]

That the English have allowed themselves to be talked into ever more institutional solutions to complex problems is strange, for theirs is a culture in which, historically, individuals used to take great pride in their own, frequently perverse and often idiosyncratic, but sometimes brilliant, creativity. That England should be so enthusiastic about extending institutional schooling is even more curious given many an English person's antipathy towards schooling when they were children themselves.

Stranger still when research shows the critical importance of those open learning situations only to be found in the emotionally supportive environment of the home, or the naturally complex if unpredictable nature of the informal community. Stranger again to historians who know that great inventors, politicians and shapers of public opinion have often been the odd-balls, the children who didn't fit comfortably into any form of institutional provision. Einstein didn't start talking until he was four, or write until he was six. By current educational arrangements, the greatest scientist of his time would have found himself on the Special Needs Register! Charles Darwin failed to qualify for a degree at both Edinburgh and Cambridge Universities; Gregor Mendel, the founder of modern genetics, failed every exam to become a high school teacher in Austria; and Bill Gates was virtually withdrawn from formal classroom work at the age of thirteen. Successful adolescents are more in need of space to be themselves than they are of more classrooms to sit in and more exams to take.

8

What Kind of Education for What Kind of World?

The crowd was excitedly waiting for the clock to sound out the midnight hour across the crowded market square, a space that had echoed long ago to the tramp of Roman legions, and seen the crowning of the first king of all the English 1,000 years ago. At the first chime a vast cheer went up; men and women, old friends and strangers, young and old, hugged each other. So many corks were pulled that a mist of champagne hung in the air. Older people looked into each other's eyes and congratulated themselves at finally having made it to the new millennium – a day in a thousand years. Excitement hung in the air, history was being made, and for a short while all seemed well in the world. We were the privileged ones who had made it to the twenty-first century.

Then, that afternoon, the BBC conducted a radio interview with Sir Martin Rees, the Astronomer Royal, later President of the Royal Society. Tell us, said the interviewer, what chance do you give the world of surviving the next thousand years, the next millennium? 'I'm not too sure about the next millennium,' he replied soberly, 'but I think I give us a 50/50 chance of surviving the next hundred years.' The interviewer, obviously shaken, asked, 'Why . . . why do you say that?' 'Well,' replied Sir Martin, 'I fear that the speed of man's technological discoveries is outpacing our wisdom and ability to control what we have discovered . . . what happens here on Earth, in this century, could conceivably make the difference between a near eternity

185

filled with ever more complex and subtle forms of life, and one filled with nothing but base matter.'[1]

Could it really be as grim a prospect as that – the extermination of humanity through our inability to control our excesses? The warning was stark and uncompromising. If Rees was right, then every aspect of how we organize our lives would have to change – from an economy based on escalating levels of consumption, to the way we value personal relationships and educate our children.

It is an issue of such apparent complexity that, Stone Age thinkers that we still are, we long to push it back to the furthest, darkest corners of our minds. 'We have a built-in cognitive filter for bad news,' commented a leading neuroscientist in 2005,[2] which probably goes part of the way to explain why humans are forever hopeful . . . but find facing problems head-on so very difficult. The evidence, however, is stacking up. Soon we were to be shaken by the events of 9/11 in New York and Washington; by the failed diplomacy that led to the wars in Afghanistan and Iraq; by the devastation and starvation in Darfur; and by the destructive force of Hurricane Katrina in New Orleans. In 2002, the World Wildlife Foundation published figures that showed that if everyone on the earth's surface were to aspire to live at the same level as the citizens of the United States, this would require three more planets, the size of planet Earth, to produce the necessary raw resources without any further increase in population.[3] Then there was the realization that our recent industrial progress has come at the cost of releasing into the atmosphere over a few short years the carbon which tens of millions of previous years had laid down as deposits of oil and coal. Shockingly we now have the data that shows the inevitable consequence of this in terms of increased solar radiation which, if not halted by 2017,[4] might mean that the entire ecosystem has passed a tipping point from which climatic change on a massive scale would be unstoppable.[5]

You don't need a PhD to ask how it is that – for all our scientists, philosophers, politicians and economists and for all our technological wizardry – we have been so silly, so blind, as to have got ourselves into this muddle. As any beer-swilling philosopher holding forth in a pub will explain, it's simply because the left hand doesn't know what the right hand is doing. A ten-year-old will give you a similar answer, and then ask why it is that adults are so dumb as not to understand this. And all that the adult can say by way of lame explanation is that 'It's more complicated than you think.' Which is both true and false, and doesn't get any of us very far.

The Western world has come to see such an issue as being complicated because, to deal with the ever increasing volume of knowledge, we long ago abandoned our innate desire to understand things in their entirety (big pictures), that critical skill which earlier helped our hunter/gatherer ancestors to survive by forming a complete understanding of what was going on in the world around them. Nowadays we have traded in this skill in favour of ways of thinking that focus on manageable sub-parts of an issue. It is said that Francis Bacon was the last real polymath, a person who knew all there was to know about everything that mattered . . . and he died in 1626. An archetypal Renaissance thinker, Bacon concerned himself both with philosophic issues of the 'whys' of life as well as searching for objective explanations for the 'hows' of life. To find those scientific explanations, Bacon, followed shortly by Isaac Newton, demonstrated that any problem could be solved if it were reduced to its individual constituent parts. Scientific Reductionism (as it came to be known), by putting up boundaries around subjects, made it easier for specialists to understand the

finer points of their discipline, but it effectively prevented connections being made with other subjects. Consequently, while
today's economists might be the finest a country can produce,
by knowing nothing of the factors that maintain ecological and
human stability, they can unwittingly advocate policies that are
ultimately self-destructive.

Such ways of thinking permeate the Western mind, and
dominate contemporary university studies and virtually every
form of post-doctoral research; they shape the secondary school
curriculum, and even now are drifting into primary schools. We
live in a world of specialists. Synthesis, the drawing together of
ideas so as to give a unified explanation that takes many factors
into account, is a much more problematic process and one that
is frequently ignored.[6] Consequently, it's not just PhDs who
find it difficult to think outside their own particular box.
Children are having the same problem themselves now. While
the ten-year-old may still be open-minded enough to be dumb-
founded by an adult's inability to see things as they really are,
fourteen-year-olds will most likely already be conditioned into
thinking small, rather than big. Reductionism, by giving a clear
picture of part of an issue, diverts our attention from those
components of a complex phenomenon which are less clear, but
may be far more significant. That's why adults who read a lot,
but don't give themselves the opportunity to think enough, get
confused. People able to see the big picture, those who can
synthesize, are in very short supply – which is largely why we're
in such a muddle.

The limitations of reductionism have been known for more
than a century, ever since the development of quantum
mechanics showed that, at the most basic of levels, there is no
difference between a solid, a liquid or a gas, for the molecules
pass seamlessly from one state to another. What matters is how

each relates to the other, and how such relationships can change rapidly as the context alters. Nevertheless, so deeply embedded is the belief in Reductionism to those who favour cut-and-dried explanations, that to see education reframed by someone with the philosophical and political experience of a man like Vaclav Havel[7] who, in the year 2000, defined a real education 'as the ability to perceive the hidden connections between phenomena', is a challenge simply too great for those who find security in working within the minutiae of a sub-discipline. The problem which Martin Rees identified, is one of the Western mind's own making, because we have forgotten how to think inclusively.

It has been formal education's inability to recognize these hidden connections and place them at the heart of children's learning over the past 40 or so years that inhibits the thinking of all of us – it's not just today's children who have become dumbed down, it's been going on for such a long time that many older people just don't recognize the limitations in their own thinking. Consequently, as adults come late in the day to see the connection between the way of life we've been led to believe would give us a high standard of living, and the consequences we now see this having on the environment and our quality of life, we just don't know what to do. We seem locked onto a treadmill – running ever faster, but not getting ourselves anywhere in particular. Never was this clearer than in mid-September 2001 when President George W. Bush, sensing that the grief Americans felt following the attack on the World Trade Center might slow down the national economy, urged his fellow countrymen to borrow more money and indulge themselves in a good dose of retail therapy.[8]

* * *

Is the ability to be acquisitive really what life is now assumed to be all about – is that what we're educating children for? You won't make sense of what follows in this and the next chapter about the kind of education needed to equip youngsters to deal with the future if you don't take some time out and think this fundamental issue through for yourself. Adults live in such a busy world that they need to step aside and ask where all this busyness is actually taking children, and why it is that what should be the natural exuberance and questioning of youth has too often been replaced by youngsters who look hammered – sort of beaten into something that denies their natural state.[9] An awful question quickly arises, and is left embarrassingly unanswered: are young people now too busy to think for themselves? And is this really what parents want, or children need? Have today's politicians somehow trivialized education and effectively missed the boat that children need to catch if they are to sail into an uncertain world? In their efforts to improve their examination results, have schools been forced into so over-teaching their pupils (so as to get the grades . . . to get the jobs . . . to get the good salary) that the pupils rarely learn how to work things out for themselves? And isn't working things out for ourselves what we came into this world expecting to do?[10]

These stuff-of-life questions require deep personal soul-searching. Some of you will remember cradling your first-born the night you got back from hospital (however long ago that was) and pondering that native American proverb found in the preface to this book, 'We have not inherited this world from our parents, we have been loaned it by our children.' Babies force us to think forward in a most intimate manner. Months later, maybe pacing your bedroom in the small hours of the morning with your restless, teething child, you perhaps stepped outside into the warmth of a summer's night under a starry sky. You, a still young and nervous parent, with that precious new life now sleeping quietly in your arms, faced eternity with the light of stars falling on you from thousands of light-years away. At that moment you probably felt caught up in the ever-rolling rhythm of life. It's a moment that we all need to revisit from time to time, remembering perhaps Kahil Gibran who wrote in *The Prophet:*

> Your children are not your children.
> They are the sons and daughters of life's longing for itself.
> They come through you, but not from you,
> and though they are with you yet they belong not to you.[11]

That the rhythm of life may not roll on like this much longer is a shocking, disturbing thought. Are we now becoming such an advanced species that we could be in danger of losing our humanity? That is what makes asking 'What kind of education for what kind of world?' such an all-important question.

Parenting is no longer the common experience of many adults, yet becoming a parent is the one activity which should force people to lift their eyes above the present, and compel them to consider what they would wish life to be for future generations. Parenting reconnects us to the concerns our ancestors had for the survival of their successors – which is why you and I are actually here. In turn, having children of our own forces us to confront the selfishness of what can today be called 'liberal modernity' – the world which seems to have come about during the past half-century that references everything to its own personal advantage. Suddenly, as you looked at your baby on that memorable night, you knew that you were no longer free to do just as you pleased. Everything had changed. You had Responsibilities. Frightening as that might have been, it nevertheless felt good. You may, or may not, be conventionally religious, but at moments such as these, life has a very obvious purpose – you have a job to do.

So the question, 'What kind of education for what kind of world?' should force us to think well beyond the immediate present and see the long-term implications of our actions. If that question is too abstract, ask yourself this: to enable children to face the challenges as set out by Sir Martin Rees at the start of this chapter, do we envisage children growing up as if they were battery hens or free-range chickens?

Poultry farmers, listening carefully to their accountants, put each of their laying-hens into little wire cages and instal conveyor belts to provide constant food and water, keeping them warm and content with reassuring music (yes, really!) and dim lighting. The eggs literally roll out, frequently and regularly, while the farmer watches as his profit margins expand (rather like a headteacher pruning the curriculum of everything that is not essential to raising test scores). Through lack of use, those chickens' leg and wing muscles simply wither away. So if the farmer got the design of those cages wrong, and the hens get out, they become perfect morsels for predatory foxes to gobble up. The free-range cockerel, on the other hand, by constantly strutting around the farmyard, is so well exercised that if it senses trouble approaching (such as you), it simply dives with its sharp beak straight for your ankle and inflicts a devastating pain. In fury you may well lunge at the creature, only to find that it has flown up to the nearest beam and crows at you from the safety of a place you can't reach. Free-range chickens are adaptable, but battery hens have had adaptability bred out of them in favour of a specialized efficient function – egg-laying – and have lost the ability to survive on their own.

Put like this, the question focuses on the most serious of issues – the way we evaluate quality of life rather than simply standards of living.[12] Whereas the hypothetical parents of this chapter are concerned for the whole life of their child, the agenda of politicians is inevitably short term and always framed in the way most likely to get them re-elected. They are about more eggs – now, today.

It is very obvious that, for the past twenty or more years, politicians have been urging schools, and in particular the curriculum, to equip youngsters to thrive in a world that can be measured in terms of an ever-rising standard of living. To this end, the school curriculum, when stripped down to its basic motivation, can be seen as a curriculum for consumption. The harder you work, children have been told, and the more exams you pass, the better job you will get, the more money you will earn; with that will come a bigger car, larger house, more wine and fine clothes, and holidays regularly taken on the other side of the globe (and possibly find that you are more unhappy rich than ever you were as a struggling student). What the present curriculum is not about is strengthening pupils' all-round ability (like the wings and legs of the hens) to sustain themselves should our ways of living have to change so much that a priority is put on adaptability, not conformity. It's hardly surprising that children come to see today's school as a battery of many single-purpose classrooms, far removed from what they sense life should be all about – they can comprehend the need for sustainability better than many an adult.

That curriculum merely reflects the values of the society that has grown up around us. Without a change in those values, woe betide any school that lessens its focus on raising its exam results, or any parent bold enough to claim that for their particular child, formal education up to the age of fifteen is more than enough. Politicians are now feeling the squeeze that shortly will come on all of us as the unintended consequence of myriads of policy decisions taken in recent years fall about their necks. It is not somewhere any of us would like to be. The English Minister for Education found himself there in November 2007 when asked to explain why it was that English schoolchildren had fallen so far behind children in other countries (as shown by the PISA results) in just five years. In seeking to take the pressure off his department, he explained this in terms of parents now spending less time reading to their children. And he tried, unsuccessfully, to dodge the issue that it had been the government of which he was a part that had done so much to get mothers into full-time work, and had encouraged an economy where 13.7 per cent of all adults now work more than 48 hours a week. This same economy has been fuelled by persuading no self-respecting ten-year-old to feel themselves complete without either a mobile phone, or a television in their own bedroom. Thirty-seven percent of those ten-year-olds are now using the technological skills learned in school to spend more than three hours a day playing computer games – far more than in any other of the countries studied.[13] A day or so later, Doris Lessing, in accepting the Nobel Prize for Literature, vehemently attacked what she called 'the fragmenting culture . . . where it is common for young men and women who have had years of education to know nothing of the world, to have read nothing'.[14]

A fragmented curriculum for a fragmenting culture where people are paid good money for staying within their own boxes, at the long-term cost of never developing their real potential – a curriculum for battery hens. This is getting worse as the impact of reductionist thinking has become more dominant. 'What an amazing and chaotic thing the [secondary] curriculum is! One subject after another is pressed into this bursting portmanteau which ought to be confined to the necessary clothes for a journey through life, but becomes a wardrobe of bits of costume for any emergency.'[15] A chaotic conglomeration of discon-nected, half-worked-out ideas. That was written long ago, in the 1940s. It has got progressively worse ever since.

Children most certainly need a curriculum that will sustain them so as to be strong enough to deal with all the vagaries of life, thereby ensuring the sustainability of the entire species by being able not simply to think outside the box, but beyond. It should be self-evident that the better educated a people are, the less they need to be told what to do; the reverse is unfortunately equally true – the less educated are a people, the more govern-ments feel it necessary to issue ever-larger rulebooks. That then becomes self-perpetuating, for the more people accept being told what to do, the less they think for themselves. Government edicts can't change people – it's education that changes people, for better or worse, but it takes time.

*   *   *

That same reductionist thinking that has wrought havoc on the physical environment has largely impeded the transfer of findings from bio-medical research on human learning from being utilized within formal educational structures and prac-tices. It took more than 100 years for psychology to accept Darwin's proposition of 1859 that the human brain, as with the rest of the body, was 'a work in progress' containing within itself some functions now largely redundant, with others not yet quite finely tuned.

Psychology remained trapped until the early 1970s in the belief that the brain was, always had been, and always would be, just as it is now – a mysterious general-purpose mechanism that operated according to unchangeable rules.[16] As Chapter 5 has shown, when educationalists turned in the late nineteenth century to psychology for explanations of human behaviour, this resulted in disastrous over-simplifications based on a mechanistic view of the brain. These included the assumption that intellect and emotion were separate and unrelated phenomena; that intelligence was a fixed, general (and therefore un-learnable) commodity not related to cultural experience; that levels of intelligence could be assessed in the early teens by means of mathematically analysed formal tests; that quality education was the result of good teaching, and was not related to personal experiences; that young children had to be 'broken in' to the discipline of school by first mastering basic skills which, when they were older, would give them the tools to make sense of the world around them; that adolescence was an aberration, something which just should not happen, and from which children should be protected; and that the key to learning was extrinsic, not intrinsic motivation.

By ignoring evolution in the brain, early psychology trivialized human nature and made the theory of Behaviourism that emerged in the 1920s and 1930s inevitable, with the consequences set out earlier. Behaviourism was the ultimate in reductionist thinking. It led to education's fixation with teaching rather than learning; with the classroom rather than the home or community; and with forms of education that have effectively made generations of pupils dependent upon their teachers, rather than working things out for themselves. Such dependency has become a self-perpetuating problem; most teachers, until only a few short years ago, were still being taught by lecturers who themselves had grown up under the influence of Behaviourism. Just as that goes for teachers, so the assumption that education is what happens as a result of what schools do to you, goes for parents and adults at large. Politicians well understand this so that when they seek re-election they appeal to the deep-seated assumption of their constituents that, whatever faults there might be with children, these can all be rectified within the school.

While reductionism focused on breaking the world apart, the new sciences that are helping to explain the nature of human learning are all about ever-changing dynamic relationships. In mathematics, models based on self-referring systems reveal incredible complexity arising from simple algorithms. In physics, the study of energy flows in open systems reveal that emergent order is the complement to the principles of disorder and randomness in a system known as entropy. In other words, complex structures emerge from simple arrangements – not the other way round. In biology, co-evolution and collaboration are emerging as important as, and inseparable from, competition and the survival of the fittest. Evolution is not simply random, but is driven by natural principles of self-organization heading towards increasing complexity. Genetics don't determine everything,[17] and the role of mind (both individual and group) is critical. Furthermore, the brain is now seen not simply as the selfish, grasping creature of Darwinian theory, but the product of two deeply embedded cultures – one mutualist, and the other hierarchical and defensive. All of which challenges the assumption that has guided formal schooling for a century and more in its search to find those relatively few people with natural academic intelligence who are worthy of more extended educational opportunities, and ignored the less obvious and more diverse skills to be found widely in the majority of the population.

The traditional factory model of education is therefore incompatible with the idea that students are workers, that learning must be active, and that children learn in different ways and at different rates.[18] Consequently, if we change our representation of intelligence, learning and teaching, then we have to change the relationships between students and teachers, schools and the community, and our representation of what the classroom, the school and the community should look like.[19]

Not until society realizes the significance of the thinking of the last 30 or so years will these earlier input/output models of learning that have done so much damage to modern society be discarded. The nineteenth-century American columnist was indeed right when he said, 'It's not people's ignorance you need to fear, it's what they know which darn well ain't true any longer that causes all the problems.'[20] To clear our minds of outdated ideas is part of the challenge of writing this book. Once this is done, and space created for the serious study of recent research findings, it should be possible to release human potential in ways that nurture and form local democratic communities worldwide, and help reclaim a world supportive of human endeavour. These are the very people that society desperately needs to draw us back from the possible abyss as anticipated by Martin Rees, and instead set us on a course for the evolution of 'ever more complex and subtle forms of life'. Could there possibly be a more important cause around which individuals, families and communities could rally?

So just what principles are emerging from this research which could provide the rationale for a new form of learning that really goes with the grain of the brain, and provides better forms of education? It is clear that:[21]

1. *All life is dependent on a constant process of adaptation and change. The human brain has evolved over vast periods of time to become the most complex and finely tuned organism known in the universe; in its structures and processes it exactly reflects the natural complexity of the ever-changing world around it. The human brain*

is both empowered by the experience of its ancestors, but constrained as well. People consistently under-perform when driven to live in ways that are utterly uncongenial to their inherited traits and predispositions.

2. Humans are born to learn. The brain is driven by curiosity and the need to make sense of all its many experiences. Intelligence is more than just a general capacity to learn; it is shrewdness, clever-ness and knowledge all rolled together with emotional intuition, balance and a strong sense of practicality. Intelligence is a quickness to apprehend and the capacity to act wisely on the thing compre-hended.

3. Learning is essentially a reflective activity that enables us to draw upon past experience to understand and evaluate the present, so as to formulate deeper understandings and far more effectively to shape our futures. The greatest incentive to learn is personal, it is intrinsic, something that so grabs the individual's attention that they stick at it with a personal dedication that sees any failure to resolve an issue, not as something to blame on somebody else, but a personal challenge to find another way of re-framing the problem.

Inquisitiveness drives human learning. It is through forming questions that we construct knowledge, and we do this best when we are able to meander or to browse, when we set off with a general goal and plenty of opportunity to stop and explore alternative routes. We learn when we are excited and involved, when we feel we are getting somewhere that matters to us. Nature has to be primed, to be activated, by nurture. The asking of questions is, for the brain, what strong, vigorous exercise is to the athlete – it strengthens the brain's neural-networks, and makes cognitive processes far more effective. Insights from evolutionary science describe a range of biologically shaped social and intellectual predispositions. These predispositions are best described as encoded sets of processes, ways of thinking, or of doing things which, through a set of mechanisms and processes as yet only partially understood, represent a set of inherited appropriate practices which are transmitted from generation to generation in the form of time-limited software. Whether or not these predispositions are used within a specific generation depends entirely on the environmental challenge, and other intrinsic motivations.

4. Predispositions open up like windows of opportunity at stages of life which evolution has found are the most appropriate to the individual's development. If not used at that stage, then the opportunity fades, the easy option is lost, and the brain grows in a different way.

Human babies are born with an innate ability to learn languages (any language) through 'immersion' in the first four or five years of life. They have particular predispositions to learn social and collaborative skills by age seven or eight and, we suspect, to carry out calculations shortly thereafter. We have evolved big brains so we are able to talk a lot, share ideas and develop fields of knowledge in common. Consequently, the broader and more diverse the experiences are when very young, the greater are the chances that, later in life, the individual will be able to handle open, ambiguous, uncertain and novel situations. It has been nicely said that we start life as question marks, but if we lose our inquisitiveness our lives end as full stops.[22]

5. Children's search for meaning starts young. It is the children who are already anxious to make sense of issues that matter to them in their own private lives, who come to formal schooling anxious to use whatever it can offer them to help meet their personal objectives. Not the other way round. That is why a caring, thoughtful, challenging, stimulating life – a life of manageable child-like proportions – in the greater community is so vitally important. That is why streets that are unsafe for children to play around are as much a condemnation of failed policy, as are burned-out teachers or inadequate classrooms.

Constructivism is the theory that explains how we progress from inquisitiveness to new knowledge – be we children or adults. In learning we never start from a position of total ignorance, for we build new ideas on top of earlier ideas which may well be changed in the process. We always see something new through eyes that have become accustomed to earlier sights. Constructivism is about progressively deepening earlier understanding, and joining ideas together. Let me tell a personal story to illustrate this. Like many teachers I was slow twenty years ago in coming to terms with the use of the computer. It was not so for my then nine-year-old son Peter who, from the moment we bought him a computer to use at home, quickly learned to manage a range of sophisticated programs. He either taught himself, or learned to solve problems through working these out with his friends. At an early stage, teachers asked for his help as more computers were put into his school. A common enough story, repeated time and time again. Young people, as young as eight or nine, learn an immense amount when deeply engaged in tasks that fascinate them. What is equally fascinating is that they are also innate teachers.

A year or so later my second son, David, three years younger than Peter, decided that he too wanted to use the computer. To start with, Peter was immensely patient as a teacher, and David learned fast. But then I noticed something curious. Peter sensed that David was coming to rely too much on him to explain new processes, rather than using what he already knew to find the answer for himself. One evening, Peter's frustration erupted. 'Dad, David's being lazy; by asking me to tell him what to do he'll never learn to solve problems for himself. That's the only reason why I know what to do – because I had to work it out for myself. If David doesn't learn to work it out like that, he'll never learn!'

That wise observation came from a boy who had never heard of the theory of Constructivism, but who understood exactly that by bringing all his experience to bear on a new problem, he could construct his own novel solution by applying things he had already learned. Even as a nine-year-old he had learned to listen intently to everything he had heard, and noted everything he saw because he realized that it was he, and he alone, who could ultimately shape his own learning. To learn like that is to go so completely with the grain of the brain that you learn very fast.

6. *'Doing it for yourself' is a deeply ingrained human instinct, something built up in the human genome over millions of years that increases our ability to survive. It's about resilience, the determination that the more you can do for yourself, the more in control of your future you believe yourself to be. Learning in such a fashion enables you to shape your future, for it gets to the heart of what it means to be human.*

Constructivism is much more than the flip-side of good teaching and conventional schooling. It is through experience mixed with reflection that humans actively weave their own understanding and knowledge of the world into unique patterns. We create that knowledge by asking questions, exploring and assessing what we know. That is why, when children ask good questions, it is better not to give your explanation but, by prompting further questions back to them, let them experience the thrill of working it out for themselves. That is when their brains really do start to work well. Constructivism sees the role of the teacher as a 'guide on the side' rather than the conventional 'sage on the stage'. Such guides empower children to be their own teachers. The more children can do this, the stronger they become; it is a bad teacher whose pupils remain dependent on him.

7. *Learning is a delicate but powerful dialogue between genetics and the environment; the experience of our species from aeons past interacts with the experiences we have during our lifetime. Learning is a network of patterns, rather than the linear progression of single ideas; complexity becomes an advantage, not a disadvantage.*[23]

Rather than thinking of the brain as a computer waiting to be programmed, constructivists favour a far more flexible, self-adjusting, biological analogy – the brain as a living, ever-changing organism that grows and reshapes itself in response to challenge, with elements that wither through lack of use. The more the brain is used, the more it shapes the way it will be able to handle further information. Consequently no two people will ever learn in the same way, and no learning is ever actually objective, as new ideas are always processed through lenses shaped by previous experience. Every new fact or experience is assimilated into a dynamic web of understanding that already exists in that person's mind. The balance between emotion and logic, the role of intuition, and the relationship between intrinsic and extrinsic motivation are all part of what is now called a *complex adaptive system* that most easily describes the brain's remarkable ability to deal with the messiness of everyday life situations constantly inspired by its intrinsic desire to make sense of what is going on around it.

The young brain has so much learning to do in the first six or seven years of life if it is to activate its evolutionary predispositions, that evolution has given it a clone-like nature. In the earliest years, the young child doesn't have to rationalize what it does, it simply automatically emulates the successful strategies of those adults around it. Yet, as in times long past, if a child had only the skills and attitudes of its parents, it wouldn't succeed years later when it had to deal with very different kinds of situations. Consequently, while evolution makes us all clone-like learners in our earliest years, the evolutionary experience of our ancestors has gone on to create adolescent brains that reverse those earlier forms of learning and forces every youngster to be suspicious of what it is told by somebody else. Adolescence forces youngsters to learn through finding their own solutions. In that sense, adolescence is a kind of biological shock treatment.[24]

8. *The adolescent brain, being 'crazy by design', is a critical evolutionary adaptation that has built up over thousands of generations, and is essential to our species' survival. Adolescence forces young people in every generation to think beyond their own self-imposed limitations, and exceed their parents' aspirations.*

No longer content simply to be sat down and talked at, yet not skilled enough to earn their own living, adolescents yearn to get out and experience life for themselves. Here the reactions of parents and teachers are similar for, having spent years leading a not-unwilling youngster, they suddenly feel that if they are no longer in control, they are not doing their job properly. Adolescence is essentially a struggle for control as parents and teachers attempt to enforce their wills on youngsters, and so clash with the adolescent's deeply felt need to take control for himself or herself. Political systems make the same mistakes when they try to micro-manage people by preventing them from thinking for themselves. Back in the 1930s, communist leaders in Eastern Europe sought to forbid any discussion critical of party dogma; when Catholics appealed to the Pope for help, he responded with a powerful statement that is the definition of the word 'subsidiarity':

9. *'Subsidiarity; it is wrong for a superior body to hold to itself the right to make decisions that an inferior is already able to make for itself.'*

Think about this carefully. Subsidiarity has, I believe, a deep significance for what should be the evolving relationship of child to adult within the educational process. It's the shortest of the fifteen principles, but it is possibly the most profound because it applies to all aspects of life. Subsidiarity is not the same as delegation, that much-used concept beloved by today's administrators as a critical component of management by objectives. To delegate is to assign a pre-designed task to a junior to carry out on your behalf, largely in the way you have defined, and then to be answerable to you at some stage to show

how well they have completed the task to your satisfaction. The achievement (as such) rebounds on you, the person who did the delegating. The person to whom you delegated the task remains tied to you. If they don't succeed, by the standard you set, you simply cut them loose. Subsidiarity could not be more different. Just as parents have to let go of their children, and a shipbuilder has to have faith in how he built a yacht which may well sail into seas he knows not of, so subsidiarity is a relationship of trust, not control. Subsidiarity is absolutely basic to worthwhile learning. If, as an adult or an inquisitive young person, you equip yourself to be able to do something, and then you are constantly over-ruled or micromanaged, you fast lose your motivation as control is taken away from you. Subsidiarity is what adolescents demand if they are eventually to become functional adults. People fester if they are denied the opportunity to act on their own knowledge.

Think what could happen if children were taught how to think responsibly in everything that they did. Especially think what it could be like if the youngest children were to receive an education that consistently sought to give them a progression of skills and attitudes which, as they grew older, would put them more in charge of their own learning, and so return to them that deep-seated urge to be really responsible for themselves. Go further, and speculate on what it would mean if the more lavish resources normally allocated to secondary schools were given instead to the primary schools, and if the lower staffing allocations of the secondary sector were to go to the classes of the youngest pupils. Try allocating those resources on a mental rule-of-thumb principle that no class should be larger than twice chronological age; ten at the age of five, twelve at the age of six, twenty at the age of ten.[25] Do this, not to make the job of the teacher easier, but to ensure that all children are able to so master basic skills that, as they get older, steadily they will have the confidence to do more and more for themselves. 'Ah! Now I get it,' someone exclaimed a while ago, 'that means it would be the children who would be tired at the end of a term, not the teachers!'[26]

Subsidiarity is the antidote to endless overdoses of Frederick Winslow Taylor's scientific management, both in education and in civic life in general. We all want to feel we are good enough not to have to be told what to do.

Here is the absolute conflict with behaviourism, which asserts that learning has always to be under the control of the teacher, as has the learning environment. We have to rid ourselves of such thinking once and for all. A multi-disciplined graduate research programme in the late 1990s ought to have sounded the death knell to behaviourism when it concluded:

> The method people naturally employ to acquire knowledge is largely unsupported by traditional classroom practice. The human mind is better equipped to gather information about the world by operating within it than by reading about it, hearing lectures on it, or studying abstract models of it. Nearly everyone would agree that experience is the best teacher, but what many fail to realize is that experience may well be the only teacher.[27]

All of which can be summarized in a single sentence: 'Behaviourism is to battery hens, what constructivism is to free-range chickens,' a statement which led a much experienced administrator to remark ruefully, 'Our problem is that we were all trained as behaviourists, so we're not well equipped to lead a pedagogic revolution that necessitates a deep understanding of constructivism – it's a question of the blind leading the blind.'

10. *This much we now know; the brain works best when it is building on what it already knows. When it is working in complex, situated circumstances. When it accepts the significance of what it is doing. When it is exercised in highly challenging but low-threat environments. Children learn spontaneously. What they need, however, is help from experts in how to learn better – how to upgrade their own self-designed but restrictive capacity for acquiring information, and creating experience.*[28]

Discovery learning does not imply that students can be left to discover everything for themselves, nor that all learning can be acquired by doing, with no formal instruction. Left to their own devices, novices reach a kind of plateau where to climb to new heights they need the help of an expert – someone who has been there before them and can demonstrate new ways of thinking about how to solve more complex problems. Expertise is complicated; it is not simply obtained by following the rules, for it also requires the experience to know when to break or bend the rules – to know when a subjective judgement is more logical than a logical conclusion. Niels Bohr, the Danish Nobel scientist, once remonstrated with a student, 'You're not thinking, you're just being logical.'

Experts start off as specialists by knowing an awful lot about their own subjects, but they have a further vital attribute – they are able to get outside their own subject. This makes them ask, search and propose uncomfortable questions. Experts tackle problems that increase their expertise, whereas specialists tend to tackle problems for which they do not have to extend themselves by going beyond the rules and the formulae which they comfortably accept. Experts indulge in progressive problem-solving; that is, they continually reformulate a problem at an ever-higher level as they achieve at lower levels, and uncover more of the nature of the issue. Experts are the real pioneers, out there on their own, totally immersed in their work, increasing the complexity of the activity as they develop new skills, taking on new challenges, and formulating new rules.

11. *Given the inherent limitations of schooling, it seems essential for a child to have an intellectual life outside school. It gives the child a chance to develop personal knowledge, building goals and techniques for incorporating new information in ways that advance towards those goals. Thus equipped, the child is in a position to use schooling as a source of learning opportunities without being drawn into short-cut strategies that work well for handling school tasks but that lead nowhere in the lifelong development of expertise.*

The creation of conditions in which expertise can develop needs both the practice of constructivism, and the rigours of subject-specific disciplines. It also needs far more than what schools can provide. In a book published for parents in 1948 about the relationship between them, their children and the school, it stated:

Parents can do a great deal to make the pupil's path less hard . . . it's not so much a question of heavy-handedly checking on homework but it does mean doing all you can to see that he or she is exposed to influences which are likely to assist in developing intellectual curiosity, form standards of judgment, and delight in high standards of achievement. It means curbing your enthusiasm for light music as a background to the evening conversation . . . above all, it means behaving as if you respect your child's efforts to find truth, and sympathizing with his difficulties; in other words it means parents going on with their own education.[29]

Expertise is a frame of mind that starts forming in the nursery, begins to grow in the primary school and should mature in the secondary school. Remember this, the brain works in terms of wholes and parts simultaneously, that is why human learning really is a complex, messy and non-linear process that we codify at our peril.

12. *Apprenticeship was an education for an intelligent way of life, a mechanism by which adolescents could model themselves on socially approved adults, so providing a safe passage from childhood to adulthood in psychological, social and economic ways.*[30]

You can't learn how to learn, without learning something; but just to measure what is being learned does not say much about how the learning actually happens. 'Learning is not something that requires time-out from productive activity; learning is at the very heart of productive activity.'[31] Which is why apprenticeship is such an appropriate response to the adolescent brain. Apprenticeship was based on the process of weaning young people off their dependence on the craft master. Throughout the process, the master coaches. He selects appropriate tasks to be tried, gives hints, guards against failure, evaluates and encourages the apprentices to evaluate themselves; the master challenges, encourages dialogue, gives feedback, works on weaknesses and structures new tasks. What is important is that the task and the process of achieving it are made highly visible from the beginning. The goal is known. Learners have access to expertise in use. They can sometimes watch several masters and then appreciate that there is not simply one way. They watch each other, understand the incremental stages and have real benchmarks against which to measure their progress.

13. *Cognitive Apprenticeship*[32] *merges knowledge of the cognitive processes emerging from the scientific study of the brain, with what is known from observation and historic data about the practices of apprenticeship, so as to develop a form of instruction that makes thinking visible. Cognitive Apprenticeship provides structures by which constructivist learning leads to deep understanding, sense-making, and the potential for creativity and enterprise.*

Research from the biological sciences shows the innate nature of these collaborative, higher-order skills and attitudes, and how with appropriate stimulation at an early age (as would have been the case in pre-industrial apprenticeship times) youngsters quickly develop. Today, children are born with all these latent predispositions enabling them to function collaboratively, but formal schooling has struggled, in the absence of real-time professionals as role models, to provide appropriate simulation of real-life situations. From a constructivist's perspective, schooling can only ever meet with partial success because the limitations of the learning environment can only stretch part of a young person's intellectual and social predispositions. For all those who have succeeded in the de-contextualized setting of the school, there are so many more for whom schooling has made very little impact. Today's schools go by rules that defy both serious research findings and common sense.

14. *Learning is an immensely complex business, so, to put faith in a highly directive, prescriptive curriculum, is to so 'go against the grain of the brain' that it will inhibit creativity and enterprise . . . the very skills needed in the complex, diverse community for which we need to prepare our children.*

Formal education imposes someone else's meaning upon students rather than encouraging them to construct meaning for themselves. Reality is modified by the teacher, and the obedient student commits it to memory. An efficient education process, it is assumed, imparts knowledge much as an efficient factory instals parts on its assembly line. Academics extol the virtues of solitary study, uninterrupted work often on a single subject, much written material, and a highly analytical ability. The world beyond the gates of the school, the world the school should be preparing children for, involves working with others, constant distractions, multi-tasking and multi-disciplinary study, verbal rather than written skills, as well as problem-solving and decision-making.

Which surely means that we should be asking far deeper questions about the very institution of schooling than have so far been raised in the school reform movement with its short-term panaceas of more accountability, site-based management, standardized tests, prescribed curriculum, vast new school buildings, and longer hours for teachers and students. We have to be much smarter than this and accept that we are dealing with a deep systemic crisis. Constructivism merged with cognitive apprenticeship collides head-on with so many of our institutional arrangements for learning.

15. *Over thousands of generations, the aim of good parenting, as of good teaching, has been to so inculcate in the growing child a range of skills, attitudes and behaviours that, at an appropriate time (sooner rather than later) the child can be progressively weaned of its dependence, so that parents take pleasure and great reassurance that their child is now 'well launched' to go wherever and however it needs.*

When will we ever learn! All of twenty years ago it was stated: 'The reforms that deal with the fundamental stuff of education – teaching and learning – seem to have weak, transitory and ephemeral effects; all those that expand, solidify and entrench school bureaucracy seem to have strong, enduring and concrete effects.'[33] Quite simply, administrators find it much easier to talk about numbers of schools, teachers, and pupils, and the management of revenue and expenditure, than they do about what those teachers are actually doing, or what schools are for, and how they might assist children to take control of their future. Precious little seems to have changed. Indeed, it has probably got worse. In America, a regime of continuous testing has still further reduced what was already a dull and politically correct curriculum to an experience likened to a dose of medicine which, if taken at the correct intervals, will eventually enable each student to eventually graduate, and so attend the school Prom.[34] It's all about sticks and carrots. In England, a curriculum for two-year-olds prescribes how rusks should be eaten, while the school day has been so lengthened that, twelve hours after getting there, the little child returns home ready to go straight to bed. For years it has been known that an overdose of concentration on a single subject, and an over-emphasis on analytical skills, rather than the skills of synthesis, may well be inimical to the creation of those essential skills needed in today's world.

A still more shocking thought (to those who can bear to comprehend this) is that the ever-increasing number of dysfunctional parents were themselves pupils in these schools only ten, twenty or thirty years ago. And it is slowly coming to be realized that, by providing ever more school-based solutions to such problems, schools have progressively sucked the lifeblood out of community – lifeblood that was already haemorrhaging because, at humanity's basic level of the family, the assumption that the search for economic well-being should take precedence over cultivating and sustaining personal relationships, has become the dominant thought of politics.

It is not simply a crisis in schools that has to be faced, for this is but the symptom of a much more serious disease – the collapse of family, and the emasculation of community. Then there is the issue of radical developments with information and communication technologies that are disrupting hierarchies and encouraging the growth of non-institutional, ever-shifting networks of learners.

Formal schooling, therefore, has to start a dynamic process through which students are progressively weaned from their dependence on teachers and institutions, and given the confidence to manage their own learning, collaborating with colleagues as appropriate, and using a range of resources and learning situations. The challenge now is for communities to begin building new organizations for learning that handle both the skills of the past and enable the understanding and co-ordination of constant change, lifelong learning, diversity and complexity, so as to prepare young people to participate in a vibrant and democratic civil society.

How is this to be done?

9

Knowing What We Know . . . What's to be Done?

These are undoubtedly extraordinary times, rich in opportunity yet loaded with uncertainty. They are destabilizing times as well, alternately exhilarating and terrifying. What is most troubling, from my perspective, is that I'm less confident now than I was as a schoolboy in the 1950s that education will win out over catastrophe. I fear that, as ever busier individuals, we have become so distracted by our technological progress that we have been blinded to the threat that people who have been overschooled but undereducated pose to the well-being of civilization.[1]

The truth has to be that, the more confused adults feel themselves to be about the big issues of life, the less willing they are in their turn to give their adolescent children the space in which to work things out for themselves. Uncertain adults breed uninvolved, inexperienced adolescents: a society that has to rediscover reasons for its faith in the future is a mean place in which to bring up children.

It seems that we, collectively as well as individually, have lost sense of what life should be all about, and where we fit in. Two narratives compete for our support. The stronger, more apparently attractive and certainly the most strident since the 1980s, is that life is improved by maximizing your wealth so as to participate as fully as possible in the good life.[2] The second, upon which the future of our planet and the survival of the human race may depend, has emerged quickly over the past five years; it is about the need to adjust individual life aspirations so as to achieve ecological and social sustainability.[3] These are very different narratives – the first argues for the rights of the individual, the latter for inter-dependence and community.

This struggle is being fought over the remains of much older narratives, well known in their different guises to our ancestors. These older narratives had been about moderating and civilizing the competing drivers of human behaviour that would otherwise bring chaos to individuals and societies by establishing a sense of the common good. 'Honour thy father and thy mother,' said those narratives that it has recently become fashionable to decry as restrictions on personal freedom; 'Love thy neighbour as thyself; respect your environment, forgive your enemies, don't be greedy, be generous to the poor, and let not your ambition mock your useful toil.'[4] In our determination to move forward ever faster, we have forgotten the social significance of those spiritual traditions which in the past sought to 'bind'[5] the individual and community together for mutual benefit[6] and create a sense of meaning, without which individuals feel cast adrift in space.

With the weakening of commonly agreed codes of behaviour and morality with which to shape our everyday personal decisions, governments have seen it necessary to prescribe in ever finer detail what we must, and must not, do. In a travesty of what should be a civilized society, governments assume that the best way to avoid anti-social behaviour is to play on people's fear of being caught on one of the country's four million closed-circuit television cameras, while the natural instinct to rescue a drowning child has to be curbed by a Chief Constable's warning to the public: 'Don't do anything that you have not been certified as competent to do.'[7] What has life become if we are so reduced to doing what we are told to do, that we cannot rise to the challenge of being personally responsible?

A whole new way of doing things has to be found. We have to start thinking strategically, and that involves analysing problems in depth by separating symptoms from causes, appreciating other people's perceptions, and above all avoiding the temptation to set up short-term panaceas that simply detract from long-term solutions. That is what this book seeks to do – make clear what can too often seem utterly overwhelming to parents arguing with their child about homework or a late-night curfew; to a magistrate dealing with a dysfunctional family; to a government minister faced with balancing resources; or to an exasperated teenager who just cannot see any point in what school is forcing him to do.

Is it within anybody's power to bring about such a massive change in both attitudes and behaviour? The answer has to be 'Yes', for we are intelligent beings. But it won't be 'Yes' if parent, child, teacher, magistrate or politician thinks they can act alone. Nothing can change without a fundamental change of heart. That means constructing a persuasive, alternative vision which is so compelling that the contemporary narrative is shown up for what it is – something shallow, utilitarian and demeaning to the grandeur of the human intellect. It's not enough for just a few people to understand this. As any military commander (and the strategy has to be planned as carefully as any military campaign) will immediately agree, the tougher the struggle is likely to be, and the more complex the plans, the more essential it is that every man and woman is so well briefed as to the overall mission that each is able to act independently in the field. A campaign to reverse an overschooled but undereducated society cannot be masterminded by any single brilliant strategist. It requires distributed leadership, and for that to be effective, everyone needs to be really knowledgeable about why they are involved, and the 'rightness' and the urgency of the cause.

This book is a kind of briefing for what I call Responsible Subversives, those people from all walks of life ready to face up to the tragic consequences of our society's failure to recognize that by failing adolescents we are actually screwing up the whole education system and, indeed, our very future. This book has drawn together research from the biological and social sciences, and from systems and complexity theories, so as to escape from the endless short-term sticking-plaster initiatives of recent years. Instead, future proposals should be based firmly on the emerging science of learning and what is known about the effective functioning of human societies. Do this, and it should release human potential in ways that nurture and form democratic communities worldwide, so making it possible to reclaim and sustain a world supportive of human endeavour. That makes the future full of exciting possibilities.

The first chapter described the wonder of human learning as a reminder that humans weren't born dumb, for the natural human default position is to be inquisitive – dumbness is something imposed on us by an inappropriate environment. The chapter that followed explained the curious way in which humans, the most vulnerable of all mammals at birth, evolved over several millions of years to become the planet's pre-eminent learning species. But simply to understand the neurological processes of the brain isn't sufficient to account for the complexity of human behaviour. The chapters subsequently showed that it is nurture that fine-tunes and personalizes our basic human natures, and creates the cultural diversity around us. We must understand nurture properly because the recent history of education is full of gut-reactive, badly thought through and disjointed initiatives launched by politicians in a hurry to apply quick-fix solutions to symptoms that leave the essential cause of the problem unchanged.

You don't need to be a history buff to be fascinated with how biological and cultural evolution conspired in the late seventeenth century to create in England the finest-ever balance between the internal mechanisms of the brain, and a manageable but always challenging environment. That practical self-starting and self-correcting creativity was the greatest asset England ever possessed. It was the loss of the greater part of that asset in the social melt-down that followed the Industrial Revolution that sociologists, economists and politicians and, yes, theologians as well have struggled to correct ever since.

Reading further into the nineteenth century, it was obvious that secondary education was effectively hijacked to reinforce the power and influence of the emerging upper middle classes, while elementary education was reduced to a functional preparation for a lower-class existence in factory, mine or mill. The political tensions between those who regarded education as a private gain and those who saw it as a public good became obvious. These tensions remain to this day, for history repeats itself for those who don't understand its lessons. Take the Monitorial Schools as an example; with several hundred pupils in a room with one teacher and as many as twenty assistant monitors, they don't look too dissimilar from the current proposals for fewer qualified teachers with many more classroom assistants, a proposal of which Charles Dickens' Mr Gradgrind would surely have approved. The Payment By Results scheme, which plagued elementary schools for much of the nineteenth century, led Matthew Arnold (son of Dr Arnold of Rugby and the first-ever Inspector of Schools) to remark in a way that echoes so much of today's criticism of excessive testing: 'In a country where everyone is prone to rely too much on mechanical process and too little on intelligence, this gives a mechanical turn to school teaching, and a twist to inspection, that must be most trying to the intellectual life of a school.' That was in 1859. Have we learned anything since?

This book has not sought to be politically correct, neither has it gone out of its way to dodge emotive issues. It has set out an argument that large numbers of people need to make their own if they are to reclaim their democratic responsibility for shaping a social agenda to which politicians should respond. For more than twenty years, however, that process has gone the other way. With the passing of the 1988 Education Act in England (and similar legislation in other jurisdictions) education has increasingly become an arm of political and economic policy rather than a reflection of the people's expressed needs for their children. Significantly, government has limited the teaching of the history and the philosophy of education to teachers in training simply to that 1988 Act, with the result that much of what is contained in this book will simply not be known to newly qualified teachers. Having only the flimsiest understanding of where the school system has come from, and why as teachers they are required to teach as they have been instructed to do, it is no wonder that so many quickly leave the profession. Few have confidence in going beyond the bare bones of what is required within the National Curriculum. The result is dire, for teachers who are not expected to be inquisitive will not respond kindly to the child who is any kind of an alternative thinker.

*   *   *

The strategy to be adopted by Responsible Subversives needs to be shaped by a strong sense of direction, for without that sense of direction, the various bits and pieces in a young person's life simply fail to come together and leave teachers and parents as confused as the pupils as to what really matters. Long ago,

William of Wykeham was very clear about what should be the direction for his College at Winchester: 'Manners makyth man,' he said – what matters most is the way we treat each other. Not a bad aspiration. Hugh Oldham, when he gave his motto to the grammar school in Manchester in 1515, said, '*Sapere Aude*,' which translated means, 'Dare to be wise' – as splendid a challenge to youngsters in the sixteenth century as it is now in the twenty-first century for young people struggling to understand the majesty and complexity of life. When, as a pupil, I was struggling with that essay on education and catastrophe back in the late 1950s, my teachers were beginning to be concerned that education was ceasing to be thought of as a 'whole process in which mind, body and soul are jointly guided towards maturity for, without this a child's personality would not necessarily be developed'.[8] Teachers instead were starting to make the dangerous assumption that education was the by-product of the efficient teaching of subjects, so that by an over-concentration on academic performance they were losing sight of the diversity of human capability.[9] The rot goes back many years.

How things have accelerated in the past half-century! Those earlier overarching aspirations were replaced in 2001 by the statement that 'the work of the Department of Education and Employment fits with a new economic imperative of supply side investment for public prosperity'. Three years later a government spokesman explained: 'We want to make children and young people happy and healthy, to keep them safe, to give them a top class education and help them to stay on track.'[10] Just what track is that, we should be asking, and is being over-protective the best way of keeping young people safe? As far as raising expectations is concerned, another spokesman said in March 2008, 'the goal is to improve the skills of England's young people to create a workforce of world-class standard'.[11]

A post-modern society denies that there is such a thing as a shared moral code, and that makes virtually impossible the definition of an all-embracing vision bigger than the immediate, the materialistic, and the individualistic. I found the expectations of the *No Child Left Behind* legislation in the United States as utilitarian and instrumental as England's *Every Child Matters*. As mission statements, no one could disagree. But what exactly did they mean? 'Matter' in what way, or 'left behind' in what race? Was it the race between education and catastrophe or the race to be the next celebrity? Neither stirs any feeling for the grandeur of human potential. 'Being healthy, staying safe, enjoying and achieving, making a positive contribution and economic well-being' are worthy objectives, but they fail to satisfy the natural expectation of parents that their children grow up to be thoughtful and helpful citizens ready in their turn to be parents in the next generation. Instead, these seem like a list (which I suspect they are) which, once checked off by an Ofsted inspector in today's *performability* Britain, can be used to evaluate one school against another.[12] Real life isn't to be found in checklists. Simplistic, politically correct statements that reflect only the lowest common denominator squeeze the life out of education, and dull the vigour of pupil and teacher alike.

For young people to utilize their powers to the full, they need a curriculum that will sustain them (that means giving them the inner security of believing in themselves) so as to be strong enough to deal with all the vagaries of life. Of all the attempts to define this in ways that inspire and excite the imagination, it was the statement made a long time ago in 1644 by John Milton, one of the two greatest English poets, that I believe best exemplifies the finest aims of education. Like ourselves, Milton lived in rapidly changing and turbulent times; born six years before Shakespeare died, he was a leading Puritan intellectual during the Civil War, becoming Oliver Cromwell's Minister of Foreign Affairs during the years in which England experimented with becoming a republic. A man of towering intellect and much practical common sense, Milton spoke from a time before reductionism sought to undermine the glory and the complexity of what being human could mean. He gave a definition of education nearly four centuries ago that we need to rediscover:

> I call therefore a complete and generous education that which fits a man to perform justly, skilfully and magnanimously, all the offices both public and private, of peace and war.[13]

Ponder Milton's choice of words – an education that was *complete* and *generous* (no half-measures here), that *fits* (like a tailor making a bespoke suit), so as to *perform* (not just talk) *justly* (so requiring a fine appreciation of ethics), *skilfully* (Milton's definition of skills included the practical as well as the theoretical), and *magnanimously* (with a big heart and empathy with others), *and not only in his private affairs but publicly* when things were going well as well as badly. There you have it. The rounded person, the adaptable, free-range person, not the efficient and single-purpose battery hen.[14] The person who can think for himself, however complex the situation. Could you wish anything better for a child of your own, or for that other child who, years later as an adult, your son or daughter might wish to marry, do business with, or contend with as a political opponent?

Above all else, Milton was talking about the creation of civil society – that place where so many of us would like to be, where people are sufficiently educated, thoughtful and responsible that the need for government intervention and prescription are reduced to an absolute minimum.[15] That is the kind of education needed now for the kind of world for which we should be planning. These are the kinds of people who possess what Professor Howard Gardner, the finest of modern educational thinkers, has recently described as 'the five minds of the future' – the disciplined mind, the synthesizing mind, the creating mind, the ethical mind and the respectful mind.[16]

Milton had been much influenced by the Czech philosopher Jan Amos Comenius[17] who, in 1638, had published *The Great Didactic* in which he wrote:

> Following in the footsteps of nature we find . . . that the process of learning . . . will be easy if it begins before the mind is corrupted; if it proceeds from the general to the particular, from what is easy to what is more difficult; if the pupil is not over-burdened by too many subjects, and if the intellect be forced to nothing to which its natural bent does not incline it.

Milton readily accepted such thinking, for it resonated with his own experience, and he went on to make two truly radical proposals. He proposed to Cromwell that a republic, which Parliament sought to create after the execution of Charles I, would require providing what today we would call primary schools in every village in the country – this at a time when only about two villages in five had a 'petty' or 'dame' school. Convinced that education was as much for the good of society as it was of value to the individual, Milton proposed that the cost of such schools should be met by a tax on every household, and so free to the individual child. His second proposal was even more perceptive: noting that the grammar schools, already several hundred years old, had become too academically elite and ungrounded in daily realities, he proposed the setting up of academies of some 150 young men between the ages of twelve and twenty-one in most of the market towns of England. In these, the skills of artisans, craftsmen, fowlers and farmers would be studied alongside those of classicists, statesmen, lawyers and theologians. Milton sought a unity of thinking and doing, and refuted the earlier teaching of Roger Ascham that theory was always more important than learning from experience.

Milton subsequently invited Comenius to come to England to help set up such academies, while Cardinal Richelieu invited him to France, and John Winthrop, the Governor of Massachusetts, invited him to Boston to become the first president of Harvard University. It was at this point that history played its problematic hand. Cromwell died before Comenius could reach England, and the new King, Charles II, had no interest in egalitarian education, and so Comenius accepted the invitation of the King of Sweden to go to Scandinavia which then included Finland, Norway and Denmark. The English grammar schools were never reformed, and as we know, by the end of the eighteenth century many of them were close to packing up. Until the recent research in cognition, neurology and evolutionary studies started to appreciate the significance of Comenius's insights, his ideas had been almost completely forgotten in England. But not in Scandinavia, a saga to which we will return shortly.

*   *   *

To establish a national vision of education in terms similar to that of Milton has to be the starting point for a national strategy that reverses our overschooled but undereducated society. It should be self-evident that the better educated people are, the less they need to be told what to do. Unfortunately, the reverse is equally true, for the less educated people are, the more governments feel it necessary to issue even larger rulebooks. That then becomes self-perpetuating, for the more people accept being told what to do, the less they think for themselves. Which is the point England now seems to have reached. We have become so overtaught that we have lost the art of thinking for ourselves. How do we break out of this self-repeating cycle?

The second part of the strategy involves acting upon that research into the learning process that, starting with the insights of Comenius, has now been reinforced by findings from neuro-biology and cognitive science. This gives a whole new way of looking at the evolved grain of the brain, and calls for a pedagogy that works to progressively wean the growing child away from its dependence on instruction. That pedagogy has to honour the principle of subsidiarity at every point. Just as parents have to let go of their children, so subsidiarity has to be a relationship of trust, not control. Subsidiarity is absolutely basic to worthwhile learning. If, as an adult or an inquisitive young person, we equip ourselves to be able to do something, and then are constantly overruled or micromanaged, we fast lose our motivation as control slips away from us.

Third, England, as with many other nations, needs an education system that would reverse the priority that Dr Arnold gained for secondary education in favour of seeing the primary sector as the time and place where the essential foundations for lifelong learning are built. Secondary education would then involve schools sharing with the greater community the responsibility for providing adolescents with a range of in-school as well as community-based learning opportunities. This is hugely challenging both to the current structures of education, and to the public's perception that school should be the place to do with children what adults now think they are too busy to do for themselves.

Both the need to do this, and the difficulties that would be encountered in so doing, were all too well demonstrated when I accepted an invitation to explain this to the Policy Unit in Downing Street in 1996 and the senior adviser commented, 'Much to my surprise, I can't really fault your theory. You are probably educationally right; certainly your argument is ethically correct. But the system you are arguing for would require very good teachers. We are not convinced that there will ever be enough good teachers. So, instead, we are going to a teacher-proof system of organizing schools – that way we can get a uniform standard.'[18] Horrifying as was that conclusion, it has only got worse since. 'The Conservatives told us *what* to teach,' said a disillusioned education officer eight years ago, 'now New Labour is telling us *how* to teach.' Politicians by their dabbling, and confused by educationalists who failed to clearly define the problem, have between them made a mockery of quality education.[19]

A clear vision that links self-starting individuals to the needs of dynamic communities, based on a form of learning that goes from cradle to grave and is practised as much beyond the walls of the school as it is within classrooms, would rapidly reinvigorate the youth of England (as it would in other countries). Quickly they would accumulate the skills and wisdom necessary to direct mankind's technological discoveries in ways, as proposed by Sir Martin Rees at the Millennium, that 'would lead to a near eternity filled with evermore complex and subtle forms of life' rather than 'one filled with nothing but base matter'.[20] The challenge subsequently has become even more stark, immediate and uncompromising.

How is it to be done? Let me return to that analogy which likens education to the balance that can be achieved by a three-legged stool, however uneven the floor. The legs, college lecturers explained years ago, represent the family, the community and the school – emotional development, inspirational ideas and intellectual growth.[21] If any leg were too short or too long, the stool couldn't balance. Be careful, people once said, don't let schools in the future take over the roles which are the natural responsibilities of home or community, for if that happens neither will any longer be able to offer the growing child that diversity of experience so essential for their balanced all-round development.

Evolutionary studies show that it was the invention of the family that made it possible for the human race to progress beyond simply surviving to the point where we have the imagination to see stars and dream of eternity, and hearing birds to make music, and touching tools to transform the earth. An amazing achievement. But what is the connection of that with the family? Simply this: from the moment that human brains grew too large for all brain development to take place within the womb, women had to find mates who would commit to providing succour for their children for very many years. Humans survive and grow through collaboration. Babies have their own well-honed biological strategies to achieve this which are sufficient (most of the time) to entice adults to love and cherish them – chunky cheeks, angelic looks, and a scent all their own.[22] Adults, in their turn, are biologically primed to be captivated by such engaging behaviour. Turning naturally promiscuous males into responsible fathers, however, has challenged women for several million years before anyone – priest, philosopher or lawyer – attempted to define this relationship as a moral principle.

It was not long into the evolutionary story that families started to come together into larger, non-genetically affiliated groups for mutual support and protection. This tendency is deep seated within us, for psychologists have found that no one of us is likely to grieve deeply for more than about a dozen people; it is as if the roots of human empathy cannot stretch too far. In numerous studies of indigenous peoples, it has been noted that, when the tribe grows beyond about 150 people (roughly equivalent to twelve families of mother and father, four or five children, a grandparent or two and a few other relatives) the tribe fractures and falls apart through internecine strife.[23] Even in pre-industrial England, the great majority of people lived within units of between thirteen and fifteen people, on family farms, in craftsmen's workshops, bakeries etc.[24] Which may explain why now there are eleven people in a cricket or soccer team, twelve people on a jury and fifteen people in a rugby team. Humans, it seems, have a natural affinity for small groups.[25]

All this means that we have fewer evolved predispositions to socialize within communities than we do within families, and have still fewer to deal with the numbers of other children we first encounter as five-year-olds in the school playground. Which isn't surprising, for in evolutionary terms schools are an extremely recent innovation. Not that any reader will any longer see learning as necessarily being coterminous with schools, for the development of our exquisite practical and theoretical skills goes right back into the mists of time when our ancestors learned interactively as they struggled together to achieve common tasks. Through such intellectual processes a predisposition for cognitive apprenticeship developed in the human brain. Learning together within the security of the family, before sharing and testing more complex issues within a larger community, is what is most natural to the brain – a progression from emotional to inspirational and on to intellectual development.

Adolescence and the family

Since the beginning of time, children have learned to become adults by observing, imitating and interacting with members of their own family. The Hadza of Tanzania are typical;[26] the tribesmen teach their sons and daughters to read the natural signs around them with all the care that parents in Boston, England or Boston, Massachussetts, show as they help their children learn to decipher printed text. Storytelling to an aboriginal father, be he Australian or a Cree from northern Canada, is as essential to those societies' existence as were bedtime stories in England until very recently when many parents are deciding to save time by putting a TV in their child's bedroom. Play to the Hadza, as it is to an English child, is about experimenting and learning how to correct mistakes in a moderately safe environment.[27] A child experiencing his or her first visit to a pantomime begins to understand the varying and interchangeable roles people play. Some researchers have concluded that 50 per cent of a person's ability to learn is developed in the first four years of life – not half their eventual knowledge, but shaping half of all the brain cell connections that he or she will use in their whole life.

What is going on? It is still more about that essential balance between nurture and nature, for the key to a successful transition from adolescence into adulthood lies, like so much else, in the earliest stages of life. There is no period of parenthood with a more direct or formative effect on a child's brain than the last three months of pregnancy when, if the mother's emotions are under stress, she is malnourished or taking drugs, the growth of the foetus's brain is severely restricted. Evidence shows that breastfed children develop greater verbal, quantitative and memory abilities earlier in life than do non-breastfed babies, not simply because of the quality of the mother's milk but because of the intense early child/mother relationship expressed through intensive eye bonding as each explores the other's feelings. Because the neural structures that manage emotions only start to develop in the second year of life, how we are treated as babies and toddlers determines the way in which *what we are born with* becomes *what we turn into*. Which explains why research that compared the relative influence that families, communities and schools had on subsequent performance levels at the age of eighteen concluded that factors outside the school were four times more important in determining future performance.[28] The most significant determinant of all these was the quantity and quality of dialogue in the child's home before the age of five.

Of all the games that children play, it is when they are pretending to be mothers and fathers that we can see if they're internalizing the skills we think are important to families.[29] With often devastating insight, their acting out is based on what they perceive to be our own apparently extraordinary behaviours! Functional families are based on parents whose love and respect for each other matures and grows to embrace their children in ways that liberate all of them. Families are strengthened the more they do things together – anything from tidying up the toy box, to family cycle rides, cutting down trees and organizing barbecues around the bonfire, or patiently helping an aged relative to endure a difficult end with dignity. Family activities create the stories that become our individual, lifelong reserve rations, which give context to the problems of every day.[30] Such families practise subsidiarity (learning to do it for yourself) even though most of them have never heard of it, because it simply feels right to treat each other in such a way.[31]

Such relationships require much time – not the hour or so some set aside as quality time when they turn off their mobile phones (and then fret that they might miss an important call), but simply being available at that spontaneous moment when a child's question opens up an opportunity for the two of them to share an explanation. Functional families treasure the nooks and crannies of daily life which host interesting conversations, be it overlooking a herd of gazelle on the plains of Africa, babysitting with a friend or watching Manchester United at Old Trafford. They set boundaries not to be restrictive but to ensure that their children don't move into broader pastures without learning first how to negotiate the home turf; too much choice and too few boundaries make family life nearly impossible. Good parents are consistent; their 'No' means '*No*', and their children know why. Parents who have themselves experienced some of the vagaries of life recognize the need for the child to develop resilience – the ability to keep going when knocked over and come up with another option. Consequently, responsible parents will not so wrap up their children in all the safety straps and the proverbial cotton wool of health and safety regulations that they leave it too late for the child to discover that to survive in anything they have to know how to take calculated risks.

Functional families are based on parents who are thought-through people, people who naturally pause and reflect on what life is all about, and share their thoughts with their children. Fortunate is the child whose own parents were earlier taken by their parents to watch the dawn of the day from a mountain top and, years later, still thrill to the memory of the sun's rays picking up the summit of a distant hill that for a few seconds seemed like an island set in a sea of mist. Whatever the reason, such parents know that there are more things in heaven and earth that their children need to experience than are dreamt of in today's essentially materialistic philosophy. Just because traditional religion may not have satisfied them personally, they are far from dismissing the search for spiritual meaning and are never ones to accept any form of dogmatic fundamentalism. Parents who are on a lifelong search of that kind breed children who won't ever feel it necessary simply to be politically correct.[32]

But here is the caution: the more at risk the family as an institution becomes, the more vulnerable and fragile society finds itself, for fewer families succeed in giving their children the positive emotional support in the early years that are the essential foundations for the mind's growth.[33] From as long ago as when the Jews were struggling to survive in the desert, through all the countless generations that have followed them, the reason for marriage until the last two or three generations (the last two or three minutes on that year-long evolutionary clock) was the raising of children, and the security that that brought to parents in their old age. As infant mortality rates fell in the latter part of the nineteenth century, the emphasis began to shift towards marriage as the basis for mutual support. Not all couples are able to conceive children, and not all adults feel themselves competent to be parents, while increasing numbers of couples rapidly lose patience with the prospect of 'till death us do part'. In 1901 there were 581 divorces in England and Wales, while in 2007 there were 157,000. Roughly one in two marriages now ends in divorce, with 31 per cent of marriages not surviving the first ten years. Nearly one child in two is now brought up by a single mother, up from one in eight in 1980.[34] While it is true that significant numbers of adults are able to move from a collapsed marriage into forms of extended and blended marriages that really do provide the love and nurture that the different relationships of their joint children need, far too many fail abysmally to give their children the emotional security necessary to form strong relationships when they are older, and so a disproportionate number later get divorced.

Very many men today are losing out by not becoming functional fathers, and too many women are exhausting themselves trying to do everything. Nothing in the social topography of England has changed as much as marriage, once deemed to be the very foundation of society. When I started teaching in the mid-1960s I was not aware of any child coming from a divorced family, and even as a headmaster twenty years later divorce was rarely given as a reason for bad behaviour. But it is today, for it has been the collapse in family relationships, fuelled by government's determination to make wealth creation the main driver of the economy, which has exacerbated the problem by coercing more and more young parents to go back into the workforce when their children still need them. For this reason alone it can no longer be taken for granted that there will be sufficient responsible and reflective adults in the future to maintain a free, democratic society.

Accepting the importance late in the day that early-years emotional development matters, governments have rushed to build chains of nursery centres admitting children as babies only a few months old, and seeing these as essential correctives for what parents are no longer doing for their own children. One such centre in Toronto is especially well equipped and offers, I was told in 2006, just about every activity that good parents, if they had the time, would themselves like to provide. Politicians from many countries have lauded this and pledged to provide something as good, if not better, in their own societies, including Britain. Such centres look good, sound good and seem to make sense because, expensive as they are, by enabling mothers to get back into work these costs are more than compensated for by way of greater national productivity.

But is that really true? Talking informally with the highly competent woman in charge of that Canadian nursery, she admitted to a real fear that might well undermine the whole scheme. She explained that she had several grown-up children of her own, each of whom had had a somewhat difficult adolescence. It had been in those bad times, when the going was really rough, that she and her husband frequently recalled the great moments they had had when their children were younger, and this gave them the patience and the energy to stick together. This they had succeeded in doing and everything was eventually fine but, that woman stressed, the energy to do that had come from those early family memories. 'When I see the smiles of the children in the centre, and hear their shouts of joy when they have done something special, and they rush up to me for a cuddle, I get very worried for their parents who don't know their own children anything like as well as I do. When their children go into adolescence, the parents will have none of the memories that I have of different and easier times to keep them going.' It is not only the adolescents who suffer when fragile families fall apart. Parents who are encouraged to leave their children at an ever earlier age actually damage themselves by not having the opportunity to grow up alongside their children, and as such they develop a sentimental but not necessarily deep relationship across the generations.

Adolescence and the community

It is at that moment when a springboard (and a safety net) is needed for youngsters leaping into adolescence that the family has to be ready to share both its problems and its opportunities with the wider community.[35] Just as the growing Stone Age child built up sufficient confidence to wander into another family's cave, so should today's children be able to wander down the street and into a neighbour's house to discover for themselves that not all adults behave like their parents, so experiencing the more open, fluid and often contradictory social affairs of the community. As children approach adolescence, the more important it becomes for their horizons to be broadened, for adolescence is that special time in life in which both mind and body need to be stretched by involving youngsters in complex issues.[36] Our ancestors knew that, in the satisfaction of a job well done, lay the motivation to reach out for something even more challenging and demanding of more advanced skills.

Evidence for this comes from some recent archaeological findings. In 1607, the year before Milton was born, 107 men set sail from London in three ships, one no bigger than a school bus, and the larger having a volume only of a modern delivery truck. The voyage across the Atlantic lasted four-and-a-half months before reaching Virginia and establishing the colony of Jamestown, the first continuously occupied English settlement in North America.[37] Completing an archaeological analysis of the site in time to celebrate the four-hundredth anniversary of what is now seen to be the birth of modern America, revealed some extraordinary findings.[38] Those small boats, it seems, could be likened to school buses in a more literal way, for careful analysis of some of the skeletons recovered from the graves of those who died within three years of landing showed some to have been only sixteen, seventeen or eighteen years old, with many in their early twenties – probably having been crazy teenagers with confused synapses when they enrolled on the expedition back in London. The youngest boy was only nine years old. The founding of modern America had been something of a school field trip minus the health and safety regulations.

The excavations showed something else remarkable – within three weeks of landing, twenty of the colonists (most likely to have been the younger unskilled ones) had erected a stockade over 300 feet long to create a fort large enough to encircle the colonists and their supplies. Archaeologists confirm that the trees cut down and erected in that stockade would have weighed up to a third of a ton each and stood ten or twelve feet tall. This meant that each of the men/teenagers chopped down on average two trees every day, trimmed them, lugged them to the fort and then erected them – all the while dodging the arrows of the Indians, living on near-starvation rations, and working in an intense heat and humidity. Film-makers recently built a replica of that fort; they were just able to do it in three weeks with twenty grown men, but only because they had chainsaws and tractors to help them, no poisoned arrows to dodge, no mosquitoes to avoid and plenty of well-cooked food.

Think of those early colonists when you next encounter a confused teenager, unengaged by school, bored with having no space to take on a meaningful task, and fast becoming obese through inactivity. It's not their fault. Adolescents need the opportunity to be out and about and proving themselves. Not for nothing is it now argued that it is the energy and sheer bloody-mindedness of adolescence that normally drives human development by forcing young people in every generation to think beyond their own self-imposed limitations and to exceed

their parents' aspirations. In countless instances over the generations it has been adolescent muscle linked with a determination
to break any limitations that others may put in their way that
have pushed forward the boundaries of civilization. Those early
teenagers in Jamestown were simply doing what came naturally,
and without them the colony might never have been established.

Back in England in the year 2007, that understanding was
totally lacking in the confusion of current educational thinking.
Secondary schools, the media widely reported, were becoming
increasingly concerned that the present generation of sixteen-
and seventeen-year-olds were so unsocialized and ill-disciplined
that, leaving the school at lunchtime to visit the local fish and
chip shop, they caused mayhem. Headteachers pleaded with the
Minister to provide money for extra teachers so as to prevent
pupils from leaving the school site in their free time. Incredible
as it might seem (remember those earlier teenagers hacking their
way through the Virginian forest?) the Minister actually agreed
and also proposed a ban on anyone setting up fast-food shops
near to schools.

It was that overschooled but undereducated issue all over
again – together with a pathetic vision of children as battery
hens. Thirty years before, as an inexperienced headteacher
myself, I had been in danger of making the same mistake until
my chairman of governors, an extremely wise and experienced
man, rebuked me with words I will never forget: 'Shame on
you. Have you so little faith in the education you're giving your
youngsters that you can't trust them out of your sight even for
ten minutes for fear they won't know how to control their
behaviour without you?' He was absolutely right. To me it was
the rebuke I needed just at the moment when my cockiness (I
had been getting on pretty well in my job) needed the savage

reminder that the whole purpose of education is to prepare youngsters to become good and useful citizens, not simply compliant pupils who only know how to behave when told exactly what to do. Wise old men like him who had known the struggle of pulling themselves up by their bootstraps during the pre-war depression years knew there was no future for battery hens – education had to be robust enough to accept the challenge of training free-range children.

Community, as an almost accidental voluntary coming together of people, has suffered over recent years from society's infatuation with privacy and the rights of the individual. This has robbed communities of that which once gave them their vitality and made their pavements, town squares and backyards the spontaneous location for intergenerational conversations and purposeful apprenticeships. Communities have now lost that sense of togetherness which we now call Social Capital.[39] Social capital is about those intangible substances that count for most in the daily lives of people – goodwill, fellowship, sympathy, and the recognition that you have both something to give and something to receive from your neighbour. Social capital is the sum of numerous, fortuitous social interchanges that various kinds of evidence suggest decrease the chance of a stroke or developing cancer, make people happier in their work, and reduce juvenile delinquency, child abuse and teenage pregnancy. A wonder drug, it would seem, that is needed everywhere. The kind of involvement that makes people feel good about themselves, develop an optimistic attitude towards life and makes them available to their neighbours.

Yet today's children live in a world of vastly depleted social capital, for technology has, all unwittingly, destroyed many of the circumstances that once created social capital. It happens all too easily. An extreme example comes from the deep south of

America in the 1930s where families were accustomed to sitting out on the front porch of an evening, fanning themselves and talking loudly to their neighbours across the street. Their children would play on the pavements under the benign supervision of several dozen pairs of eyes. All this changed with the invention of air conditioning. Families retreated from the common space of the porches and the streets into their front rooms and shut the windows tight, only to discover long afterwards that they had forgotten how to talk to their neighbours and that there was no one looking after the children. This same thing may be happening to children in the house next to you who have become so involved with social networking sites on the worldwide web that they have lost interest in playing with their friends. They no longer have any inclination to spend time with their grandparents who would dearly welcome the opportunity to share a lifetime's wisdom with the younger generation before it's too late. It may be happening in your own home, to your own children; it may even be happening to yourself.

Because of society's preoccupation with efficient productivity, we have stripped out of many communities the opportunity for young people to learn in a hands-on manner either as formal apprentices or working alongside skilled people whom they respect.[40] In this vacuum where youngsters are given pocket money to spend to fill up the hours that their ancestors would have spent working and perfecting their skills, adolescents all too often have a most difficult time. The values of mutuality and reciprocity that were once an important part of our culture have been replaced by a shoulder-shrugging individuality that seems to excuse most adults and society as a whole from what used to be the adults' responsibility, freely given, of nurture and support. Rather than being sensitive to the needs of adolescence, we shift the responsibility for managing life onto their still young shoulders, and discard them when they become too much trouble. It is social capital that prevents adolescents from becoming a tribe apart.[41]

Adolescence and the school

I was early attracted to the analogy of the three-legged stool as it explained a deficiency in my own education. At the age of thirteen and a half I had been sent away to boarding school and so stopped playing for the local boys' football team, singing in the church choir and lost my connection with old Mr MacFadgen who had taught me to woodcarve. I immediately appreciated my new school's extended sports and musical opportunities, found many of my teachers fascinating, but each time I returned to my parents' home for the holidays, I realized that I was losing contact with my former friends who were now caught up in new friendships that didn't involve me. I began to feel a stranger in my own town, more emotionally committed to my school than to the place I had come from.

Years later that analogy helped me understand why my own education had seemed unbalanced – the community leg had got too short and the school leg had over-compensated. In my case my school was made up predominantly of boys like me so that, as with many other public schoolboys, I didn't really understand where I had come from, and arrogantly looked down on the local community's football teams and church choirs as being merely amateurish. Being enthusiastic for my school, I had become alienated from my community.

Studying education a few years later, I came to recognize just how wrong that was. Now, looking back over more than 40 years of teaching,[42] I have mixed and contradictory memories. I remember with affection the enormous energy of inspired teachers each trying in their own ways to improve the opportunities for children – either with the experiential primary school curriculum in the late 1960s, or with the new courses developed in the 1970s for the so-called non-academic pupils, or for those men and women who forged Britain's early lead in integrating computers into education. I have admired the way teachers extend their children's education by taking them away on field trips, and the hours they give up to directing school plays and supervising sports teams. But as a headteacher trying to direct teachers' enthusiasms in ways which strengthened rather than weakened the unique contributions of home and community, I found it extraordinarily hard. Schools readily develop a momentum of their own and all too easily swamp those other aspects of a child's potential experience that are so essential to a complete education.

By the mid-1980s I was becoming increasingly frustrated with politicians' simplistic belief that there wasn't much wrong with young people that couldn't be fixed by placing increased responsibility on schools and requiring teachers to work harder, and stick more tightly to what government advisers told them to do. But simply working harder doesn't necessarily mean working better, neither does it give children the skills they actually need.[43] Over the years I noticed that fewer teachers were willing to become headteachers, and for me that was the writing on the wall – when those closely involved with education didn't want to take personal responsibility for what was going on in school, something was very wrong. Politicians and administrators became preoccupied with more and more testing, rather than any great thirst for pupil knowledge. As an American educator said as he recalled his childhood on a farm in the Midwest, 'If you want to fatten hogs, you feed 'em, you don't weigh 'em.' The cart really had been placed before the horse. The whole education system in which we were trapped had become so out of date that it was no longer fit for purpose.

I started to describe this as being upside-down and inside-out.[44] Upside-down because more money was spent on secondary education than on primary schools (and that meant more teachers for secondary schools than primary schools, and lower pupil–teacher ratios for the older pupils), and inside-out because by inflating the importance of schools, teachers and politicians had forgotten the significance of children's informal learning and were remorselessly appropriating to the school the time which should be left for families to enjoy their children. There was something else – England has a greater percentage of its children attending independent schools (mainly the public schools) than any other nation, and those children seemed to do so much better later on than state school pupils; virtually half the places at Oxford and Cambridge go to the 7 per cent of pupils from independent schools. Why is that? Is it simply because they have better teachers, better resources and higher self-esteem? Or is it something even more fundamental, a structural fault that might run through every state school in the country? Increasingly I came to believe that it was. I refer to the decision in 1902 to follow the public schools in their assumption (based on Plato's belief that children below the age of thirteen didn't matter very much) that schooling should be split into two parts, primary and secondary.

Take your thinking back to the mid-nineteenth century, to that point where the new public schools had cornered the upper-class market for what we would now call secondary education. They looked disparagingly at those elementary schools being developed by philanthropists for the great majority of the population, as much concerned with saving their souls as they were in developing functional skills and maintaining social order. This was the two nations of which Disraeli spoke between whom there was virtually no social discourse – the one nation receiving its education through the rates as a public good, the other at liberty to invest vastly larger sums to ensure that their sons' education brought them a private gain. The 1870 Education Act (known originally as the Education of the Poor Act) which sought to improve elementary education by establishing board schools, provoked the public schools to make a unilateral declaration of independence, arrogantly dismissing any form of state education as being of no concern to them.

Thirty years on, however, by providing an inclusive education for all children to the age of fourteen, and for those who wanted it onto sixteen or even seventeen, the board schools became very popular. They attracted more pupils and gained impressive qualifications. By 1902, the Establishment was put on its guard, for here was a possibility that the ordinary people of England might receive a more relevant education than the sons of the gentry received in the public schools. Parliament prepared to put a stop to such competition, being resolved to limit elementary education to children below the age of fourteen. Remember that Herbert Asquith (later to be Prime Minister) harangued the House of Commons: 'If you vote for this proposal you'll put an end to the existence of the best, the most fruitful and most beneficial educational agencies that ever existed in this country.' To England's lasting shame, Asquith and his colleagues failed, and by the Act of 1902 elementary education was stopped at the age of fourteen, making secondary education as delivered by the public schools associated with social privilege. When the Victorians and Edwardians thought of schooling, they had two contrasting visions – elaborate and very expensive public schools, and elementary schools which, because they were provided on the rates, were looked down upon by anyone who sought to improve their social status. Some of these attitudes remain today.[45]

Jump forward to the last years of the Second World War and the recognition that post-war England would demand some form of secondary education for all. Parliament's commitment to elementary education, still tainted by early Victorian attitudes, withered as pressure mounted to divert funds into the new secondary education that the 1944 Education Act proposed to establish. It is here that today's school child is still paying the price for the horrible compromise that was about to be made. Persuading itself that the old elementary school curriculum hadn't mattered very much, and that the new secondary school was where the action would be, government decided with virtually no consultation that three years would be shorn off the old elementary school curriculum to create the new primary schools which would require achieving in six years what the earlier elementary school had done in nine. This would provide the time, and the money, for four years of secondary schooling, with the hope that sooner rather than later the leaving age would be raised to sixteen, thereby making secondary education last five years.[46]

I know of no research that justifies the age of eleven as a suitable time for transfer. Certainly, the public schools have held tenaciously to thirteen-and-a-half as being the most developmentally appropriate stage. To transfer to 'big school' often plunges physically diminutive pupils a year or so before puberty into large secondary schools, and often at a considerable distance from their home. So, over the past 60 years, English pupils' experience of primary education has been rushed and incomplete. Reduced to its simplest terms, youngsters now spend less of their time with primary teachers whose belief it is that they teach children, and more of their time with secondary teachers who are convinced that they are teaching subjects. The possibility of teachers from the earliest years through to the sixth form agreeing that the whole of schooling should be organized to go with the grain of the brain was so remote as to be unimaginable. Teachers in secondary schools used to the advantage of small classes would be most reluctant to surrender them. The pedagogy that this book has argued for would require the system to be front-loaded by swapping the more generous funding of secondary schools with those of the primary school, so that the secondary teachers became more concerned to support children's self-learning.

In a system divided into primary and secondary, such an understanding just does not fit on a teacher's radar screen, and certainly not in the policy considerations of administrators or politicians. In its place has grown up the assumption that the job of primary schools is to prepare children for secondary school, and that secondary schools, suffering from any sense of a moral imperative to educate youngsters to be fit to perform justly, skilfully and magnanimously, see the justification of their curriculum as fitting 'the new economic imperative of supply-side investment for national prosperity'.

There is something else. The old grammar schools up to the early years of the nineteenth century, as with elementary schools well into the twentieth century, were all located within the heart of the community, meaning simply that children were in daily contact with the hustle and bustle of everyday life. School, home and community were interchangeable in the course of a short walk. It was the boarding public schools that changed that, as it did for me in the 1950s.[47] While the 1944 Act largely acknowledged that children below the age of eleven needed to remain in their communities by building lots of small local primary schools, the new secondary schools had no such scruples – children had to spend considerable time travelling to much larger schools because each served a very much larger catchment area. This travel time came, not out of the pupils' school hours, but from the time that would otherwise have been spent in the home or community. Research that has some bearing on this comes from the study showing that, for every ten minutes of extra commuting time, adults cut their commitment to community activity by 10 per cent – children probably do the same.[48]

Dr Arnold and the others in the public schools saw in the encouragement of extra-curricular activity a way of using up youngsters' excessive energy in controllable ways.[49] However, by failing to appreciate that adolescents have a fundamental need to use that energy in productive ways, they effectively reduced the life of an adolescent simply to that of a game. And that was all wrong. Butler, as the Minister who introduced the 1944 Education Act, thought so too. In his memoirs he talked of his own experience as a child in a public school and quoted a cousin who said, 'The penalty of belonging to a public school is that one plays before a looking-glass all the time and has to think about the impression one is making. And as public schools are run on the worn-out fallacy that there can't be progress without competition, games as well as everything degenerate into a means of giving free-play to the lower instincts of men.'[50] And if that was the problem of the boarding school, then it still casts its shadow over today's secondary schools. They have taken such a huge chunk of a child's life away from the home and the community that they have reduced the child's understanding of life to something of a game of which they are observers, not participants.

So that is what you see when you look at the current primary and secondary school – a system that has emerged through a whole series of accidents and false assumptions.

A tale of three nations

In a world obsessed with statistics, it is Finland, a country whose education system is the least dominated by testing, that comes out on top in reading, mathematics, science or in the quality of life enjoyed by its students. With only six million people scattered thinly over a landscape of lake and forest, Finland is a high-tech economy with one of the world's highest per-capita incomes. Unlike the English, the Finns don't believe their children are mature enough to go to school until they are seven, by which time home and community have given every child a broadly based yet emotionally rich start to life. Finnish schools are an integral part of their communities, built so that most children can walk to school or go by bike, along paths totally separated from traffic. These are all-through schools – not large, for few have even as many as 750 pupils, where children go for nine years from the age of seven to sixteen.[51]

Finnish teachers are required to have both a three-year honours degree in a specific subject, together with a three-year pedagogic degree in educational theory and practice. They know what they are doing and why, and are respected figures within the community, so much so that government delegates to the individual school the design of its own curriculum, and leaves individual teachers to decide on appropriate teaching styles. With a varied and stimulating life outside school, the classrooms are strictly functional places concentrating on developing rigorous and thoughtful young minds. There are no external assessments until a single exam at the age of sixteen which is used to help decide with parents, child and teacher what form of further education is most appropriate. Only 3 per cent of students drop out at the age of sixteen, and two years later between 60 and 70 per cent of them go on to higher education. Finland is an easy land to visit as most nine- and ten-year-olds will inevitably put you at your ease by talking comfortably with you in English.

This is the land (once part of Sweden) to which Comenius came in the mid-seventeenth century when Milton was unable to bring him to England. Three hundred and fifty years later the concept of a complete and generous education thrives in Finland. If anything goes wrong with children's lives, the first question asked is 'What's gone wrong in the community?', not what might have gone wrong in the school. Education is a social concern, not a political issue. That idea runs deep, for Finland retains much of its thoughtful and non-ostentatious Presbyterian work ethic, and the Finns retain a simplicity in their lifestyle – to own a log cabin on the side of a lake complete with a sauna in which you can entertain your friends, is heaven enough to most people, with only SAD syndrome (Seasonal Affective Disorder) spoiling otherwise high levels of mental stability. To spend time with Finnish youngsters is to appreciate Milton's expectation for the English all those years ago.

A further comparison of national education systems in 2007 surprised observers by showing South Korea now level-pegging with Finland in top place.[52] South Korea is very different from Finland. A traditional Confucian society mixed with Buddhism and evangelical Christianity, the country was devastated by war in the 1950s. Subsequently America provided a massive reconstruction programme including the near universal application of the American five-to-eighteen school system split into its three parts of junior, middle (twelve- to fourteen-year-olds) and high school. Because the Koreans retain a traditional deference to parents, elders and teachers, Korean children simply do as they are told, for family honour is at stake. While American youth pursue the latest fashions and follow their baseball teams,

South Korean children quietly walk out of the school gates each afternoon and into hours and hours of extra tutoring that helps them get the grade levels of which American parents can only dream. It is not a way of life that would appeal to many Europeans. Two professors in Seoul were quoted in 2003 as saying, 'Public education has been degraded to a system incapable of bringing any intellectual or emotional stimulus to children,' and another added, 'If children get a standardized education like that of battery chickens, they can't develop their own personality and then make themselves unhappy.'[53]

Raw statistics can't explain everything. Which one of these countries is your heaven or your hell will depend on what kind of education you think is appropriate for what kind of world – is it to be the predictable world of the overschooled child, or the more open world in which a child whose education has been complete and generous will thrive?

In that same analysis of international performances, England, the country that has spent billions upon billions of pounds in the past twenty or so years in creating a complex, centralized and top-down system of schooling, has slipped over four years from seventh to seventeenth place in reading levels, and from twelfth place to twenty-fourth in mathematics. To compound the nation's sense of dismay, the UNICEF Report showed that Britain was in bottom place for the quality of relationships within the family, for the use its children make of drink and drugs, and was in next-to-bottom place for recorded levels of happiness. It was in only seventeenth place for the quality of education.

Government's response has been to renew its commitment to its performability agenda – such failures had to mean that its measurement of intermediate levels of performance were not yet sophisticated enough to give early warning of problems.

Consequently what was needed was to combine education with social services into a single system. While any headteacher or member of a social services team will readily appreciate that while education and social services need to support all programmes that help children, this does not mean that the two services are the same or are interchangeable. Education and social services are very different in their specialized knowledge and their procedures.

The relationship between education and social services is, at its best, platonic – each appreciating the other professionally – but is not based on an emotional relationship. There is nothing to be gained by politicians forcing a marriage between such different creatures. If they were to produce offspring, the probability is that they would be sterile, like an ass born to a horse and a donkey. By combining education with social services into new Directorates of Children's Services, government has misunderstood the nature of both agencies. In many parts of the country an education officer is now a second-tier appointment answerable to a director whose professional expertise could as well be in social services as it is in education. In a sense it is comparable to the relationship between history and geography as school subjects; while it goes without saying that it is helpful for a child studying the one to have some understanding of the other, when schools 30 years ago amalgamated the two subjects into a single Humanities, it proved a near disaster as geographers found themselves teaching the history that they didn't understand, while historians often made bad geographers. It has taken many years for a new discipline of humanities to emerge with its own rigorous discipline and standards, but in the meantime history and geography, which were once highly popular subjects with students, have lost their appeal because they lost their professional expertise.

At this moment of crisis in English education, the government is placing its faith in a totally new discipline, or a new way of doing things, which is ill-defined and untested. I stress my commitment to both highly competent social services, and highly competent school administrators, as well as my commitment to ensure that both of them work collaboratively. But a premature forced marriage leads to the most serious misunderstanding both of the nature of education and of the loosely knit world in which social services have to operate. The roughness of England's dilemma was reinforced when *Time* magazine published in April 2008 an article entitled 'Unhappy, Unloved and Out of Control'. This showed how an epidemic of violence and crime among adolescents (27 teenagers were murdered in London in the previous year) as well as drunkenness (27 per cent of fifteen-year-olds claim to have been drunk more than twenty times) was sweeping Britain.[54] It was caused, at least partially the article suggested, because the English had come to see their children as an entirely separate species which they preferred to disown.

So which road will England take (or for that matter Canada, which stood at thirteenth out of twenty-one countries in the Well-being Report, or the United States that came out as twentieth, just above Britain)? Will it be the road and strategy that was plotted out 350 years ago by Milton? If, on the other hand, you believe in the force-feeding approach of South Korea, I suggest you are doomed, for, as most of us know in our hearts, we English never were a rule-abiding society, deferential to elders and parents – and certainly not so to politicians. The English were once the ultimate free-range chickens. That is still there in our genetic and cultural make-up. We want to be what Milton suggested we could be.

*   *   *

This book was conceived through six international conferences held at Wingspread, the beautiful conference centre on the shores of Lake Michigan in Wisconsin. Sixty people – eminent researchers, former Ministers of Education, highly placed civil servants, teachers, lecturers, bankers and diplomats, from fourteen different countries – laid the foundations for a synthesis[55] of the research emerging from the social and biomedical sciences into the nature of learning. It was no easy task – as we moved backwards and forwards between the world of pure research and the realities of everyday life, we found ourselves too often wallowing in the troughs of decisions taken long ago which, if unchallenged, pre-condition society to reject any new ideas that challenge the status quo.

As the last conference came to its conclusion, an American participant[56] put her finger firmly on the crux of the matter. 'Knowing what we now know,' she said with passionate conviction, 'we no longer have the moral authority to carry on doing what we have always done.' I was deeply impressed. Here was a statement, rich in meaning, that contained a profound truth that might not have been obvious to everyone. Analyse that statement – the word 'we' occurs three times, and the statement and punchiness lies in the high-sounding expression 'moral authority'. *What does this mean? Who are we? Who has such 'moral authority', and what is the nature of that 'civil society' in which individuals personally accept responsibility for the common good?*

It was a statement that comes more easily from an American than it does from a Briton, an Australian or a Canadian. Americans think differently about society, the nature of authority, and have a different appreciation of what they mean when they speak of 'we' from other English-speaking countries. When Thomas Jefferson drafted the Declaration of Independence in that Philadelphia boarding house in June 1776,[57] he had in mind the kind of covenant that the Pilgrim Fathers had signed on board the *Mayflower* 150 years previously: 'We whose names are underwritten . . . solemnly and mutually in the presence of God and one another, *covenant and combine our services together in a civil body politic.*'[58] Each of those embryonic Americans swore loyalty to each other when they were literally all in the same boat together. There is a massive, yet subtle, difference between a covenant and a contract. Englishmen understand contracts with their clearly defined boundaries beyond which neither party may tread. Covenants, however, go beyond the legal boundaries set out in contracts to embrace a never-ending commitment to each other.[59] It was to such an idea of covenant that John F. Kennedy appealed when he said, 'Ask not what your country can do for you, ask what you can do for your country.'

In a covenantal relationship, no amount of shoulder-shrugging, no anguished appeal to politicians, no recourse to blaming other people's inertia, can ever excuse the knowledgeable individual's responsibility to get up and do it for themselves. Some English and Americans will remember the words of the General Confession written not long after the Pilgrim Fathers landed in Massachusetts: 'We have left undone those things which we ought to have done, and done those things we ought not to have done . . . and there is no health in us.'[60] To fail to do something which you are required to do is one thing, but to fail to do something which you know ought to be done makes us equally culpable in a covenantal relationship of letting other people down.

As the earlier English sense of society became ever less convincing as a way of thinking about human relationships in the latter part of the century, so the country-house metaphor for assimilation which had given way to the idea of a hotel as a model for multiculturalism, also failed.[61] Effectively both denied what we now know from evolutionary psychology, that humans are born with an innate predisposition to mistrust those who, for many reasons, don't seem to be members of the same tribe. This becomes the critical point, for without deep, trusting relationships we can never establish a sense of civil society, or work on a common task. We have to stop building walls that divide us, and build instead bridges that unite our diversity. People who sweat together, stick together (don't take that too literally!). It is the 'doing things together' – however menial the task – that is the biggest antidote to tribal prejudice. We have to respect our differences, and delight in variety, just as a builder uses stones of different shapes, textures and colours to create future homes that reflect the individuality of separate families. And it is the homes that we build together that have to replace, metaphorically, the featureless, anonymous housing estates of the mind that imprison us. A recent arrival in Toronto from Sri Lanka said of his first year on such an estate what can be re-echoed in every city across the world: 'In my homeland we lived within people, here we live within walls.'[62] And it will be in the rebuilding of civil society that we will create together a home 'we can all share, based not on laws, but on fraternity'. Most of all, we must snap out of our infatuation with the material, and discover anew the love that comes from relationships that extend to each an acknowledgement that we need the other because none of us is sufficient unto ourselves.

The reason that assimilation and multiculturalism have failed is that policy-makers have forgotten that a state, to be fully functional, cannot simply be defined in terms of a government that makes and administers the laws within which individuals are then left free to do their own thing, and compete with one another.

Most day-to-day activity has nothing to do with law; it's about getting on with our neighbours and creating a quality of life that depends on our access to people we trust, like, admire and find fun. Children need to learn this everywhere – from their mother's knee, to the nursery and the playground, the school and in all their interactions with members of the community. Apart from the odd speeding ticket, the vast majority of us don't come up against the law, yet our lives are full of social interactions totally unmediated by government. That is a more glorious achievement than the law could, or should ever attempt to, deliver. Just to live within the law means very little; but to live within the law and have a sense of civil society is to create a great place in which to live. We have to remind ourselves that society is 'an aggregate (something formed from a mass of loosely-connected fragments) of people living together in more or less orderly communities'. To learn that lesson well is the social justification for investing in schools. It holds together through its own natural procedures, and is impossible to manage in a logical and legalistic way. Being an aggregate is society's strength; or put another way, society is the aggregate of what people think for themselves.

Which makes civil society the location for moral authority. Society is about the quality of human relationships, it is where people have to accept responsibility for the consequences of their action, it's where the micro meets the macro issues. Society is where one can find the human face – not in the laws, not in the operation of economic theories of life, nor in nebulous philosophies. Society is down-to-earth. It is the seat of our greatest ambitions. It is where we want to be, because it feels right. It is the equivalent of our Stone Age campfire, where all generations share the stories of the past and their hopes for the future.

The state, on the other hand, is central and impersonal; it

levies taxes, and provides services, but there is nothing voluntary about this – you can't opt out because the state, by definition, is all-embracing. It uses power, not goodwill, to achieve this. It uses a metaphorical GPS system to find the way, not the individual's skill in finding alternative routes through good map reading. If the role of the state grows, it is always at the cost of reducing the significance of civil society. When taxes replace generosity, and social workers replace caring neighbours, something precious within the organic nature of society withers. Without that precious *something*, life becomes colourless.

Civil society is about the quality of human relationships implied by covenant; it is where people have to accept responsibility for the consequences of their actions. Civil society, however, has become a greatly weakened concept, and because education has now become micro-managed by the state so as essentially fitting 'with a new economic imperative of supply-side investment for national prosperity', the revitalization of education has to proceed in sequence with the recovery of civil society. That may not be as impossible a task as it might have seemed a few years ago. The belief in *performability*, of management by objectives, is at long last starting to falter, and it's faltering for very human reasons. Humans are a collaborative species – it is how we are. We are driven to think for ourselves; it's how we survive. Remember that, and we have everything that we need to deal with the problems facing world society.

*   *   *

If this book has done its job properly, this last paragraph becomes the opening for the story to be told by those who, daring all, will shake education out of its two-centuries-old inertia. Just as the rising sun heralds the promise of another day, so the natural exuberance of youth predicts the arrival of fresh potential. In the saga of the ages, if a generation fails, the fault lies squarely with the previous generation for not equipping them well enough for the changes ahead. The most immoral thing that any man can ever say is, 'This will last out my time.' We were once all adolescents; those of us who have done well enough to read through to this point have done so, not on the strength of our own muscle or brain power, but because we have been privileged to walk with older men and women who have stiffened our sinews and stretched our minds. Do that right now, and generations yet unborn will give thanks that we returned adolescence to its rightful place of enabling young people to go beyond their self-imposed limitations, and exceed their parents' aspirations. That is what adolescents do naturally – *given the right opportunity.*

APPENDIX A

The 21st Century Learning Initiative

The 21st Century Learning Initiative grew out of the Education 2000 Trust that had been established as a recognized charity in 1983. Education 2000 was founded by Sir Bryan Thwaites and Christopher Wysock-Wright who had been working together since 1970 on the impact of computers on education. They founded it in conjunction with a large number of chairmen and chief executives of major British companies because they realized that the education system was failing this country. The Patron was His Royal Highness Prince Philip and the President Sir Keith Joseph.

It was founded on the following three assumptions:

1. The structure and methods of education must help to sustain the traditional values of society while also responding adequately to current and future rates of cultural, social, industrial and technological change;
2. Such radical changes will require every individual to have access to educational opportunities throughout life;
3. As the typical lead time for major educational change is twenty years, no time should be lost in formulating proposals.

At a conference held at Westfield College in July 1983 under the patronage of the Duke of Edinburgh, *A Consultative Document Hypothesis for Education in AD 2000* was published.

259

Two years later John Abbott, then headmaster of Alleyne's School, Stevenage, had produced a Feasibility Study on *A Curriculum Appropriate for Secondary Education in the 21st Century* for Hertfordshire County Council. This was the result of a nine-month secondment jointly sponsored by the Prudential Assurance Company and the Manpower Services Commission. In 1985 John Abbott joined the Trust as its first (and only) Director. Starting in 1986, Education 2000 developed the first of its nine community-wide projects in Letchworth in Hertfordshire where, among other things, it pioneered the large-scale introduction of computers into education by setting, and achieving, a target of one computer to every seven pupils when the national average was one to 120. This work attracted much interest from charities and national commercial sponsors. Within nine years, 39 companies had contributed a minimum of £25,000, with many donating more than £100,000, and one £500,000.

In 1987 the Director was invited to give the opening keynote speech to the Annual Conference of the Confederation of British Industries (CBI). In the months that followed, there was intense political interest in the Trust's ideas, and several times the Director was invited to meetings in Downing Street. In the previous year Sir Keith Joseph who, as Secretary for Education, had been most supportive of both Education 2000 and of John Abbott's feasible study, retired from politics and, as Lord Joseph, then became the President of Education 2000. By the time of the CBI Conference, the new Secretary for Education, Kenneth Baker, was already shaping up his proposals for the Education Reform Bill of 1988. Despite his lengthy visit to Letchworth and his much-publicized endorsement of what Education 2000 was doing, the nature of the legislative changes he proposed meant that the Trust and government were set on very different courses – the Trust emphasizing the progressive development of the individual's skill in learning, intellectual weaning and stressing the importance of home and community, and national government increasingly moving towards standardized forms of instruction and assessment and the pre-eminence of the school. The difference was to grow ever greater with time (with the exception of a brief period in 1996 towards the end of John Major's premiership).

From 1988 onwards the work of Education 2000 attracted more interest in overseas English-speaking countries than it did within this country (see *Educational 2000: Educational Change with Consent* published in 1990 by Cassell). This had the incidental advantage of drawing John Abbott into addressing increasing numbers of major educational conferences in many other lands, from Scandinavia through to Australia, and from the Americas to Africa. Through this he became acutely aware of the possibilities for research emerging from neurobiology and cognitive science to contribute a powerful explanation for what psychologists and learning experts had noted for years, but which they had lacked the neurological knowledge to explain. The Trust coined the phrase 'Learning that goes with the grain of the brain'. Increasingly, the work of Education 2000 was transformed as it sought to build a synthesis to bridge the biomedical and social sciences. In early 1995 the Director was invited to address a representative group of senior officials in the Department of Education and Science who declared themselves to be ill-equipped to appreciate the significance of such findings for the formal structuring of schools.

In December 1995 John Abbott accepted the invitation made partly by the Johnson Foundation in Wisconsin, and by the most articulate, influential and determined of the academics in the United States and elsewhere who invited him to go to

Washington DC to transform Education 2000 into the transnational 21st Century Learning Initiative. The Initiative was pledged to extend the idea of synthesis so that it might facilitate the emergence of new approaches to learning that would draw upon a range of insights into the human brain, the functioning of human societies, and learning as a self-organizing activity. This, the Initiative believed, would release human potential in ways that would nurture and form local democratic communities worldwide, and would help reclaim and sustain a world supportive of human endeavour. In December 1996, after the first three conferences, the Initiative published *The Synthesis: A Work in Progress*. This was widely distributed, extensively discussed and much applauded. One of several Papers described the Initiative's work and published in various journals was selected for inclusion as one of the four best articles of that year on cognitive process in the annual edition of *Psychology* for 1988/9 ('To be Intelligent', first published in *Educational Leadership* by ASCD in 1997). Following further extensive discussions and a number of other conferences, *A Policy Paper: The Strategic and Resource Implications of a New Model of Learning* was published in mid-1999. In this it concluded:

There is too much evidence now available for us to continue deceiving ourselves. Our present community and school structures are finely tuned to outdated assumptions about how humans learn. These new understandings simply undermine the old assumptions on which the present structures gain their authority. If we are to capitalize on these new understandings and opportunities we must recognize that the changes necessary are of such a scale that the normal processes of instrumental innovation are totally inadequate. The conventional units of change (a single school or state-wide government) are no longer appropriate; new, intermediate units which correspond more closely to human expectation and community needs have to be developed.

This idea and the reasoning behind it caught the personal attention of the United States Secretary of Education, former Governor of North Carolina, Dick Riley, who at the end of an extensive session said,

These are such fundamental issues that I need to know and understand them far better. I imagine the issues were similar across the advanced countries. We will all need to support each other. If you could call a meeting of Secretaries of Education from particular countries so that we can discuss the possible political, logistic and strategic implications of all this, not only would I come, I would encourage the others to do the same.

What a fantastic opportunity appeared to be opening up!

But that meeting never took place, for the defenders of the status quo were well organized. One of our most generous sponsors, an American foundation in New York, took violent exception to those very conclusions that had so appealed to the Secretary of State, and defined them as being so idealistic that they undermined the validity of the rest of our work. This was a terrible shock that could have meant the death of the Initiative – as I still believe that that is what such foundations wanted to happen. Then, as now, the proposals that the Initiative drew from the synthesis of the research findings really did upset the status quo. It is said that managers do things right, but leaders do the right things. And the difference is enormous. Back in

1999 the Initiative was almost killed by managers of a foundation who passed as leaders, and who listened too carefully to educational administrators. They could not conceive of a solution as radical as the Initiative believed the research required.

From late 1999, however, the Initiative, having relocated its base back in England, began to thrive more than ever before. *The Child is Father of the Man: How Humans Learn and Why*, was published in 1999, and *The Unfinished Revolution: Learning, Human Behaviour, Community and Political Paradox*, was published in 2001. For five years the Director crossed and re-crossed England addressing conferences in nearly all of the 140 local education authorities, and running training courses in several. Conferences were addressed in many locations across Canada, the United States and Europe, in Ghana, Nigeria, Ethiopia, Tanzania, Namibia and South Africa – as well as in South America, Australia, Japan, Malaysia and Indonesia.

In late 2005 the Initiative was given a contract to take these training programmes and develop them within Canada through the sponsorship of the Canadian Council on Learning over an initial four-year period. This led to conferences and workshops in many parts of British Columbia, Saskatchewan, Manitoba, Ontario, Ottawa and New Brunswick. It was in 2006 that, at a lecture in Toronto, Heather MacTaggart asked if her organization, Classroom Connections, could eventually become the delivery unit for the Initiative within Canada. This is proving to be a most beneficial arrangement, not least in the production of this book.

Interesting and fundamental systemic change, the Initiative has come to realize, is cyclical; from early 2007 there was a dramatic decrease in invitations to address teachers' conferences in England because, as one headteacher said bitterly,

Why bother to listen to something we can't aspire to? We have grown accustomed to such a strict specification by politicians of what education is meant to be about, that we have developed the kind of teacher who is very good at doing what he or she is told to do, but to consider other ways of doing things is just not on their agenda. Furthermore, we couldn't justify the cost of running a conference which was not directly linked to raising examination results, or implementing new health and safety regulations.

Hence the reason for this book, which has grown out of a quarter of a century of one small, independent organization's attempt to work out exactly what course should be set for the future of education and (to maintain the nautical analogy) what are the necessary instructions to pass down to the engine room.

This has now to become the stuff of vigorous national debate. I personally believe that civilized society depends upon it.

APPENDIX B

Synthesis

The art of drawing together findings from the biological and social sciences into a single statement of ideas presents many difficulties. It was most powerfully stated by Professor Ervin Schrödinger in his classic short treatise, *What is Life*, published in 1944. In this he said:

A scientist is supposed to have a complete and thorough knowledge at first hand, of some subject, and therefore is usually expected not to write on any topic of which he is not a master. This is regarded as a matter of *noblesse oblige*. For the present purpose I beg to renounce the noblesse, if any, and to be freed of the ensuring obligation. My excuse is as follows.

We have inherited from our forefathers the keen longing for unified, all-embracing knowledge. The very name given to the institutions of highest learning reminds us that from antiquity and throughout many centuries, the *universal* aspect has been the only one given full credit. But the spread, both in width and depth, of the multifarious branches of knowledge during the last hundred-odd years has confronted us with a queer dilemma. We feel clearly that we are only now beginning to acquire reliable material for welding together the sum total of all that is known into a whole; but on the other hand, it has become next to impossible for a single mind fully to command more than a small specialized portion of it.

I can see no other escape from this dilemma (lest our true aim be lost for ever) than that some of us should embark on a synthesis of facts and theories, albeit with a second-hand and incomplete knowledge of some of them – at the risk of making fools of ourselves . . .

So much for my apology.

I don't think anyone subsequently has articulated the issue more clearly. In the 60 years that have followed, the difficulty with synthesis has become immensely more difficult, yet at the same time immensely more important.

APPENDIX C

Prophets of a Future Not Our Own

There have been many occasions at the end of conferences when it has seemed appropriate to raise people's expectations to appreciate that only by many people pulling together and doing the right things will these problems ever be solved. John Abbott has often found it useful to quote the last prayer of Oscar Romero, the Archbishop of San Salvador, that was found on his body when he was murdered on the steps of his cathedral in 1980.

This is what we are about. We plant seeds that one day will grow. We water seeds already planted, knowing that they hold future promise. We lay foundations that will need further development. We provide yeast that produces effects far beyond our capabilities.

We cannot do everything, and there is a sense of liberation in realizing that. This enables us to do something, and enables us to do it very well. It may be incomplete, but it is a beginning, a step along the way, an opportunity for the Lord's grace to enter and do the rest. We may never see the end result, but that is the difference between the master builder, and the worker.

We are workers, not master builders, ministers, not Messiahs. *We are prophets of a future not our own.*

Notes

Because this book is largely a work of synthesis, it draws upon ideas and arguments developed in often large and extensive texts, so the references in this text are normally to these books in general, and only to specific pages for direct quotations.

Introduction

1   Wells, H. G., *The Outline of History* (1920, Vol. 2, Chapter 41).

2   Rorabaugh, W. J., *The Craft Apprentice: From Franklin to the Machine Age in America* (Oxford University Press, 1988); and Laslett, Peter, *The World We Have Lost – Further Explored* (Routledge, 1992).

3   The 21st Century Learning Initiative is an educational charity, set up in 1996, which grew out of the earlier Education 2000 Trust established in 1983. The Initiative's essential purpose is to facilitate the emergence of new approaches to learning that draw upon a range of insights into the human brain, the functioning of human societies, and learning as a self-organizing activity. The Initiative believes that this will release human potential in ways that nurture and inform local democratic communities worldwide, and will help to claim and sustain a world supportive of human endeavour. www.21learn.org.

4   The Johnson Foundation at Wingspread, Wisconsin, cultivates ideas that sustain community – people living in harmony with one another and their environment. www.johnsonfdn.org.

5   Abbott, John, *Learning Makes Sense: Recreating Education for a Changing Future* (Education 2000, 1994) and *The Child is Father of the Man: How Humans Learn and Why* (The 21st Century Learning Initiative, 1999); and Abbott, John and Ryan, Terry, *The Unfinished Revolution: Learning, Human Behaviour, Community and Political Paradox* (Network Educational Press Ltd, 2001 and Association for Supervision and Curriculum Development [ASCD] Virginia, USA, 2001).

271

6 The Canadian Council on Learning (CCL) is a Canadian national, independent and non-profit corporation that is committed to improving learning across the country and across all walks of life. It is a catalyst for lifelong learning, promoting and supporting evidence-based decisions about learning throughout all stages of life, from early childhood through to the senior years. www.ccl-cca.ca.

7 See Appendix A.

8 Bingham, Harry, *This Little Britain: How One Small Country Built the Modern World* (Fourth Estate London, 2007).

9 Synthesis – the combination of ideas to form a connected whole which resolves the tensions that otherwise exist between any of the separate bits. See Summary of Schrödinger's Paper 'What is Life' in Wyller, Arne, *The Planetary Mind* (MacMurray & Beck, 1996).

10 Laszlo, Ervin, *The Whispering Pond: A Personal Guide to the Emerging Vision of Science* (Element Books Ltd, 1996).

Chapter 1: A Fable: The Whole Story in Fewer Than 2,500 Words

1 Allport, Susan, *The Natural History of Parenting* (Harmony Books, 1997).

2 Tattersall, Ian, *Becoming Human: Evolution and Human Uniqueness* (Harcourt Brace & Co., 1998).

3 Wills, Christopher, *The Runaway Brain: The Evolution of Human Uniqueness* (HarperCollins, 1994).

4 Ehrlich, Paul R., *Human Natures: Genes, Cultures and the Human Prospect* (Island Press, 2000).

5 Lawrence, Paul R. and Nohria, Nitin, *Driven: How Human Nature Shapes Our Choices* (Jossey-Bass, 2002).

6 Hall, Granville Stanley, *Adolescence: Its Psychology and its Relations to Physiology, Anthropology, Sociology, Sex, Crime, Religion and Education* (D. Appleton & Co., 1904).

7 Hine, Thomas, *The Rise and Fall of the American Teenager* (Avon Books Ltd, 1999).

8 Handy, Charles, *The Future of Work: A Guide to a Changing World* (Basil Blackwell, 1984).

9 Carson, Rachel, *Silent Spring* (Mariner Books, 2002); and Lovelock, James, *Gaia: A New Look at Life on Earth* (Oxford University Press, 1995).

10 Wilson, E. O., *The Future of Life* (Little, Brown, 2002).

Chapter 2: The Wonder of Learning

1 Hart, Betty and Risley, Todd R., *Meaningful Differences in the Everyday Experience of Young American Children* (Paul H. Brooks, 2003).

2 Diamond, Jared, *Guns, Germs and Steel: A Short History of Everybody for the Last 13,000 Years* (Vintage, 1997); and *Collapse: How Societies Choose to Fail or Succeed* (Viking Penguin, 2005).

3 Quote from a teacher at the Villiers High School Conference in Ealing, West London, on 27 September 2002.

4 Eliot, Lise, *What's Going on in There? How the Brain and Mind Develop in the First Five Years of Life* (Penguin Group, 1999); and Gopnik, Alison, Meltzoff, Andrew N. and Kuhl, Patricia K., *The Scientist in the Crib: Minds, Brains, and How Children Learn* (William Morrow & Company, 1999).

5 Farnham-Diggory, Sylvia, *Schooling* (Harvard University Press, 1990).

6 Barrow, John, *The Artful Universe Expanded* (Clarendon Press, 2005).

7 Freeman, Charles, *Egypt, Greece and Rome: Civilizations of the Ancient Mediterranean*, 2nd edn, (Oxford University Press, 2004) specifically Chapter 2.

8 Shlain, Leonard, *The Alphabet Versus the Goddess: The Conflict Between Word and Image* (Viking, 1998).

9 Boardman, John, Griffin, Jasper and Murray, Oswyn, *The Oxford History of Greece and the Hellenistic World* (Oxford University Press, 2001).

10 Gardner, Howard, *The Unschooled Mind: How Children Think and How Schools Should Teach* (Basic Books, 1991).

11 Kotulak, Ronald, *Inside the Brain: Revolutionary Discoveries of How the Mind Works* (Andrews & McMeel, 1996).

12 Calvin, William H., *How Brains Think* (Basic Books, 1996).

13 Caine, Renate and Geoffrey, *Making Connections: Teaching and the Human Brain* (ASCD, 1991).

14 Sylwester, Robert, *A Celebration of Neurons: An Educator's Guide to the Human Brain* (ASCD, 1995); and Greenfield, Susan, *Brain Power: Working Out the Human Mind* (Element Books Ltd, 1999).

15 To American participants at the Young President's Organisation Annual European Conference, Venice, July 2002.

16 Participant at the Tameside Headteachers' Conference, Autumn 2006.

Chapter 3: Human Nature: A Brain for All Times

1 Darwin, Sir Francis, *The Autobiography of Charles Darwin* (Watts & Co., 2003).

2 Wright, Robert, *The Moral Animal* (Little, Brown & Co., 1995).

3 A house in Bath, not 100 yards from where this book was written, has carved over its central window 5792 as its date of building, which is curious for in fact it was 1788 by our calendar, but the builder sought to date it from what he thought was the formation of the earth according to Archbishop Usher.

4 Wills, *The Runaway Brain*.

5 Jolly, Alison, *Lucy's Legacy* (Harvard University Press, 1999).

6 Sterkfontein (Afrikaans for *Strong Spring*) is a set of limestone caves of special interest to paleo-anthropologists located in Gauteng province, northwest of Johannesburg, South Africa. A number of early hominid remains have been found at the site over the last few decades. Sterkfontein was declared a World Heritage Site in 2000 and the area in which it is situated was named the Cradle of Humankind. www.southafrica-travel.net.

7 Snowden, David, *Aging with Grace* (Fourth Estate, 2002).

8 Zohar, Donah and Marshall, Ian, *SQ – Spiritual Intelligence the Ultimate Intelligence* (Bloomsbury, 2000).

9 Enoch Powell, 1946, quoted in Wiener, Martin J., *English Culture and the Decline of the Industrial Spirit: 1850–1980* (Oxford University Press, 1983).

10 Nicholson, Nigel, 'How Hardwired is Human Behaviour?' (*Harvard Business Review*, July/August 1998).

11 Gardner, Howard, *Frames of Mind: The Theory of Multiple Intelligences* (Paladin Books, 1983).

12 Goleman, Daniel, *Emotional Intelligence: Why it Can Matter More Than IQ* (Bantam Books, 1995).

13 Ridley, Matthew, *Nature Via Nurture: Genes, Experience and What Makes Us Human* (Fourth Estate, 2003).

14 Kellogg Foundation, State of Michigan Survey, quoted at the White House Conference on Early Learning, 1997.

15 Edelman, Gerald M., *Bright Air, Brilliant Fire* (Basic Books, 1992); *A Universe of Consciousness* (Basic Books, 2000); and *Wider than the Sky: The Phenomenal Gift of Consciousness* (Penguin Books, 2004).

16 *The Guardian*, 18 March 2003, 'African click language holds key to

origins of earliest human speech'.

17 Ackerman, Diane, *Deep Play* (Random House, 1999).

18 Jamison, Kay Redfield, *Exuberance: The Passion for Life* (Alfred A. Knopf, 2004).

19 Mithen, Steven, *The Prehistory of the Mind: The Cognitive Origins of Art, Religion and Science* (Thames and Hudson, 1996).

20 Lewis-Williams, David, *The Mind in the Cave* (Thames & Hudson, 2002).

21 Conversation, reported through interpreter, when camping with the Hadza in 2005 in the region of Lake Eyas in Tanzania.

22 As 20 above.

23 *The Guardian*, 4 March 2003.

24 *The Daily Telegraph*, 25 April 2003.

25 *The Guardian*, 26 April 2003.

26 Birmingham LEA Enquiry, spring 2003.

27 Wade, Nicholas, *Before the Dawn* (Penguin Press 2006).

28 Wells, Spencer, *The Journey of Man: A Genetic Odyssey* (Random House, 2003); and Olson, Steve, *Mapping Human History: Genes, Race and Our Common Origins* (Mariner, 2003).

29 Abbott, John, *Adolescence: A Critical Evolutionary Adaptation* (The 21st Century Learning Initiative, 2006).

30 Sykes, Bryan, *The Seven Daughters of Eve* (Bantam Press, 2001).

31 Sykes, Bryan, *The Blood of the Isles* (Bantam Press, 2006).

32 Strauch, Barbara, *The Primal Teen* (Doubleday, 2003); and New York Academy of Sciences, Vol. 1021, *Adolescent Brain Development: Vulnerabilities and Opportunities*, 2004).

33 Diamond, Marian and Hopson, Janet, *Magic Trees of the Mind: How to Nurture Your Child's Intelligence, Creativity, and Healthy Emotions from Birth Through Adolescence* (Dutton, 1998).

34 Greenspan, Stanley I., *The Growth of the Mind and the Endangered Nature of Intelligence* (Merloyd Lawrence, 1997).

35 Gerhardt, Sue, *Why Love Matters: How Affection Shapes a Baby's Brain* (Routledge, 2004).

36 Hall, *Adolescence*.

37 Brownlee, Sharon, *Inside the Teen Brain* (US News); and *Mysteries of the Teen Years* (10 May 2005).

38 Bogin, Barry, *The Growth of Humanity* (Wiley-Liss, 2001).

39 Quote by a mother at the Luanda International School, Angola, in

October 2005.

40 Csikszentmihalyi, Mihaly and Larson, Reed, *Being Adolescent: Conflict and Growth in the Teenage Years*; and *Becoming Adult: How Teenagers Prepare for the World of Work* (Basic Books, 1984).

41 Csikszentmihalyi, Mihaly, *Flow: The Psychology of Optimal Experience* (Harper & Row, 1990).

Chapter 4: Nurture and Culture

1 Pupil at a school in Bath, England, September 2007.

2 Hillsdon, Paul, pupil in Vancouver, letter of 25 November 2006.

3 Palmer, Sue, *Toxic Childhood: How the Modern World is Damaging Our Children and What We Can Do About It* (Orion Books, 2006); and Schor, Juliet, *Born to Buy: The Commercialised Child and the New Consumer Culture* (Scribner, 2004).

4 James, Oliver, *Affluenza* (Vermillion, 2007).

5 Dennis, Norman and Erdos, George, *Families Without Fatherhood* (IEA, 1993); Morgan, Patricia, *Farewell to the Family: Public Policy and Family Breakdown in Britain and the USA* (IEA, 1995); Kirby, Jill, *The Nationalisation of Childhood* (Centre for Policy Studies, 2006); and Hewlett, Sylvia Anne and West, Cornel, *The War Against Parents: What We Can Do for America's Belief in Mums and Dads* (Houghton Mifflin, 1998).

6 Putnam, Robert D., *Bowling Alone: The Collapse and Revival of American Community* (Simon & Schuster, 2000); Kohn, Alfie, *Unconditional Parenting: Moving from Rewards and Punishments to Love and Reason* (Atria, 2005); and Freely, Maureen, *The Parent Trap: Children, Families and a New Morality* (Virago, 2000).

7 Ozment, S., *When Fathers Ruled: Family life in Reformation Europe* (Cambridge, 1983), p. 132, quoted in Cunningham, Hugh, *Children and Childhood in Western Society Since 1500* (Pierson, 1995).

8 Lawrence, Paul R. and Nohria, Nitin, *Driven: How Human Nature Shapes Our Choices* (Jossey-Bass, 2002).

9 Lawrence and Nohria, *Driven*, Chapter 1.

10 Fiske, A., *Structures of Social Life: The Four Elementary Forms of Human Relationships* (Free Press, 1991), as quoted in Lawrence and Nohria, *Driven*.

11 Fiske, A. (1991), quoted in Lawrence and Nohria, *Driven*, p. 163.

12 Hardy, Sarah Blaffer, *Mother Nature: A History of Mothers, Infants and*

Natural Selection (Pantheon Books, 1999).

13 Sykes, Bryan, *The Seven Daughters of Eve* (W. W. Norton & Co., 2001).

14 Lewis-Williams, David and Pearce, David, *Inside the Neolithic Mind* (Thames & Hudson, 2005); and Mithen, Steven, *After the Ice: A Global Human History 20,000–5000 BC* (Weidenfeld & Nicolson, 2003).

15 Castle, E. B., *Ancient Education and Today* (Penguin Books, 1961).

16 Barrow, Robin, *Greek and Roman Education* (Bristol Classical Press, 1996).

17 Cribiore, Raffaella, *Gymnastics of the Mind: Greek Education in Hellenistic and Roman Egypt* (Princeton University Press, 2005).

18 Lee, Desmond (transn), *Plato The Republic* (Penguin Books, 1986).

19 Barrow, *Greek and Roman Education*, p. 13.

20 Castle, *Ancient Education*.

21 Boardman, John, Griffin, Jasper and Murray, Oswyn, *The Oxford History of the Roman World* (Oxford University Press, 2001).

22 Orme, Nicholas, *Medieval Schools: From Roman Britain to Renaissance England* (Yale University Press, 2006), p. 28.

23 Cahill, Thomas, *How the Irish Saved Civilisation* (Scepter, 1995).

24 *Bede, The Venerable* as quoted by Stenton, F., *Anglo-Saxon England* (Oxford University Press, 1971).

25 Pollard, Justin, *Alfred the Great: The Man Who Made England* (John Murray, 2005).

26 Bartlett, Robert, *England Under the Norman and Angevin Kings 1075–1225* (Clarendon Press, 2000).

27 Hunt, H., as quoted in Bartlett, *England Under the Normans*, (2000), p. 130.

28 Bartlett, *England Under the Normans*, p. 507.

29 Castle, *Ancient Education*, p. 131.

30 Orme, Nicholas, *Medieval Children* (Yale University Press, 2001) quoting the Harley Manuscript in the British Museum, p. 254.

31 Harriss, Gerald, *Shaping the Nation: England 1360–1461* (Clarendon Press, 2005) especially Chapters 5 and 6.

32 Collinson, Patrick, *The Reformation 1580–1680* (Weidenfield & Nicolson, 2003).

33 Williams, Penry, *The Later Tudors: England 1547–1603* (Oxford University Press, 1995).

34 Shakespeare, William, *As You Like It*, Act II, Scene 7.
35 Kermode, Frank, *The Age of Shakespeare* (Weidenfeld & Nicolson, 2004).
36 Ackroyd, Peter, *Shakespeare, The Biography* (Chatto & Windus, 2005).
37 Wrightson, Keith, *English Society 1580–1650* (Unwin Hyman Inc., 1982).
38 Laslett, Peter, *The World We Have Lost – Further Explored* (Routledge, 1992).
39 Pollock, Linda A., *Forgotten Children: Parent–Child Relations from 1500 to 1900* (Cambridge University Press, 1983).
40 *Oxford Dictionary of Quotations*.
41 Shakespeare, William, *The Winter's Tale*, Act III, Scene 3.
42 Ozment, S. (1983), also quoted Cunningham, *Children and Childhood*, p. 27.
43 Dawkins, Richard, *The God Delusion* (Bantam Press, 2006).
44 McGrath, Alister, *The Dawkins Delusion* (SPCK, 2007).
45 Ficher, David Hackett, *Albion's Seed* (Oxford University Press, 1989).
46 Genesis 1.26.
47 Wright, W. A., *Roger Ascham: English Works* (Cambridge University Press, 1904).
48 Wright, *Roger Ascham*, p. 45.
49 Langford, Paul, *A Polite and Commercial People: England 1727–1783* (Oxford University Press, 1989) especially Chapter I.
50 Bunyan, John, *The Pilgrim's Progress* (1678) (Penguin Books, ed. Sharrock, Roger, 1965).
51 Langford, *A Polite and Commercial People*, especially Chapters 4, 7 and 9.
52 Hoppit, Julian, *A Land of Liberty? England 1689–1727* (Clarendon Press, 2000), especially Chapter 13.
53 Chesterfield, The Earl of, *Letter to his Son*, 4 October 1746, as quoted in Livingstone, Sir Richard, *The Future in Education* (Cambridge University Press, 1941).
54 Carter, G., as quoted in Langford, *A Polite and Commercial People*, p. 81.
55 Hoppit, *A Land of Liberty*, p. 171.
56 Uglow, Jenny, *The Lunar Men: The Friends Who Made the Future 1730–1810* (Faber & Faber, 2002).

57 Hobsbawn, Eric, *Industry and Empire* (Penguin Books, 1969), especially Chapters 1, 2 and 3.

58 Aspin, Chris, *The Water-Spinners* (Helmshore Local History Society, 2003).

59 Watson, J. Stephen, *The Reign of George III 1760–1815* (Clarendon Press, 1960), especially Chapter XX.

60 Hilton, Boyd, *A Mad, Bad, and Dangerous People? England 1783–1846* (Clarendon Press, 2006).

61 Smith, Adam, *Wealth of Nations*, originally published 1776, Penguin Books, 1999.

62 Raikes, Robert, Letter to *The Universal Magazine*, 5 June 1784, as quoted in Jones, M. G., *The Charity School Movement in the XVIII Century* (Cambridge, 1937) p. 145.

63 Jones, *The Charity School Movement*.

64 Scott, Anne, *Hannah Moore: The First Victorian* (Oxford, 2003); and Hilton, *A Mad, Bad, and Dangerous People?*, especially pp. 354/5/6.

65 Green, Andy, *Education and State Formation* (MacMillan, 1990) especially pp. 265/6/7.

66 Bell, Andrew (1753–1832), the originator of the Monitorial School System based on an orphanage established in Madras, also known as the Madras System.

67 Giddy, Davies, speech in Parliament, in Cobbett Parliamentary Papers, 13 July 1807, p. 798.

68 Lovett, William, *Chartism: A New Organisation of the People* (1841) quoted in Simon, Bryan, *The Two Nations and the Educational Structures 1780–1870* (The Camelot Press, 1960).

69 Lovett, *Chartism*.

70 Lovett, *Chartism*, pp. 89–90; see also Lovett, William, *The Lifet and Struggles of William Lovett* (R. H. Tawney MacGibbon & Kee, 1967).

Chapter 5: Hands-on Apprentices to Hands-off Pupils

1 Hobsbawn, Eric, *Industry and Empire* (Penguin, 1968, revised 1999); and Simon, Brian, *The Two Nations & The Educational Structure, 1780–1870* (Lawrence & Wishart, 1974).

2 Dickens, Charles, *Oliver Twist* (1838), Chapter 2.

3 Hughes, Thomas, *Tom Brown's Schooldays*, first published 1857 (Oxford University Press, 1989).

4 Bamford, T. W., *The Rise of the Public Schools* (Nelson, 1967),

especially the comment of the Second Duke of Wellington in 1859, pp. 28–9.

5   Vincent, Edgar, *Nelson: Love & Fame* (Yale University Press, 2003).

6   Warner, Rex, *The English Public Schools* (Collins, 1945), p. 25.

7   Arnold, Thomas, *Letter* of 9 May 1836 quoted in Bamford, T. W., *Thomas Arnold* (1960), see p. 120.

8   Parkin, G. R., *Life and Letters of Edward Thring* (MacMillan & Co., 1898) p. 67.

9   Roberts, S. C., *A History of Brighton College 1957*, quoted in Bamford, T. W., *The Rise of the Public Schools* (Nelson, 1967).

10   Woodward, Sir Llewellyn, *The Age of Reform 1815–1870* (Oxford University Press, 1962), pp. 486–9.

11   Tocqueville, Alexis de, *Journeys to England and Ireland*, ed. Mayer, J. P. (Faber and Faber, 1958), pp. 107–8.

12   Briggs, A., *Victorian Cities* (Penguin Books, 1982), p. 116.

13   Disraeli, Benjamin, *Sybil 1845* (Book 2, Chapter 5).

14   Woodward, *The Age of Reform*, quoting *The Newcastle Commission Report*, Book 4, Chapter 2.

15   Lowe, Robert, First Viscount Sherbrooke, Vice President of the Privy Council and Education 1859–64. *The Revised Code* 1862 (see Hoppen, Theodore, *The Mid-Victorian Generation 1846–1886* (p. 47 for The Revised Code and Payment by Results), *Hansard Report* (Volume C1XV, p. 229, February 1862).

16   Lowe, Robert, see above.

17   Dickens, Charles, *Hard Times* (1854, see Chapter 2).

18   Smiles, Samuel, *Self-Help*, 1859 (reprinted Penguin Books 1986).

19   Smiles, *Self-Help*, p. 19 and others.

20   Smiles, *Self-Help*, p. 22.

21   Smiles, *Self-Help*, p. 39 and others.

22   Hoppen, *The Mid-Victorian Generation*, Chapter 12.

23   Hoppen, *The Mid-Victorian Generation*, Part 4: England and beyond; also Eric Hobsbawn, *Industry and Empire* (Penguin, 1999), chapter 7.

24   *The Public Schools Report*, normally referred to as the Clarendon Report. The Commission had been first proposed by Lord Brougham as long ago as 1818 as being *An Enquiry into the Abuse of Charities Connected with the Education in England and Wales.* The House of Lords objected to the nine Great Schools being involved in that enquiry, delaying their inspection until 1861–4 .

25 *Report of the Public School Commission* (Volume 1, p. 56).

26 *The Schools Enquiry Commission*, normally known as the Taunton Commission *'to enquire into the state of education for those large classes of English society which are comprised between the humblest and the very highest'*.

27 Bamford, *The Rise of the Public Schools*, Chapter 9.

28 Clark, H. L. and Wwech, W. M., *History of Sedbough School 1925* (pp. 98–9, quoted in Bamford, *The Rise of the Public Schools*).

29 Dickson, George, one-time Lord Mayor of Birmingham, as quoted in Simon, Brian, *The Two Nations and the Educational Structure 1780–1870* (Lawrence and Wishart, 1960), pp. 325–36.

30 Hoppen, *The Mid-Victorian Generation*, pp. 597–600.

31 Parkin, G. R., *Letters of Edward Thring* (MacMillan, 1898), Volume 1, p. 169.

32 Bamford, *The Rise of the Public Schools*, Chapter 9.

33 *Hansard*, 17 February 1870 (465–6).

34 Hoppen, *The Mid-Victorian Generation*, p. 599–600.

35 Parkin, *Letters of Edward Thring*, Volume 2, p. 261.

36 Disraeli, speech in House of Commons, 15 June 1874.

37 Ross, Elizabeth. *Private Papers* relating to the second infant school to be established in Birmingham at Jenkins Street, 1873.

38 Boughton, Fred, quoted in Burnett, John, *Destiny Obscure* (Routledge, 1994).

39 Burgess, F. W., 'The Practical Retail Draper' (1912, quoted in Searle, G. R., *A New England? Peace and War 1886–1918* (Clarendon Press, 2004).

40 Dilke, Sir Charles, *Greater Britain Beyond the Seas* (1868), quoted in Woodward, *The Age of Reform*.

41 Ensor, Sir Robert, *England 1870–1914* (Clarendon Press, 1936), see Chapters V and X.

42 Gordon, Peter, Aldrich, Richard and Dean, Dennis, *Education and Policy in England in the 20th Century* (Woborn Press, 1991), see Chapters 1 and 2.

43 Allen, B. M., *Sir Robert Morant: A Great Public Servant* (Macmillan, 1934).

44 Eaglesham, E. J. R., *The Foundations of 20th Century Education in England* (Routledge, 1972).

45 Butler, R. A., quoted in *The Art of the Possible* (Hamish Hamilton,

1971), Chapter 5.

46 Bamford, *The Rise of the Public Schools*, see especially 'Contributions of the Public Schools of the Victorian Era' and p. 261.

47 Hartley, L. P., *The Go Between* (Penguin Classic, 2004).

Chapter 6: Lest We Fail to Learn from Our Mistakes

1 The Prince of Wales, later to become George V, in a speech made after an extensive tour of the Dominions.

2 Marshall, A., who attributed Britain's loss of industrial leadership to the lethargy and self-complacency of the late Victorian generations for the sons of the earlier entrepreneurs 'worked shorter hours, and they exerted themselves less to obtain new practical ideas than their fathers had done, and thus a part of England's leadership was destroyed rapidly'. Printed in 1908 as a White Paper, No. 321, and quoted in Ensor, Sir Robert, *England 1870–1914* (Clarendon Press, 1936), see pp. 501, 522–4; and Howard, Michael, *The First World War* (Oxford University Press, 2002).

3 Based on a speech by George Wyndham quoted in *The Times*, 29 March 1909.

4 Waugh, Alec, *The Loom of Youth* (Grant Richards, 1921), pp. 255–307.

5 Thorndike, E. L. (1874–1949), *The Principles of Teaching* (1906), and *Education* (1912).

6 Latin, at ordinary level of the General Certificate of Education (GCE), remained a compulsory subject for entry to Oxford and Cambridge into the 1960s, regardless of the discipline to be studied.

7 Kanigel, Robert, *The One Best Way: Frederick Winslow Taylor and the Enigma of Efficiency* (Viking, 1997).

8 Taylor, F. W., *The Principles of Scientific Management* (1911); and Abbott, J. and Ryan, T., *The Unfinished Revolution: Learning, Human Behaviour,* Community and Political Paradox (Chapter 5), from Postman, Neil, *Technopoly: The Surrender of Culture to Technology* (Vintage Books, 1992), p. 51.

9 Pritchet, Henry, President of the Carnegie Foundation for the Advancement of Teaching.

10 Watson, John Broadus (1878–1958), quoted by Pinker, Steven, *The Language Instinct: The New Science of Language and Mind* (Penguin, 1994) pp. 406–7.

11 Binet, Alfred (1857–1911), *The Development of Intelligence in Children* (1916, reprinted Arno Press, 1973).

12 Burt, Cyril L., *The Causes and Treatment of Backwardness* (London University Press, 1964); his earlier reputation as one of England's first psychologists was marred by his later work in which he was accused by many psychologists of having cheated on his data; and Hearnshaw, L. S., *Cyril Burt: Psychologist* (Hodder & Stoughton, 1979).

13 Hall, *Adolescence*.

14 Hine, *The Rise and Fall of the American Teenager*, Chapter 9.

15 Baden-Powell, Robert, *Scouting for Boys: A Handbook for Instruction in Good Citizenship* (1908), republished by the Scout Association with useful introduction.

16 Sunday Schools in nineteenth- and early twentieth-century England.

17 Springhall, John, *Youth, Empire and Society: British Youth Movements 1883–1940* (London, 1977), quoted in Cunningham, H., *The Invention of Childhood* (BBC Books, 2006).

18 Dewey, John (1859–1952), *The School and Society* (1899), *The Child and the Curriculum* (1902), *How We Think* (1910), *Democracy and Education* (1916), and *Experience of Education* (1938).

19 Livingstone, Sir Richard, *The Future in Education* (Cambridge University Press, 1941).

20 Livingstone, *The Future in Education*, p. 3.

21 Livingstone, *The Future in Education*, Chapter 2 and Postscript.

22 Livingstone, *The Future in Education*, p. 28, and following.

23 Livingstone, Sir Richard, *Education for a World Adrift* (Cambridge University Press, 1949).

24 Butler, R. A., *The Art of the Possible* (Hamish Hamilton, 1971), p. 90.

25 Butler, *The Art of the Possible*, p. 10, quoting Sorley, Charles, *Letters from Germany and the Army*.

26 Butler, *The Art of the Possible*, Memo from Winston Churchill, 12 September 1941.

27 Holmes, Sir Maurice (1885–1964), an archytypal civil servant of whom Butler said, 'Brilliant, yet derisive of many of the persons and fatuities that came his way, yet acute in ideals and practice' (Butler, *The Art of the Possible*, pp. 93 and following).

28 Norwood, Sir Cyril (1875–1956), a classical scholar and formerly headmaster of Marborough College. Chairman of the Norwood Committee established in 1943 which combined the teaching of

Plato with the recommendations of the *Spens Report* (1938) that pupils could be classified into three types.

29   Fleming Commission set up to investigate the future of the public schools in 1943, but did not report until later in 1944 after the Education Act had been approved. This Report achieved little, as neither did that of the Public School's Commission of 1965.

30   The school-leaving age was to have been raised to fifteen on 1 September 1939, but this was cancelled with the outbreak of war; eventually raised to fifteen in 1947, and sixteen in 1973.

31   A pass was required to enter grammar school; in some parts of the country there were only places for some 10 per cent of eleven-year-olds, while in other parts of the country it was as high as 50 per cent.

32   Wilkinson, Ellen (1891–1947), fought her way from a working-class home to Manchester University where she became a member of the Communist Party, but resigned in 1924 to become the only woman Labour MP in the parliament of that year. In 1935 she became Labour MP for Jarrow, and led the Jarrow March in 1936 (Ellen Wilkinson, *The Town that was Murdered*, Left Book Club (Victor Gollancz Ltd), 1939). Politically determined, she was intensely patriotic and was the only Labour MP to give Churchill a sympathetic cheer when he entered the House of Commons after defeat of the General Election of 1945. Her early death was thought to have been brought on by extreme overwork.

33   Jones, Ken, *Education in Britain 1944 to the Present* (Polity, 2003), p. 28.

34   A decision made, ironically, by R. A. Butler when he had become Chancellor of the Exchequer.

35   *Half Our Future* (Ministry of Education, 1963), Chapter 22, Sections 265–8.

36   *The Woodworker*, 'Chips from the Chisel' (late 1948).

37   Cunningham, Hugh, *The Invention of Childhood* (BBC Books, 2006), see Chapter 6.

38   Spock, Dr Benjamin, *The Common Sense Book of Baby and Child Care* (1946).

39   *Times Educational Supplement*, 'What should school leavers know?', 18 September 1948.

40   Professor Crawford, 1966–7, Trinity College, Dublin.

41   Newsom, J. H., *The Child at School* (Penguin Books, 1950), pp. 11,

25/26 and 98/99.

42   McKenzie, R. F., *State School* (Penguin, 1970), pp. 17/18/19.

43   Hutchinson, Michael and Young, Christopher, *Educating the Intelligent* (Penguin Books, 1962), see p. 43; and Davis, Robin, *The Grammar School* (Pelican, 1967), especially Chapters 1 and 4.

44   Pedley, Robin, *The Comprehensive School* (Pelican, 1963), especially Chapter 5.

45   DES, Circular 10/65 (July 1965), p. 16.

46   Phillips, Mike and Phillips, Trevor, *Windrush: The Irresistible Rise of Multi-racial Britain* (HarperCollins, 1948), see Chapter 15, School Days: 1960–70.

47   Sacks, Sir Jonathan, *Recreating Society: The Home We Build Together* (Continuum, 2007). I am much indebted to Dr Sacks for ideas contained within this part of Chapter 6, and subsequently small sections in Chapters 7 and 9.

48   Mill, John Stuart, *Utilitarianism, On Liberty, and Considerations on Representative Government* (Dent, Everyman's Library, 1984), p. 78, and quoted in Sacks, *Recreating Society*, p. 39.

49   Sacks, *Recreating Society*, p. 47–8, 'Where Conversation Ends, Violence Begins'.

50   Sacks, *Recreating Society*, Chapter 2, 'Society's Country House, Hotel or Home?'

51   Conway, David, *A Nation of Immigrants? A Brief Democractic History of Britain* (Civitas, 2007).

52   Church of England Information Board, *Faith in the City* (1981).

53   Powell, Enoch (1912–98), speech at Conservative Political Centre Birmingham, April 1968, 'As I look ahead, I am filled with foreboding. Like the Roman, I see the "River Tiber foaming with much blood".' (Virgil, Book 8).

54   Education 2000, *Learning Makes Sense* (1994).

55   Wilson, James Harold (1916–95), Prime Minister. Slogan developed during the spring 1974 election.

56   Professor Alan Ross of Birmingham University in the 1950s proposed that language could be divided into two categories: U, which was correct, upper-class usage; and non-U, reserved for the rest of the country. This became a fashionable game of social blunders epitomized by John Betjeman's prize-winning poem, 'How to get on in Society', and popularized by Nancy Mitford.

Chapter 7: Adolescents Left Out

1   The *Princeton Review*, Spring 2001.

2   Campbell, Sir Menzies, *The Guardian*, 16 October 2007.

3   Ferrie, Joseph P., *Yankeys Now: Immigrants in the Antebellum US, 1840–1860* (Oxford University Press, 1999).

4   Powel, Arthur G., Farrar, Eleanor and Cohen, David, *The Shopping Mall High School* (Houghton Mifflin, 1985); Sizer, Theodore R., *Horace's Compromise: The Dilemma of the American High School*; Sizer, Theodore R., *Horace's School: Redesigning the American High School* (Houghton Mifflin, 1992); Boyer, Dr Ernest, *High School* (Harper & Row, 1st edn, 1983); and Bloom, Allan, *The Closing of the American Mind* (Simon & Schuster, 1987).

5   Conversation in Pittsburg, October 1984.

6   Introduction to *The Excellency Report*, Washington DC, 1983.

7   James Callaghan, Prime Minister 1976–79, speech delivered at Ruskin College, Oxford, October 1976.

8   Boyer, Dr Ernest, President of the Carnegie Foundation for the advancement of teaching, in response to *The Excellency Report* in 1983.

9   Hart, Betty and Risley, Todd, *Meaningful Differences, and the Everyday Experience of Young American Children* (Paul Brooks, 1995); and Harris, Judith Rich, *The Nurture Assumption* (Bloomsbury, 1998).

10 Christian Socialism, a social reform rooted in Christian theology. Much associated in the 1930s with Archbishop William Temple (see Wilson, *After the Victorians*, pp. 305–17). Central to Non-conformist church teaching (Ellen Wilkinson) and the Labour Party. Similar to today's Liberation Theology in South America (Archbishop Oscar Romero – Appendix C).

11 David, Robin, *The Grammar School* (Pelican, 1967), especially Introduction.

12 Holden, Andrew, *Makers and Manners: Politics and Morality in Post-War Britain* (Politico's, 2004).

13 Weiner, Martin J., *English Culture and the Decline of the Industrial Spirit 1850–1980* (Cambridge University Press, 1981), especially Chapters 5, 7 and 8.

14 Luke 10.30–7.

15 Matthew 25.14–30.

16 Rae, Dr John, Headmaster of Westminster School and Chairman of the Council for Education and World Citizenship.

17 The State of the World Forum, under the Chairmanship of former President Mihale Gorbechev, met annually to discuss those major issues that politicians were loath to put on the agenda.

18 Sacks, *Recreating Society,* p. 78.

19 Story told at educational conference in February 2008.

20 Seventeen-year-old student at Gulf Islands Secondary School (GISS), British Columbia, September 2007.

21 Wright, Robert, 'Evolution of Despair' (*Time* magazine, 1995); and Darwin, Charles, *The Moral Animal.*

22 Wilson, D. S. and Wilson, E. O., 'Evolution: Survival of Selflessness' (*New Scientist*, 3 November 2007).

23 Hennessey, Beth and Amabile, Teresa, *The Nature of Creativity* (Cambridge University Press, 1997), 'People will be most creative when they feel motivated primarily by the interest, enjoyment, satisfaction, and the challenge of the work itself – not by external pressures'; Layard, Richard, *Happiness: Lessons from a New Science* (Penguin, 2005); and Noddings, Nell, *Happiness and Education* (Cambridge University Press, 2003).

24 Beeching, Dr Richard, *The Reshaping of British Railways* (HM Government, 27 March 1963). Government's attempt to reduce the cost of running the railway system of the UK. The Report concluded that much of the railway network carried little traffic and should be closed down. His report proposed a massive closures programme which would involve 5,000 miles of track and 2,363 small stations being closed, which came to be known as the Beeching Axe.

25 Hersch, Patricia, *A Tribe Apart: A Journey into the Heart of American Adolescence* (Fawcett Columbine, 1998).

26 Student at British Columbia Superintendents' Association Annual Conference, Victoria, November 2007.

27 Baker, Kenneth, Secretary of State for Education, May 1986 to July 1989.

28 Collins, Allen, Brown, John Seely and Holum, Anne, 'Cognitive Apprenticeship: Making Thinking Visible' (*American Educator*, Winter 1991).

29 Bullock, Sir Alan, *A Language for Life* (December 1974), a personal summary of the significance of his Report given at a private meeting

in 1988.

30 Cockcroft report (HMSO, 1982).

31 Red Book, *Curriculum 11–16, working papers by HM Inspectorate* (March 1978) with *Curriculum 11–16: A Review of Progress*, a joint study by HMI and five LEAs (HMSO, 1981).

32 Comment made by chemistry teacher at school in Stevenage at staff meeting.

33 Wilby, Peter and Crequer, Ngaio, *The Independent*, 28 July 1988.

34 Baker, Kenneth, Introduction the Education Bill in the House of Commons in December 1987. Hansard (Volume 123).

35 Dearing, Sir Ron, who stated in his final report, 'My concern is, rather, to release more of teachers' energies teaching; (the proposed reduction) will lift the burden of anxiety felt my many teachers.'

36 Blatch, The Baroness, on BBC Radio 4, 2 August 1993, as commented on by Chitty, Clyde, *The Education System Transformed* (Baseline Books, 1999).

37 A former teacher from Birmingham, Marie Jennings, speaking in Bath in November 2006.

38 State of the World Forum, New York, 2001: a participant in a discussion on the impact of globalization.

39 Cheney, Dorothy and Seyfarth, Robert, *Baboon Metaphysics: The Evolution of the Social Mind* (University of Chicago Press, 2007), especially Chapter 5; and Goodall, Jane, *In the Shadow of Man* (revised edn, 1988; and Hauser, Mark, *Wild Minds: What Animals Really Think* (Allen Lane, 2000).

40 Following a lecture given in the Estonian city of Narva in October 1998, an English-speaking Russian-educated teacher asked John Abbott, 'Who are you? You in the West persistently misunderstood us dissidents. When we tore down the Berlin Wall we did so because we wanted to be free to make decisions for ourselves. But you thought we did this because we wished to replace communism with capitalism. Now it looks as if we are replacing one tyranny with another. When the Berlin Wall was there, you in the West defined yourself negatively: you were against communism. Now that communism is no longer a threat to you, your reason for being seems empty. Surely you in the West are about more than just money?'

41 Tony Blair, on becoming Prime Minister on 2 May 1997.

42 Performability is rooted in the assumption that it is both possible and

desirable to measure performance against absolute standards, and has come to dominate government policy. It has led to an obsession with performance, assessment and accountability, and to the belief that if this does not provide the results needed, it is because the measurement tool is not yet perfected, rather than that the situation is impossible to effectively quantify.

43 Blunkett, David, Secretary of State for Education, speech to the Institute for Economic Affairs.

44 Purvis, Libby, *The Times*, June 2002.

45 Victoria Climbié.

46 Blair, Tony, Foreword as Prime Minister to the *Every Child Matters* White Paper (2003).

47 Kirby, Jill, *The Nationalisation of Childhood* (Center for Policy Studies, 2006).

48 There are upwards of twelve bodies to whom headteachers are now directly responsible beyond the school – Ofsted, The Department of Children and Schools and Families, The General Teaching Council for England, the Health and Safety Executive, National Statutes for Literacy and Numeracy, governing bodies, school councils, extended services, employment tribunes etc.

49 'How the well-being of British children compares' (*The Independent*, 14 February 2007).

50 Currie, Elliott, *The Road to Whatever: Middle-class Culture and the Crisis of Adolescence* (Metropolitan Books, 2004), p. 13; and especially Chapters 3 and 6 and pp. 262 and 272.

Chapter 8: What Kind of Education for What Kind of World?

1 Rees, Martin, *Our Final Century: A Scientist's Warning: How Terror, Error and Environmental Disaster Threaten Humankind's Future in this Century – On Earth and Beyond* (Heinemann, 2003).

2 CBC Radio interview in late 2007 with Dr William Reese, Professor at UBC School of Community and Regional Planning, who developed the concept of Ecological Footprint.

3 Martin, Claude, Director General of the World Wildlife Foundation International in article contributed to the *International Herald Tribune* in 2002.

4 National Center for Atmospheric Research (NCAR) news release, 11 December 2006.

5 Gladwell, Malcolm, *The Tipping Point: How Little Things Can Make a Big Difference* (Abacus, 2002).

6 Lawrence and Nohria, *Driven*. p. 13. Putting together a panel that combines experts from each of these fields would only have generated endless arguments with no coherent advice, making matters even worse . . . what is really needed is a well-rounded, seasoned general practitioner for an entire human society, an expert, to use an old-fashioned term, in applied political economy.

7 Capra, Fritjof, *The Hidden Connection: A Science for Sustainable Living* (HarperCollins, 2002); and *The Web of Life: A New Scientific Understanding of Living Systems* (Anchor Books, 1996).

8 The same policy was followed in April 2008 when Congress, with the full endorsement of President Bush, exalted Americans to indulge themselves in 'retail therapy' as a way of stimulating the falling markets, and made a tax-free gift of $600 to every taxpayer.

9 Taylor, Laurie and Matthew, *What Are Children For?* (Short Books, 2003).

10 *The Woodworker*, August 1948: 'Chips from the Chisel'.

11 Gibran, Khalil, *The Prophet* (Heinemann, 1926, republished by Pan Books, 1991).

12 Abbott, David, book review on Initiative website, *How Should One Live? Rejecting the Perfectibility of Man* (May 2008).

13 *The Guardian*, 29 November 2007, 'England plunges in rankings for reading'.

14 Lessing, Doris, *On Not Winning the Nobel Prize*, speech following acceptance of Nobel Prize in Literature on 7 December 2007.

15 Livingstone, Sir Richard, *The Future in Education* (Cambridge University Press, 1941), p. 113 (today's equivalent of a portmanteau is an overnight case).

16 Plotkin, Henry, *Evolution in Mind* (Allen Lane/The Penguin Press, 1997).

17 Ridley, Matthew, *Nature via Nurture: Genes, Experience and What Makes Us Human* (Fourth Estate, 2003); and Cavalli-Sforza, Luigi Luca, *Genes, Pupils and Language* (Allen Lane/Penguin Press, 2000).

18 Shanker, Dr Albert, comment made in presentation to Education 2000 in 1988.

19 Bruer, John, *Schools for Thought: A Science of Learning in the Classroom* (MIT Press, 1993), especially Chapter 3.

20 Billings, Josh, American humorist, 1818–85.

21 The ideas contained within the principles each come from many places. The following titles add to the books already enumerated: Bird, Richard J., *Chaos and Life: Complexity and Order in Evolution and Thought* (Columbia University, 2003); Blakemore, Sarah-Jayne and Frith, Uta, *The Learning Brain: Lessons for Education* (Blackwell, 2006); Bloom, Paul, *Descartes' Baby: How the Science of Child Development Explains What Makes Us Human* (Basic Books, 2004); Boyer, Pascal, *Religion Explained: The Human Instincts That Fashion Gods, Spirits and Ancestors* (William Heinemann, 2001); Boysson-Bardies, Bénédicte de, *How Language Comes to Children: From Birth to Two Years,* trans. by M. B. DeBevoise (MIT Press, 1999); Brooks, Jacqueline and Brooks, Martin, *In Search of Understanding the Case of Constructivist Classrooms* (ASCD, 1993); Caine, Renate and Geoffrey, *Education on the Edge of Possibility* (ASCD, 1997); Caine, Renate and Geoffrey, *Making Connections: Teaching and the Human Brain* (ASCD, 1991); Delors, Jacques, *Learning: The Treasure Within* (UNESCO Publishing, 1996); Egan, Kieran, *The Educated Mind: How Cognitive Tools Shape Our Understanding* (University of Chicago, 1997); Elman, Geoffrey and others, *Rethinking Innateness: A Connectionist's Perspective on Development* (MIT Press, 1999); Freeman, Walter, *How Brains Make Up Their Minds* (Weidenfeld & Nicholson, 1999); Gazzaniga, Michael S., *Nature's Mind: The Biological Roots of Thinking, Emotions, Sexuality, Language and Intelligence* (Penguin, 1992); Gluckman, Peter and Hanson, Mark, *Mismatch: Why Our World No Longer Fits Our Bodies* (Oxford University Press, 2006); LeDoux, Joseph, *The Emotional Brain: The Mysterious Underpinning of Emotional Life* (Simon & Schuster, 1996); *Synaptic Self: How Our Brains Become Who We Are* (Viking, 2002); Lieberman, Philip, *Toward an Evolutionary Biology of Language* (Harvard University Press, 2006); National Research Council, *How People Learn: Brain, Mind, Experience and School* (National Academy Press, 1999); Perkins, David, *Outsmarting IQ: The Emerging Science of Learnable Intelligence* (Free Press, 1995); Pinker, Steven, *How the Mind Works* (W.W. Norton & Co., 1997); Pinker, Steven, *The Blank Slate: The Modern Denial of Human Nature* (Allen Lane/Penguin Press, 2002); Pinker, Steven, *The Language Instinct: The New Science of Language and Mind* (Allen Lane/Penguin Press, 1994); Pinker, Steven, *The*

Stuff of Thought: Language as a Window Into Human Nature (Penguin, 2007); Pinker, Steven, *Words and Rules: The Ingredients of Language* (Weidenfeld & Nicholson, 1999); Roberts, A. C., Robbins, T. W. and Weiskrantz, eds, *The Prefrontal Cortex: Executive and Cognitive Functions* (Oxford University Press, 1998); Schwartz, Jeffrey M. and Begley, Sharon, *The Mind & The Brain: Neuroplasticity and the Power of Mental Force* (Regan Books, 2002); Senge, Peter M., *The Fifth Discipline: The Art and Practice of the Learning Organisation* (Doubleday, 1990); Shanker, Stuart and Greenspan, Stanley I., *The First Idea: How Symbols, Language, and Intelligence Evolved from Our Primate Ancestors to Modern Humans* (Da Capo Press, 2004); Sylwester, Robert, *A Celebration of Neurons: An Educator's Guide to the Human Brain* (ASCD, 1995); Tomasello, Michael, *The Cultural Origins of Human Cognition* (Harvard University Press, 1999); and Zohar, Danah and Marshall, Ian, *Spiritual Intelligence: The Ultimate Intelligence* (Bloomsbury, 2000).

22 Paper by Tomislav Reskovac, teacher of philosophy from Croatia, published by the Open Society Initiative in Eastern Europe, *Debate Was the Question Mark, School Was the Full Stop* (September, 2005).

23 Coveney, Peter and Highfield, Roger, *Frontiers of Complexity: The Search for Order in a Chaotic World* (Faber & Faber, 1995); Cauffman, Stewart A., *The Origins of Order: Self-organisation and Selection in Evolution* (Oxford University Press, 1993); and Waldrop, Mitchell, *Complexity: The Emerging Science at the Edge of Order and Chaos* (Simon & Schuster, 1992).

24 Abbott, A. J., *Adolescence, A Critical Evolutionary Adaptation* (The 21st Century Learning Initiative, 2006); Adelson, Joseph, *Inventing Adolescence: The Political Psychology of Everyday Schooling* (Transaction Books, 2008); Annals of the New York Academy of Sciences, *Adolescent Brain Development: Vulnerabilities and Opportunities* (Volume 1021, 2004); Ainley, Patrick and Rainbird, Helen, *Apprenticeship: Towards a New Paradigm of Learning* (Kogan Page, 1999); Bogin, Barry, *The Growth of Humanity* (Wiley-Liss, 2001); Csikszentmihalyi, Mihalyi, *Being Adolescent: Conflict and Growth in the Teenage Years* (Basic Books, 1984); Csíkszentmihályi, Mihály and Schneider, Barbara, *Becoming Adult: How Teenagers Prepare for the World of Work* (Basic Books, 2000); Csíkszentmihályi, Mihály, *Flow: The Psychology of Optimal Experience* (Harper & Row, 1990);

Epstein, Robert, *The Case Against Adolescents: Rediscovering the Adult in Every Teen* (Quill Driver Books, 2007); and Strauch, Barbara, *The Primal Teen: What the New Discoveries About the Teenage Brain Tell Us About Our Kids* (Doubleday, 2003).

25 First proposed at a meeting between Education 2000 and the DfEE in 1995.

26 Comment made by participant at the annual conference of the Ontario Trustees' Association, 1998.

27 Schank, Roger C. and Claeve, John B., *The Mind, The Brain and Complex Adaptive Systems: Natural Learning, Natural Teaching, Changing Human Memory*, published by the Santa Fe Institute in the Sciences of Complexity (Addison-Wesley, 1994), p. 175.

28 Bereiter, Carl and Scardamalia, Marlene, *Surpassing Ourselves: An Inquiry Into the Nature and Implications of Expertise* (Open Court, 1993).

29 Newsom, J. H., *The Child at School* (Penguin Books, 1950), pp. 98–9.

30 Rorabaugh, W. J., *The Craft Apprentice: From Franklin to the Machine Age in America* (Oxford University Press, 1988), together with Laslett, Peter, *The World We Have Lost – Further Explored* (Routledge, 1988).

31 Zubboff, Shoshana, *In the Age of the Smart Machine: The Future of Work and Power* (Heinemann, 1988).

32 Collins, Allen, Brown, John Seely and Holum, Anne, 'Cognitive Apprenticeship: Making Thinking Visible' (*American Educator*, Winter, 1991).

33 The Rand Corporation, one of America's premier non-partisan research groups, in a major study on education systems in 1988.

34 The 21st Century Learning Initiative; *A Policy Paper: The Strategic and Resource Implications of a New Model of Learning* (1999).

Chapter 9: Knowing What We Know . . . What's to be Done?

1 Starr, Chester, *A History of the Ancient World* (Oxford University Press, 1992). 'Every so often civilisation seems to work itself into a corner from which further progress is virtually impossible along the lines then apparent: yet if new ideas are to have a chance the old systems must be so severely shaken that they lose their dominance,' quoted in Wright, Robert, *Non Zero: The Logic of Human Destiny*,

p. 136.

2 Capra, Fritjof, *The Hidden Connections: The Science for Sustainable Living*, Epilogue, pp. 228 and following.

3 Gore, Al, *An Inconvenient Truth: The Planetary Emergence of Global Warming and What We Can Do About It* (Rodale, 2006); Jacobs, Jane, *Dark Age Ahead* (Random House, 2004); Lovelock, James, *Gaia: A new look at life on earth* (revised, Oxford University Press, 1979); *The Revenge of Gaia: Why the Earth is Fighting Back – and How We Can Still Save Humanity* (Allen Lane, 2006); McKibben, Bill, *Deep Economy: The Wealth of Communities and the Durable Future* (Henry Holt & Co., 2007); Schumacher, E. F., *Small is Beautiful: Economics as if People Mattered* (Harper Perennial, 1973); and Wright, Ronald, *A Short History of Progress* (Canongate, 2004).

4 Davis, Paul, *The Mind of God: The Scientific Basis for a Rational World* (Touchstone, 1992); Fox, Matthew, *The Reinvention of Work: A New Vision of Livelihood for Our Times* (HarperSanFrancisco, 1994); Holloway, Richard, *Doubts and Loves: What is Left of Christianity* (Canongate, 2001); Holloway, Richard, *On Forgiveness: How Can We Forgive the Unforgivable?* (Canongate, 2002); Holloway, Richard, *Looking in the Distance: The Human Search for Meaning* (Canongate, 2004); Postman, Neil, 'Science and the Story that We Need' (*First Things*, January, 1997); and Williams, Shirley, *God and Caesar: Personal Reflections on Politics and Religion* (Continuum, 2003).

5 Sacks, *Recreating Society*.

6 Sacks, Jonathan, *The Dignity of Difference: How to Avoid the Clash of Civilisations* (Continuum, 2002); and Sacks, Jonathan, *To Heal a Fractured World: The Ethics of Responsibility* (Continuum, 2005).

7 Detective Chief Inspector Owen of the Wigan Police, *The Guardian* (21 September 2007).

8 Hutchinson, Michael and Young, Christopher, *Educating the Intelligent* (Pelican, 1962), p. 37; and see also Huxley, Aldous, *Proper Studies* (Chatto & Windus, 1927 – essay on education), especially pp. 112 and 113.

9 Vaizey, John, *Education for Tomorrow* (Penguin, 1962); Postman, Neil, *Amusing Ourselves To Death: Public Discourse and the Age of Show Business* (Matthew, 1985); Postman, Neil, *Teaching as a Subversive Activity* (with Charles Weingartner, Knopf); Postman, Neil, *The End of Education: Redefining the Value of School* (Knopf, 1995); Wolf,

Alison, *Does Education Matter: Myths about Education and Economic Growth* (Penguin, 2002).

10 Department of Children, Schools and Families. www.dfes.gov.uk, 2008.

11 Department of Children, Schools and Families, *Raising Expectations*, Consultation Document, 17 March 2008.

12 de Wall, Anastasia, *Inspection, Inspection, Inspection! How Ofsted Crushes Independent Schools and Independent Teachers* (Civitas, 2006); see also Sacks, Peter, *Standardised Minds: The High Price of America's Testing Culture and What We Can Do to Change It* (Perseus Books, 1999).

13 Milton, John, *Of Education: Essay to Master Samuel Hartlib, 1644* (published as Tractate on Education by Harvard Classics in 1909).

14 Newsom, J. H., *The Child at School*, see especially chapter 1 'Why Education?'.

15 Sacks, *Recreating Society*; see also Seligman, Adam B., *The Idea of Civil Society* (Princeton University Press, 1995).

16 Gardner, Howard, *Five Minds for the Future* (Harvard, 2006).

17 Comenius, Jan Amos (1592–1670). Comenius has often been called 'The Father of Modern Education'. Comenius lived a rough life at a time of intense religious hostility. He was a Bishop of a small Protestant sect. He was driven out of his home land at the age of 30 and wandered through much of Europe for the remainder of his life. He wrote numerous works on education and became famous throughout Europe. He wrote frequently to Milton and other European intellectuals. At a time when children were simply trained to repeat and memorize Latin vocabulary and conjugations, Comenius opened up the first serious attempt to make education about empowering the child to learn for itself.

18 Abbott, *The Child is Father of the Man*, p. 369.

19 Chief Adviser, Dudley Education Authority, 2000.

20 See Chapter 8.

21 Newsom, *The Child at School*, p. 11.

22 Bowlby, John, *Attachment* (Basic Books, 1969); De Marneffe, Daphne, *Maternal Desire: On Children, Love and the Inner Life* (Back Bay Books, 2004); and Bromhall, Clive, *The Eternal Child: An Explosive New Theory of Human Origins and Behaviour* (Ebury Press, 2003).

23 Wade, Nicholas, *Before the Dawn: Recovering the lost history of our ancestors*, see especially Chapter 8.

24 Laslett, Peter, *The World We Have Lost – Further Explored* (Routledge, 1988), especially Chapter 3.

25 Louis-Williams, David, *The Mind in the Cave*, especially Chapter 9, 'Cave and Community'; McMurry, John, *The Personal World* (Florence Books, 1996); George, R., *Communities of Collaboration: Shared Commitments/Common Tasks*, quoted *On Community* (Notre Dame University Press, 1991); Abbott, John, *Individualism, Community and Learning* (The 21st Century Learning Initiative, 2001).

26 Wannaburg, Alf, *The Bushmen* (Struik Publishers, 1979 onwards to 1991), see especially Chapter 1, *The 10,000-year Generation Gap*.

27 Abbott, John, *Master & Apprentice: Reuniting Thinking with Doing* (unpublished manuscript, 2004); Greenspan, Stanley, *The Growth of the Mind: And the Endangered Origins of Intelligence* (Addison-Wesley, 1997); Gerhardt, Sue, *Why Love Matters: How Affection Shapes a Baby's Brain* (Routledge, 2004); Diamond, Marion, *Magic Trees of the Mind: How to Nurture Your Child's Intelligence, Creativity, and Healthy Emotions from Birth Through Adolescence* (Dutton Books, 1998); Siegel, Daniel, *The Developing Mind: Towards a Neurobiology of Interpersonal Experience* (Gilford Press, 1999).

28 The Kellogg Foundation, research in the State of Michigan, quoted at the White House Conference on Early Childhood Education in 1997.

29 Leach, Penelope, *Children First: What our Society Must Do – and Is Not Doing – for Our Children Today* (Knoph, 1994); Karr-Morse, Robin and Wiley, Merrideth, 'Ghosts from the Nursery: Tracing the Roots of Violence' (*Atlantic Monthly*, 1997).

30 Purvis, Libby, *One Summer's Grace: A Family Voyage Around Britain* (Coronet Books, 1989); concluding paragraph states, 'From that experience I came to believe what anthropologists sometimes note: that the thing which human beings need more than comfort, more than possessions, more than sex or a settled home, is a good supply of stories. Through stories we make sense of the world.'

31 Ryan, Terry, *Children, Families, Social Capital and Education in Go-Go Capitalism: A Dispatch from America's Richest County* (The 21st Century Learning Initiative, 2002).

32 Coles, Robert, *The Political Life of Children* (Houghton Mifflin, 1986); *Spiritual Life of Children* (Mariner Books, 1991); and *The Moral Intelligence of Children* (Random House, 1997); and *The Secular Mind* (Princeton University Press, 1999).

33 Greenspan, Stanley, *The Growth of the Mind, and the Endangered Origins of Intelligence* (Addison Wesley, 1997); and Miles, Rosaland, *The Children We Deserve: Love and Hate in the Making of the Family* (HarperCollins, 1994).

34 *The Guardian*, 28 March 2008.

35 Csikszentmihalyi and Schneider, *Becoming Adult*; Csikszentmihalyi and Larson, *Being Adolescent*.

36 Abbott, John, *Lieutenant Peter Puget, the Grain of the Brain and Modern Society's Failure to Understand Adolescents* (Public Education in British Columbia and the World, Victoria, British Columbia, 9 March 2004).

37 Fischer, David Hackett, *Albion's Seed* (Oxford University Press, 1989).

38 Kelso, William M., *Jamestown: The Buried Truth* (University of Virginia Press, 2006).

39 Hanifan, L. J., State Supervisor of Rural Schools in West Virginia in 1916, appears to have been the first person to use that term.

40 Stein, Janice Gross, *Cult of Efficiency* (Piatkus Books, 2004).

41 Curry, Elliott, *The Road to Whatever* (Metropolitan Books, 2004).

42 I attended a pubic school, and then did a diploma in education at the Royal Dublin High School. I taught for short periods in a prep school and a secondary modern and then taught at Manchester Grammar School for seven years and was headmaster of an old grammar school going comprehensive for twelve years. Since then I have lectured to schoolchildren in several different countries.

43 Confederation of British Industry, Annual Conference, Glasgow 1987. Keynote speech.

44 *Policy Paper: The Strategic and Resource Implications for a New Model of Learning,* the 21st Century Learning Initiative (1999).

45 Simon, Brian, *The Politics of Educational Reform 1920–1940* (Lawrence and Wishart, 1974); and Grey, J., MacPherson, A. F. and Raffe, D., *Reconstructions of Secondary Education: Theory, Myth and Practice Since the War* (Routledge, 1983).

46 Chitty, Clyde, *Education Policy in Britain* (Palgrave, 2004).

47 Edward Thring, the highly successful headmaster of Uppingham who followed in the tradition of Dr Arnold, wrote in 1870: 'England has not chosen to have its education carried on at home, but deliberately prefers, when it can be had, a boarding school. As a fact beyond dispute Englishmen of the upper-classes send their children from home, and the reason why they are sent from home is not the teaching . . . (but that the boarding school provides a better place of training than the home).' Quickly such a belief permeated English society, meaning that by 1902 it was easy for Morant to suggest that the new county grammar schools should resemble, in as far as possible, the practices of a boarding public school.

48 Saguara Seminars, *Civic Engagement in America* in 2001; this went on to show that social capital reduces crime, juvenile delinquency, teenage pregnancy, child abuse, welfare dependency and drug abuse, and increases student test scores and graduation rates.

49 Bamford, T. W., *Thomas Arnold* (The Crescent Press, 1960). Arnold found it necessary to support the enthusiasm of his teachers for giving young boys plenty of opportunity before sport and physical activity as a way of using up their energy. Arnold deplored, however, the idea that a delight in physical prowess should be associated with the kind of education that he advocated. In 1940 he wrote, 'There is no earthly thing more mean and despicable in my mind than an English gentleman destitute of all sense of his responsibilities and opportunities, and only revelling in the luxuries of our high civilisation and thinking himself a great person.' Arnold never saw that his ideas would become trivialised as 'muscular Christianity'.

50 Sorley, Charles, letters from Germany and the Army (printed privately and given to a few personal friends) and quoted by Butler, R. A. in *The Art of the Possible* (Hamish Hamilton, 1971).

51 Crace, John, *Heaven and Helsinki* (an article in *The Guardian*, 16 September 2003).

52 Organisation of Economic Cooperation and Development: Programme for International Student Assessment (PISA), December 2007.

53 *The Chosun Ilbo* (South Korea), 3 October 2005, Professors Lee Tae-Woo and Dr Chung Eoyeon-Sun.

54 Mayer, Catherine, 'Unhappy, Unloved and Out of Control: An

Epidemic, Violence, Crime and Drunkeness has Made Britain Scared of its Young. What's Causing the Crisis?' (*Time* magazine, 7 April 2008).

55 *The Synthesis: A Work in Progress* (The 21st Century Learning Initiative, 16 December 1996).

56 Pace-Marshall, Stephanie, Founding Executive Director of the Illinois Math and Science Academy and one-time President of ASCD, and a member of the Presidents' Council of Science Advisers (USA).

57 Middlekauff, Robert, *The Glorious Cause: The American Revolution 1763–1789* (Oxford University Press, 1982).

58 *Chronicles of the Pilgrim Fathers*, Everyman's Library, Introduction by John Masefield (1910), p. 23.

59 Sacks, Jonathan, *The Home We Build Together: Recreating Society* (Continuum, 2007).

60 The Book of Common Prayer, 1662.

61 Sacks, *Recreating Society*.

62 *Globe & Mail*, Toronto, 13 March 2006, see also *Lost in Translation* published by The 21st Century Learning Initiative, March 2006.

Index